Erdener Kaynak, PhD
Pervez N. Ghauri, PhD
Editors

Euromarketing: Effective Strategies for International Trade and Export

Pre-publication REVIEWS, COMMENTARIES, EVALUATIONS . . .

"**U**seful to the new student and the experienced practitioner as well. The raging debate as to what euromarketing is, or even if it exists, will not be fully answered by any single source, but this book makes an important contribution to the dialogue."

Lee Dahringer, DBA
Dean,
College of Business,
Butler University

Euromarketing
Effective Strategies
for International Trade and Export

INTERNATIONAL BUSINESS PRESS
Erdener Kaynak, PhD
Executive Editor

New, Recent, and Forthcoming Titles:

International Business Handbook edited by V. H. (Manek) Kirpalani

Sociopolitical Aspects of International Marketing edited by Erdener Kaynak

How to Manage for International Competitiveness edited by Abbas J. Ali

International Business Expansion into Less-Developed Countries: The International Finance Corporation and Its Operations by James C. Baker

Product-Country Images: Impact and Role in International Marketing edited by Nicolas Papadopoulos and Louise A. Heslop

The Global Business: Four Key Marketing Strategies edited by Erdener Kaynak

Multinational Strategic Alliances edited by Refik Culpan

Market Evolution in Developing Countries: The Unfolding of the Indian Market by Subhash C. Jain

A Guide to Successful Business Relations with the Chinese: Opening the Great Wall's Gate by Huang Quanyu, Richard S. Andrulis, and Chen Tong

Industrial Products: A Guide to the International Marketing Economics Model by Hans Jansson

Euromarketing: Effective Strategies for International Trade and Export edited by Erdener Kaynak and Pervez N. Ghauri

Euromarketing
Effective Strategies for International Trade and Export

Erdener Kaynak, PhD
Pervez N. Ghauri, PhD
Editors

International Business Press
An Imprint of The Haworth Press, Inc.
New York • London • Norwood (Australia)

Published by

International Business Press, an imprint of The Haworth Press, Inc., 10 Alice Street, Binghamton, NY 13904-1580

The Haworth Press, Inc., 10 Alice Street, Binghamton, NY 13904-1580

Library of Congress Cataloging-in-Publication Data

Euromarketing : effective strategies for international trade and export / Erdener Kaynak. Pervez N. Ghauri, editors.
    p.   cm.
    ISBN 1-56024-427-5 (acid-free paper).
    1. Export marketing-Europe-Management. I. Kaynak, Erdener. II. Ghauri, Pervez N., 1948- .
HF1416.6.E85E94   1994
658.8'48-dc20   93-17363
                                                         CIP

CONTENTS

List of Tables   xi

List of Figures   xv

About the Editors   xvii

Contributors   xix

Foreword   xxi
Kenneth Simmonds

Preface   xxv
Arch G. Woodside

Introduction   xxix
Erdener Kaynak
Pervez N. Ghauri

**SECTION I. INTEGRATIVE STATEMENT
ON EUROPEAN MARKETING**

**Chapter 1. Current Status of European Marketing:
Introduction**   3
Erdener Kaynak
Pervez N. Ghauri

Background of the Book   6
Conceptual Framework   9

**Chapter 2. The Challenges of the European Community
(EC) Industrial Policy**   15
Cecilia Andersen

Introduction   15
The Community Industrial Policy for the Nineties   16
The Technological Capacity of the Community   23
Conclusion   34

Chapter 3. The European Internal Market: Between Scylla and Charybdis?   **35**
    Bert Piëst
    Henk Ritsema

Introduction   35
The Effects of Market Integration   36
Challenging the Assumptions Behind Europe 1992   37
A Framework   42
Vulnerability of the Strategies   46
Concluding Remarks   51

SECTION II. EUROMARKETING STRATEGIES: WESTERN EUROPE

Chapter 4. Consumer Behavior and Marketing Issues in the Europe of Post-1992   **57**
    Erdener Kaynak
    Pervez N. Ghauri

Introduction   57
The Environment   58
Homogeneous vs. Heterogeneous Marketplace   71
Suppliers in 1992 Europe   77
Marketing to Europe 1992–Problems and Opportunities   78
Conclusion   81

Chapter 5. Marketing Planning and 1992: Observations and Expectations   **85**
    Peter S. H. Leeflang
    Charles P. de Mortanges

Background   85
The Strategic Marketing Planning Process   88
The Possible Effects of a Single European Market   91
Conclusion   103

Chapter 6. A Model for Defensive Marketing Strategy with Examples from the Europe 1992 Context   **107**
>*Roger J. Calantone*
>*C. Anthony di Benedetto*
>*Curtis E. Harvey*

Introduction   107
Modeling Competitive Attack and Defense   109
Decision Model   112
Sample Applications   124
Conclusion   131
Appendix: Issues in Model Development   135

Chapter 7. Marketing Mix Strategies in the Europe of Post-1992   **139**
>*Gianluigi Guido*

Characteristics of the "Euro-Market"   139
A Pan-European Approach   141
Product Strategies   144
Pricing Strategies   148
Promotion Strategies   150
Distribution Strategies   155
Conclusion   159

Chapter 8. Marketing in Europe Beyond 1992: The Challenge of a Mix Between Global and Local Marketing Strategies   **163**
>*Riccardo Varaldo*
>*Andrea Piccaluga*

Effects of the Completion of the European Single Market   163
The Changing Marketing Mix   165
The Different Growth Strategies in the European Markets   165
Marketing Strategies in Europe: Global vs. Local Alternatives   169
The Mirage of the Euroconsumer   173
Global Marketing Strategies   175
Local Marketing Strategies   177

Customization vs. Standardization   178
Conclusion   179

SECTION III. EUROMARKETING STRATEGIES: EASTERN EUROPE

Chapter 9. East and Central European Marketing: 1992 and Beyond   185
Gabor Hovanyi

Introduction   185
The Hungarian Scene: Recent, Past, and Present Situation   186
The Plans of the Hungarian Government for the 1991-92
    Period   190
Marketing Concepts and Practices of the Different
    Courses of Economic Development   193
Outlook to the Other Ex-Communist Countries'
    "Marketing Potential"   199

Chapter 10. U.S./Hungarian Joint Ventures: An Opportunity for Entering New Markets   205
Robert D. Hisrich
Jan Jones

Introduction   205
Methodology   207
Findings   208
Conclusions and Recommendations   221

Chapter 11. Decision Processes in Strategic Alliances: Designing and Implementing International Joint Ventures in Eastern Europe   225
Arch G. Woodside
József Kandikó

Theoretical and Methodological Perspectives   226
Method   230
Results   241
Strategic Management Implications   259

SECTION IV. EUROPEAN MARKETING: WHAT IS HAPPENING AFTER 1992?

Chapter 12: Fortress Europe: Which Industries Are Most Vulnerable?   **267**
    Trina L. Larsen
    Robert T. Green

Background   268
Methodology   272
Findings   275
Limitations   282
Discussion   282
Conclusion   284

Chapter 13. A Normative Framework for Assessing Marketing Strategy Implications of Europe 1992   **287**
    Subhash C. Jain
    John K. Ryans, Jr.

Europe 1992 and Marketing   288
Assessing Marketing Strategy Implications   290
Toward a Research Program   305
Conclusion   309

Chapter 14. European Marketing: Future Directions   **315**
    Pervez N. Ghauri
    Erdener Kaynak

Threats and Opportunities Beyond Europe 1992   317
Europe Beyond 1992   326
Managerial Implications   333

Index   **345**

List of Tables

1.1. The Triad Profile   5

1.2. Europe and Its Sub-Markets   7

1.3. Japanese Investments in Europe   9

3.1. Preferred strategies in the internal market   47

3.2. Vulnerability of strategies in the internal market   51

4.1. Major Socio-Economic Indicators for the EC in 1990   59

4.2. Macro-Economic Consequences of EC Market Integration for the Community in the Medium Term   64

4.3. Forces in Favor of and Against European Unification   67

4.4. Foreign Languages Spoken by European Business People (%)   69

4.5. Population and Households (12 European Countries)   70

4.6. The Aging Population (10 Countries)   71

4.7. EC: Total Consumer Spending 1979-94 (ECU bn)   73

4.8. Rates of Exchange (Mid-March 1992)   75

4.9. National Income and Gross Domestic Product–1985   76

4.10. Major European Food Retail Alliances, 1990   80

5.1. Projected Changes in Selected Economic Variables   92

5.2. Overview of Some Expected Developments in Various Industries   93

6.1. Brand ratings on attributes and prices: Application 1   126

6.2. Summary of terminal market share projections   127

6.3. Profit contribution projections for Brand 1   128

6.4. Brand ratings on attributes and prices: Application 2   130

7.1.	Product Strategies in Europe of 1992	146
7.2.	Pricing Strategies in Europe of 1992	149
7.3.	Promotion Strategies in Europe of 1992	151
7.4.	Distribution Strategies in Europe of 1992	156
9.1.	Characteristic Trends of the Hungarian Economic Scene in 1980-1989	188
9.2.	Effects to be Considered by Western Companies Investing in East European Countries	200
9.3.	The Role of Economic Factors in the Development of Marketing Concepts and Activities in East European Countries	201
10.1.	Hungarian-U.S. Joint Ventures in 1989	208
10.2.	Rules Governing Establishing Joint Ventures in Eastern Europe	212
10.3.	Hungarian Joint Ventures	214
10.4.	Risk and Uncertainty Avoidance: Hungarian Managers' Responses	216
11.1.	Comparisons of Hungarian-United States and Hungarian-Japanese IJV Design Characteristics	258
12.1.	Low Vulnerability Products	276
12.2.	High Vulnerability Products	278
13.1.	Factors Determining Europe 1992's Effect on Marketing	294
14.1.	Impact of German Unification on the Growth Rate of the Other Member Countries	316
14.2.	State Aids in the European Community	319
14.3.	Cellular Radio Subscribers in Europe, June 1989	323
14.4.	Duration Structure of Unemployment (as % of labor force)	324
14.5.	Economic Growth (% annual average change in real gross domestic product)	326

14.6. Inflation Performance (% annual average change in consumer prices) 327

14.7. Exchange Rates to the ECU (as of September 16, 1991) 329

14.8. The EMS and Economic Convergence: The Inflation Example 330

14.9. Composition of the ECU 332

14.10. The West European Retail Market in 1988 334

14.11. European Retail Market, 1989 335

14.12. Firm Strategies Toward the Single European Market 338

14.13. Main Economic Indicators, 1989-1993 (Community, USA, and Japan) 341

14.14. Real GDP, Domestic Demand, and World Trade (annual % change) 342

List of Figures

1.1. Global Trade Map   4

1.2. European Trade Block   6

3.1. Effects of the elimination of non-tariff barriers   39

3.2. Strategies in the internal market   44

4.1. The Decision-Making Process in EC   62

5.1. Steps in the Strategic Marketing Planning Process   90

6.1. Three-dimensional per-dollar map: Two brand case   113

6.2. A taste-preference ray in three-dimensional space   116

6.3. Indifference curves in three-dimensional space   117

6.4. Per-dollar map: Three brands   118

6.5. Repositioning of Brand 3 and resulting indifference
      curve shifts   120

6.6. Disruptive change in industry structure   123

7.1. The Six Clusters and Their Population (1990, in 000's
      of people)   142

7.2. 1992: The Implications of Pan-European Marketing   143

8.1. Expansion and Penetration Strategies   167

8.2. Different Types of Needs and Territorial Heterogeneity   174

9.1. Outputs and Risk in the Three Types of Economic
      Development   194

11.1. Joint Venture Design Model   237

11.2. Solution-Opportunity Identification in Hungarian-U.S.
      Consumer Durable Manufacturing Enterprise   242

11.3A. Evaluation of Proposed Hungarian-U.S. Consumer
       Durable Manufacturing Enterprise   245

xv

11.3B. Evaluation of Proposed Hungarian-U.S.
Consumer Durable Manufacturing Enterprise   246

11.4. Design/Implementation of Proposed Hungarian/U.S.
Consumer Durable Manufacturing Enterprise   249

11.5. Solution-Opportunity Identification in Hungarian-
Japanese Industrial Manufacturing Enterprise   251

11.6. Evaluation Phase of Hungarian-Japanese IJV   253

11.7. Design/Implementation of Hungarian-Japanese IJV   254

12.1. Non-EC Import Growth   275

13.1. Framework for Assessing Marketing Strategy
Implications of Europe 1992   292

14.1. Enlarged Europe Beyond 2000   318

ABOUT THE EDITORS

Erdener Kaynak, PhD, is Professor of Marketing at the School of Business Administration of The Pennsylvania State University at Harrisburg, Middletown, Pennsylvania, U.S.A. Dr. Kaynak has lectured widely in diverse areas of marketing and international business and has held executive training programs before senior executives in Europe, North America, Latin America, The Middle East, The Far East including The People's Republic of China, and Australia. A prolific author, Dr. Kaynak has published 18 books and over 150 articles in refereed scholarly and professional journals. Two of his books were translated into Chinese and Japanese. He has read papers, contributed chapters to reading books and chaired panels and special sessions in more than twenty countries at over fifty conferences on five continents. Dr. Kaynak is the Executive Editor for International Business Press (IBP) as well as being the Senior Editor (International Business Press) for The Haworth Press, Inc. of New York, London, and Norwood (Australia). He also serves as Founding Editor and Editor in Chief of five international marketing/business journals as well as being on the Editorial Review Board of a dozen marketing and management journals published in North America, Europe, Asia, Australia, and Africa.

Dr. Kaynak has served as a business consultant, training advisor, and a seminar leader with a number of Turkish, Canadian, Hong Kong, Peruvian, Finnish, Groatian, Dutch, Norwegian, Colombian, U.S., Chinese, Egyptian, Venezuelian and international organizations. He has been the recipient of a number of research scholarships and distinctions, most notably: Fulbright Post-Doctoral Research Scholarship, Turkish Government Scholarship, Fellowship of the Salzburg Seminar in American Studies, British Council Fellowship, Swedish Institute Research Scholarship, German Academic Exchange Service Scholarship, Lodz University (Poland) Rector's Scholarship, United Nations Development Program (TOKTEN) Award, and Oulu University (Finland) Distinguished Researcher of the Year Award.

Pervez N. Ghauri, PhD, is Professor of Marketing in the Faculty of Management and Organization of The University of Groningen, The Netherlands. He also has a part-time position as Professor of Marketing at The University of Limburg, Maastricht, The Netherlands. Dr. Ghauri received his doctoral degree from Uppsala University, Uppsala, Sweden, where he was a faculty member for more than ten years. During 1989 through 1993, he was Provost and Pro-Rector at Oslo Business School, Oslo, Norway.

Dr. Ghauri is the author or co-author of several books on cross-cultural negotiations and international business as well as articles and book chapters for European and North American journals. He is the Editor of International Business Review, published by Pergamon Press Ltd. and sits on the Editorial Review Board of several European and North American journals.

CONTRIBUTORS

Cecilia Andersen is a professor at Antwerp University, Belgium, where she lectures MBA students on multinational management and European community policies affecting business. She is also a faculty member of Boston University, Brussels, and teaches business in the European environment.

Roger J. Calantone, PhD, is Professor of Marketing at the Graduate School of Business Administration of Michigan State University, East Lansing, Michigan, U.S.A.

Charles P. de Mortanges, PhD, is Associate Professor of Marketing at the University of Limburg, Maastricht, the Netherlands. His teaching and research is primarily in international marketing.

C. Anthony di Benedetto, PhD, is Associate Professor of Marketing, Department of Marketing at the School of Business and Management, Temple University, Philadelphia, Pennsylvania, U.S.A.

Robert T. Green, PhD, is Harkins Professor of Business at the Department of Marketing of the University of Texas at Austin, Texas, U.S.A.

Gianluigi Guido, PhD, is Professor of Monetary and Capital Markets in the Faculty of Banking Economics of The University of Lecce, Italy.

Curtis E. Harvey, PhD, is Professor of Economics at the Department of Economics of The University of Kentucky, Lexington, Kentucky, U.S.A.

Robert D. Hisrich is Professor and Bovaird Chair of Entrepreneurship, Enterprise Development Center, The University of Tulsa, Tulsa, Oklahoma, U.S.A.

Gabor Hovanyi, PhD, Budapest University, is Professor of Industrial Economics at the Janus Pannonius University, Hungary, Senior Researcher at the Research Institute of Industrial Economics of the Hungarian Academy of Sciences and Senior Adviser to the general manager of the I.V. Management Consulting Group, Budapest.

Subhash C. Jain, PhD, is Professor of Marketing at the School of Business of the University of Connecticut, Storr, Connecticut, U.S.A.

Jan Jones is Director, Venture Capital Exchange, The University of Tulsa, Tulsa, Oklahoma, U.S.A.

Milan Jurse, PhD, is Assistant Professor of Marketing and International Business at the Faculty of Business Economics of The University of Maribor, Maribor, Slovania.

József Kandikó, PhD, is Professor of Marketing at The International Management Center, Budapest, Hungary.

Trina L. Larsen, PhD, is Assistant Professor of Marketing at the Department of Marketing, College of Business Administration of Drexel University, Philadelphia, Pennsylvania, U.S.A.

Peter S. H. Leeflang, PhD, is Professor of Marketing at the Faculty of Economics of the University of Groningen, the Netherlands.

Andrea Piccaluga has finished his doctoral studies at Scuola Superiore S. Anna in Pisa. He also received an MSc from the Science Policy Research Unit at the University of Sussex in Brighton (UK) in 1991.

Bert Piëst, PhD, was a member of the Faculty of Management Science at the State University of Groningen. He is currently General Marketing Manager for AVEBA b.a. in Veendam, the Netherlands.

Henk Ritsema is currently Assistant Professor at the Faculty of Management and Organization of the University of Groningen, the Netherlands.

John K. Ryans, Jr., PhD, is Professor of Marketing at the Graduate School of Management of Kent State University, Kent, Ohio, U.S.A.

Riccardo Varaldo is Professor of Business Administration at Scuola Suporioro S. Anna in Pisa, Italy. He was Visiting Fellow at Salford University in 1977, Visiting Professor at Syracuse University in 1981 and Dean of the Faculty of Economics at the University of Pisa. He is now Director of Scuola Superiore S. Anna in Pisa.

Arch G. Woodside, PhD, is Professor of Marketing at Freeman School of Business, Tulane University, New Orleans, Louisiana, U.S.A.

Foreword

Why study Euromarketing when European markets are so diverse, and constantly changing? Surely it would be more likely to yield useable results to study single country markets, compare country markets or attempt global generalizations. Is there anything intrinsically European that would justify a distinctive concern for Euromarketing? The answer, of course, is a resounding "Yes. " There are a great many reasons for studying Euromarketing. It is a study that is long overdue.

First, Europe, and more so the European Community, presents a highly interdependent group of economies in which consumer segments can show a great deal of similarity. Across European countries, society has been shown to split into consumer groups very similar in lifestyle, aspirations, and purchasing power. There are increasingly identifiable cross-European segments. Failure to perceive such cross-European segments could lead a firm into needless expense in trying to adjust separately to each country market, and make it vulnerable to competitors who do recognize these segments.

Second, changes in the political, economic, social, and institutional elements of the European environment are all closely linked across European countries. Understanding what is changing and how these changes will affect its own marketing, is important for any business facing European competitors whether inside or outside Europe. It may be too late simply to wait until the impact of a change is felt. Foresight based on insight into the evolving social patterns is a safer strategy than reaction.

Another reason for Euromarketing as a coherent field of study is that careful thought and analysis is required for accuracy in projecting the business impact of social change. Impacts are seldom self-evident. Take, for example, the simple claim that removing internal barriers to enable a single European market will create opportunities for economies of scale and corresponding takeovers and amalgamations. As a result of tariff removals, for example, it is evident that there are firms that gain and firms that lose. Some firms will have been valued more highly in the past than they will be once the impact of the single market is understood. Other firms will be valued more highly, once the impact is recognized. They will gain relative to their competitors. Does this mean then that a firm that has a higher price earnings ratio than it will have later, will eventually be the loser and be taken over? Not necessarily. In fact, if it moves faster than stockmarket recognition of what is happening, it is in a position to use its higher price-earnings ratio to take over a firm that has a lower price-earnings ratio than it will have in the future. The about-to-be-disadvantaged firm has the advantage of a takeover target that is likely to improve. That cannot be said for its competitor. The firm about to gain from the change would not want to bid for a competitor that was still overvalued while its own shares remained undervalued. Already, Europe has seen many examples of takeovers by firms that would otherwise have lost had they waited. It would be wrong to conclude, for example, that non-European firms would end up the ultimate losers from formation of the European single market.

Perhaps the strongest reason for studying Euromarketing is that the majority of marketing research and publication has been American. A cultural bias has crept into marketing writings simply because of their predominant focus on things American. More comparative studies would reduce this bias, but comparative research is difficult and expensive. A concentration on Euromarketing will show, through comparisons, where findings do not have international applicability.

There is the possibility, too, that by stepping away from strong U.S. tradition new ideas and concepts will be formed. Research into European marketing that starts with the basic assumption that what the business survivors have done was right, because they have survived, cannot fail to give new insights. It is quite clear that industries have taken different marketing paths in Europe. Retailing in France, for example, has preserved more small stores yet actually led the U.S. in its large hypermarkets. Britain, on the other hand, has so far managed to preserve many of its High Streets. Passenger rail transport in Europe has survived the automobile and airplane. City living has not been killed by suburbia. Restaurants, cafes, and public houses, retain quite different characteristics. Patterns of education and university life are quite unlike the U.S. patterns.

It is not a matter of Europe being behind and the U.S. ahead on marketing. That would be a very naive view of the world. A more sophisticated view is that hundreds of thousands of firms competing for survival in European countries have survived by adjusting to the wishes of their consumers. Their marketing actions have been right. We need to explain how and why.

It is even possible that Europe with its internal groupings of distinct cultures and languages may give some leads to U.S. marketing. The U.S. is clearly moving more toward cultural groupings that are disinclined to integrate and more inclined to communicate in their native language and remain as an identifiable subculture.

Europe also needs more attention as a source of global market innovation. Global *market* leadership in this sense is different from Global *marketing* leadership. There are some products and services which having emerged in one market, spread across the globe into market after market. With its high incomes and grouped social characteristics, it is not unlikely that European markets will continue to lead markets in this way. Debit cards and the French video phone directories are two examples.

Another compelling reason for attention to Euromarketing is that what European marketers do will affect the welfare not only of Europeans but of millions of others outside Europe. Like their foreign competitors, Europe's marketers are trying both to protect their home markets and to supply the markets of other countries. They cannot achieve their aim in all businesses or foreign customers would not have the resources with which to buy. Exactly where they do emerge as leading competitors, however, and the terms on which they do so, are crucial to predict. Do we see a Europe leading in capital goods manufacture, financial services, and branded goods? Or do we see Europe in retail chain ownership, construction, and agriculture? To what extent is innovation in design and operations going to enable Europe with its high wage rates to keep ahead of countries with lower wage rates and rapidly increasing productivity? We all know that John Stuart Mill's concept of comparative advantage is not much help here. Nor are more recent theories of successful country strategies. Careful marketing assessment of country markets and marketing strengths are much more likely to give us reliable pictures of where Europe is heading than are theories with very shallow economic reasoning.

In sum, Euromarketing presents an academic challenge with practical significance –hence this book.

Kenneth Simmonds
Professor of Marketing and International Business
London Business School

Preface

The First Lesson in Forecasting the Well-Being of Continents

Patten (1993) emphasizes that the first lesson in forecasting the wealth of continents is to approach the task with humility. Based on prior predictions for each upcoming century, the common wisdom of intuitive selections of winners and losers turn out to be wrong. For example, Europeans surged with self-confidence in the 1890s: Europe was banker to the world; the national incomes of both the U.K. and Germany were increasing around 50% per decade. The coming twentieth century shone brightest for Europe. Who would have predicted North America to lead in economic well-being for this century? or Europe facing the brunt of two World Wars followed by 50 years of "truce by terror"?

Where Success Is Most Likely To Be Predicted Accurately

We likely will be more accurate in our predictions if we direct them at the middle, not the ends of the spectrum: safer to bet on specific nations (e.g., U.S., Germany, Japan, France, the U.K., and Italy) and industries (e.g., electrotechnologies, pharmaceuticals, space, tourism) rather than continents or enterprises (e.g., General Motors, I.B.M., Volkswagen, Disney World). Focusing our forecasts on the middle diversifies our risk, yet, permits us to cherry-pick the nations likely to continue to do best. More cherries are found in Europe than elsewhere.

"Lester Throw has reminded us that the countries that were the richest a century ago are still by and large the richest today. It is difficult to become rich. Getting into the big time demands a long haul–year after year, decade after decade, of steadily increasing growth rates. And you cannot afford to let your rate of population increase trim too much off your economic growth. Over the past 100 years, Japan grew at an average of 4% a year, almost four times the annual rate of her population increase" (Patten 1993, p. 21). In Europe, Finland grew to more than match this pattern of growth until the nation's 1990s loss of its most favored customer (the U.S.S.R.). Thus, an examination of national success factors, the wealth of nations, and the growth of industries calls our attention to Europe. This continent has seven of the world's top ten trading nations; its four biggest nations (Germany, France, Britain, and Italy) in combined exports and imports more than double the estimated world trading of the U.S.

The Kaynak-Ghauri Proposition

Data on important national success factors support Kaynak and Ghauri's central proposition for this volume, "Europe now is becoming the world's leading economic power, not only because of its size and affluence, but because of its political power and market dynamics" (see Chapter 1). Particularly relevant is the broad, forward momentum caused by the following actions and needs: the creation and implementation of the European Community; the reintroduction of democratic governments and capitalism in Central Europe nations, the developing democracies and economic reforms in Russia and the Ukraine; the continuing slide in population growth; the investments in cross-national, infrastructure projects; the strong cultural, business and government commitment to educating youth and managers in manufacturing/intellectual skills and languages; the widespread industrial adoption of new manufacturing and service technologies; the forging of strong trading links between the EC, EFTA, and Central European nations; and opportunities ahead that must be met in cleaning-up the over 40-years of environmental poisoning of the Eastern-half of the continent. Reading *Euromarketing* is particularly useful for developing knowledge and insights in many of these factors.

Why Read this Book?

By focusing all chapters on European contexts for effective marketing strategies, the editors are able to integrate the chapters effectively, and provide both macro and micro perspectives for making better marketing decisions. The focused coverage helps develop distinct European perspectives for marketing strategies. The help in gaining such a perspective is the best reason for reading the book.

What are the specific actions in implementing new European marketing strategies from the perspectives of executives and policymakers, and most importantly, customers? What are the normative issues, and implications from empirical findings to these issues, for marketing strategies in Europe? These two questions are reference points across the 14 chapters in *Euromarketing*. Each chapter includes answers to one or both of these issues. By answering these questions in substantial depth, the book serves well as a valuable environmental scan for assessing opportunities and threats for Euromarketing strategies.

Arch G. Woodside, PhD
Tulane University

REFERENCE

Patten, Christopher (1993), "Hope and Experience," *The Future Surveyed, The Economist,* September 11-17, 18, 21-22.

Introduction

Euromarketing: Effective Strategies for International Trade and Export was developed to meet the needs of academicians, practitioners, and public policy makers in the discussion of marketing issues pertaining to Europe as a whole. The book promises to increase our understanding of the strategic planning aspects of marketing in enlarged Europe and the planning aspects of the trading relationship between European and foreign firms.

Unified Europe, scheduled to be completed by the end of 1992, does create tremendous market opportunities for firms of all sizes from a variety of regions and countries of the globe. The unified Europe within the confines of the triad–North America, the European Community, and East Asia–will become even more important in the years to come. At present, these three major trading blocs represent 76% of the total world exports and 72% of the total world imports. The North American trading bloc, which consists of the U.S., Canada, and Mexico, accounted for $530 billion (17.7%) of the total world exports and $601 billion (20.7%) of the total world imports. On the other hand, the share of the European Community is $1.12 trillion (37.3%) of the world's exports and $1.21 trillion (38.6%) of the world's imports. Likewise, countries of East Asia account for $629 billion (21%) in exports and $441 billion (15.2%) in imports.

As can be seen, the European Community accounts for a major share of the total world trade. But, besides the EC, there are two other sub-trading blocs within Europe, the European Free Trade Association (EFTA) and East and Central European countries, there have been certain moves toward unifying these three sub-markets into one of an enlarged mega-Europe. So far, an agreement has been signed between the EC and the EFTA which created European Economic Space (EES) and some select number of East and Central European countries on the free movement of goods and services.

Former Socialist countries lacking the necessary infrastructure and capital resources still offer tremendous opportunities for foreign firms. If we also add the three associate EC member countries (Turkey, Cyprus, and Malta) to the European trading block, an enormous inter- and intra-trading relationship pattern emerges.

Single Europe is going to play an increasingly more important role in the global business arena, so the unique position of the bloc is certain to provide fascinating reading material for scholars, teachers, policy makers, researchers, and students of international business and marketing. This volume fosters a conceptual understanding of the European markets and marketing systems, provides analytical insights, and highlights the past, present, and future of European marketing.

This book of readings contains four major sections. In the first section, the coeditors present an integrative statement on European marketing where certain macro issues affecting Euromarketing are examined. Section II is devoted to the description and analysis of Euromarketing strategies in a number of European countries with strategic focus and orientation in mind. Because of its growing importance, Section III is allocated to Euromarketing strategies pertaining to East and Central European countries. The chapters in this section are mostly related to Hungary–the most developed and advanced country among the group, and this country has also had the longest trading relationships with the West. Another interesting characteristic of this section is that important entry strategy joint ventures and strategic alliances are the backbone of the chapters. Finally, Section IV contains chapters which are prognostic in nature. Future directions of marketing in Europe as well as what will happen in Europe after 1992 are highlighted.

During the preparation of this book, the coeditors have received help from many individuals too numerous to mention by name. We, first of all, would like to thank contributors to the volume who, along with their busy work schedules, created the necessary time to develop outstanding chapters. Our special thanks and gratuity go to Bill Cohen–Publisher of The Haworth Press, Inc. and Bill Palmer–Administrative Editor, and Patricia Malone Brown–Assistant Editor for Haworth for helping us so diligently throughout the completion of this project. Our wives and children were a constant source of help and encouragement. Without their backing and sacrifices, it would have been far more difficult to complete this project in a timely fashion.

Needless to say that any omissions or mistakes are the responsibility of the coeditors.

Erdener Kaynak
Hummelstown, Pennsylvania

Pervez N. Ghauri
Oslo, Norway

SECTION I.
INTEGRATIVE STATEMENT
ON EUROPEAN MARKETING

Chapter 1

Current Status of European Marketing: Introduction

Erdener Kaynak
Pervez N. Ghauri

On January 1, 1993 Europe became the largest international market in the world. It has the population and the economic and technological dynamism of an integrated market that allows its industry to organize on a scale big enough to compete with its main rivals in the U.S. and Japan.

During the 1980s, the global economic power was shifting from North America to the Far East. At this time, people were talking about the creation of a Pacific Century. The collapse of communism in Eastern Europe and the former Soviet Union, Western Europe's push toward a unified market and German reunification have all propelled the European continent into the economic limelight. We have witnessed the emergence of the United States of Europe where a shift has taken place from the creation of a Pacific Century to that of an Atlantic Century (see Figure 1.1).

There have been certain changes and developments in world trade and the investment climate during the last decade. The formation of the triad (Japan, U.S. and Europe) creates markets of tremendous importance. Beside a sophisticated European trading bloc, we have technologically advanced Japan and the U.S. with huge market opportunities (see Table 1.1). The formation of the triad of major trading blocs means both rapid development of free trade and rapid evolution of protectionism among blocks. Many of Europe's biggest companies, including most car makers, airlines, and computer firms, are less efficient than the U.S. and Japanese rivals within the triad (Tully, 1991).

3

FIGURE 1.1. Global Trade Map

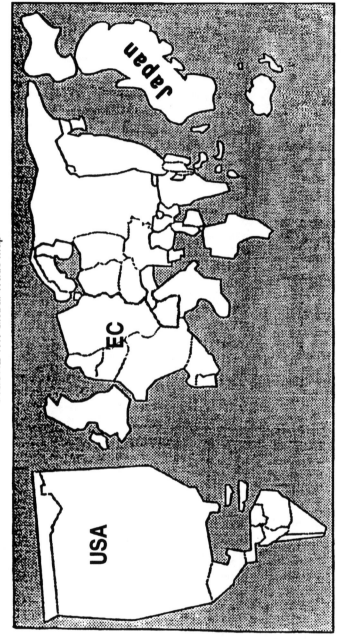

TABLE 1.1. The Triad Profile

The countries Population and Region		GDP ($billion US)	Export ($billion US)	Import ($billion US)
USA	250	5,500	448	599
Japan	125	3,200	310	224
EC	342	4,900	1,200	1,250

This so-called true triad grouping creates 80% of the world's manufacturing production and consumes 67% of the world's manufactured goods. The triad countries produce a surplus of food and produce virtually all of the raw materials they need. A further study of the available statistics indicates the huge potential and the magnitude of the triad. For instance, the U.S. accounts for 5% of the world's population and 32% of its gross domestic product (GDP). Japan accounts for 2% of the world's population but 12% of its GDP. Finally, Europe, which has the largest population base among the triad, accounts for 22% of the GDP of the world.

Within this general triad framework, Europe as a single market has a special place. The boundaries, currently defined by the 12 European Community (EC) members, contain a sprawling block of 342 million spending consumers, and may well expand to include at least 25 countries and 525 million people by the year 2000. If one includes EuroRussia in this picture, an enlarged Europe will offer a market potential of 700 million consumers (see Figure 1.2).

Europe now is becoming the world's leading economic power, not only because of its size and affluence, but because of its political power and market dynamics. The market itself comprises three different sub-markets at different stages of socio-economic, technological and market development (Table 1.2). The EC is forging links with two sub-European markets: The European Free Trade Association (EFTA) and Central Europe's three strongest economies, Hunary, Poland and Czechoslovakia. The seven EFTA countries–Austria, Finland, Iceland, Denmark, Norway, Sweden, and Swit-

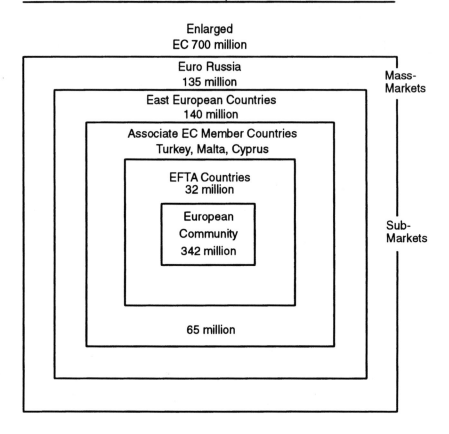

FIGURE 1.2. European Trade Block

zerland–are home to 32 million of the world's most affluent consumers. The EFTA countries have concluded an agreement to start
lifting most trade barriers with EC countries on January 1, 1993.

BACKGROUND OF THE BOOK

During the past decade, researchers, public policy makers and
students of international business and trade have increasingly turned
their attention to strategic planning aspects of international marketing. This is not a surprising move as the majority of firms on both

TABLE 1.2. Europe and Its Sub-Markets

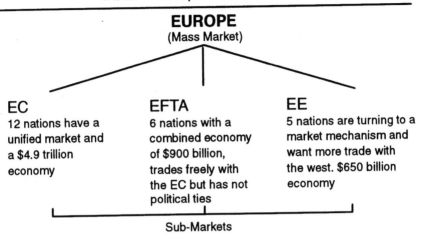

EUROPE
(Mass Market)

EC
12 nations have a
unified market and
a $4.9 trillion
economy

EFTA
6 nations with a
combined economy
of $900 billion,
trades freely with
the EC but has not
political ties

EE
5 nations are turning to a
market mechanism and
want more trade with
the west. $650 billion
economy

Sub-Markets

sides of the Atlantic are increasingly venturing into overseas markets in order to attain their profit and growth objectives. Although a substantial body of research and reading material is now available on the marketing behavior of organizations and the marketing practices of businesses in the international context, strategic planning aspects of international marketing have not yet been studied adequately. Marketing studies dealing with specific regions of the world are very scarce indeed. Whatever is available in the context of a single country, industry or a sector is examining issues in a descriptive or normative manner at best (see Dudley, 1989). Little has, so far, been accomplished in the way of synthesizing the established body of knowledge and offering managerial insights to the practicing international marketing manager by providing him with yardsticks to measure his international marketing performance across nations and in specific regions of the globe. Marketing practices, institutions and processes in various trading blocks have not been studied adequately either.

As it has already been pointed out, at the end of 1992 a single European market has emerged which will offer significant opportunities and threats for European as well as non-European businesses, consumers and public policy makers alike. Already, structuring of European industries has started and this will accelerate at a faster pace in the coming months. In particular, we have already witnessed occurrences such as ASEA-Brown Boveri merger, acquisition of BAT, a series of acquisitions by Electrolux and some mergers of advertising agencies as well as consolidation of power among manufacturing sector participants. Furthermore, we are seeing the powerful presence of giant public sector enterprises and their procurement practices, favoring local and European suppliers. The greatest benefit of EC 1992 is the fact that a manufacturer no longer must have a plant and/or warehouses in almost every country to conform to national product and transportation standards. Hence, companies are consolidating their manufacturing facilities and replacing them with warehouses and centralized highly mechanized distribution centers (Thuermer, 1992).

The emergence of glasnost and perestroika and the collapse of the USSR along with the recent developments in Eastern and Central Europe are creating newer forms of relationships and business practices for European, U.S. and Japanese firms. This, coupled with the increased trade among the triad power of North America, Europe and Japan, is creating further business opportunities and threats for Europe. Within Europe itself inter and intra trading relationships involving EFTA and EC member states as well as the most recent developments in East European countries are conducive to newer forms of business environment where competition and/or cooperation are watchwords for survival and growth. In the face of this imminent competition, firms of all sizes from a variety of countries are forming strategic alliances. Some Japanese companies are investing in various European countries in an effort to have a strong hold in a unified Europe. This is illustrated by Table 1.3.

Although 1992 Europe is in the making of a mass of 342 million European consumers and industrial markets with similar buying and purchasing characteristics, companies will have to pay attention to existing differences among member countries' consumers and purchasers. According to a recently published "The Economist Intelligence Unit" report, what is perhaps needed is a global marketing approach with a local touch. Along with these consumer related developments we will also be seeing drastic changes in product standardization, packaging, strict labelling requirements, quality assurance, pricing and warranties. All of these developments will

TABLE 1.3. Japanese Investments in Europe

Total Investment $ million	Year to March 1988	Year to March 1989	Cumulative total 1951-1989	Number of manufacturing plants
UK	2.473	3.956	10.554	92
Netherlands	829	2.359	5.525	27
Luxembourg	1.764	657	4.729	23
W. Germany	403	409	2.364	67
France	330	463	1.704	85
Switzerland	224	454	1.432	4
Spain	283	161	1.045	41
Belgium	70	164	1.027	23
Ireland	56	42	432	19
Italy	59	106	370	24

Source: *European Affairs,* "The Japanese in Europe," Volume 3, Autumn 1989, p. 98.

have far-reaching implications for research, teaching and practice of marketing as a discipline, not only in Europe but also elsewhere.

CONCEPTUAL FRAMEWORK

The book treats the subject of European marketing in four sections. In Section I an integrative statement is made for European marketing. In the first chapter the coeditors of the volume, Ghauri and Kaynak, set the tone by stating the current status of European marketing. This chapter serves as an introduction and presents a global triad profile. The changes and developments that have taken place in world trade and investment during the last decade are presented. A market of 700 million customers of an enlarged Europe is introduced. A useful comparison between the three blocks is made and Foreign Direct Investment (FDI) into EC by other blocks is highlighted.

In the second chapter, "The Challenges of the European Community (EC) Industrial Policy," Cecilia Andersen discusses the steps taken by the EC commission with respect to industrial policy. Further, the chapter relates their policy measures to electronic and information technology industry in Europe. Finally, it analyzes the expectations of the EC as regards this industrial policy. The purpose of the chapter is to make business executives understand these policy measures and how they can influence their business activities. The chapter particularly discusses the implications of the Treaty on European Union negotiated at Maastricht by the representatives of member states. The impact on industrial policy, trans-European networks, research and technological development, education and training are specifically discussed.

Chapter 3, "The European Internal Market: Between Scylla and Charybdis?" by Bert Piëst and Henk Ritsema, questions the normal proposition that establishment of an internal market would cause increased competition within EC. Moreover, the view that the most suitable strategy for EC is to produce standardized products is also challenged. The authors then present an interesting framework for strategies in the internal market. They profess that companies in the internal market may follow different strategies and still be successful. Finally, they present and discuss different strategies available to companies in the internal market.

In Section II, "Euromarketing Strategies: Western Europe," the coeditors again set the scene by providing the first Chapter (Chapter 4) on "Consumer Behavior and Marketing Issues in the Europe of Post-1992." The objective of this chapter is to examine and evaluate the implications of concepts and theories of consumer behavior on U.S.-based corporate product strategy as they are prepared to exploit the opportunities offered by the Europe of 1992. The chapter includes a review of the European environment and its recent history, its consumers, and its suppliers. This chapter also deals with the question of whether we would see a homogeneous mass market. The chapter concludes the discussion by providing suggestions for successfully managing this portentous transformation.

Chapter 5 by Peter S. H. Leeflang and Charles P. de Mortanges, "Marketing Planning and 1992: Observations and Expectations," addresses the ambivalent situation of "euphoria" and states that irrespective of the outcome of 1992, marketing planning will be influenced. The authors therefore present a framework of the strategic marketing planning process. This six-step process of marketing planning is discussed and analyzed in relevance to generic competitive strategies. This chapter believes that competition in a single European market will be intensified and it would provide strategies for the manipulation of marketing decision variables.

Chapter 6, "A Model for Defensive Marketing Strategy with Examples from the Europe 1992 Context" by Calantone, di Benedetto, and Harvey presents the use for a decision model designed to help marketing managers assess the effects of offensive and defensive marketing strategies. Its use in simple repositioning strategies and in revolutionary product innovation is discussed. The model is claimed to be applicable to oligopolistic scramble in the "single" European market of 1992 and is illustrated using empirical evidence.

In Chapter 7, Gianluigi Guido treats "Marketing Mix Strategies in the Europe of Post-1992." He claims that changes in national regulations and standards will force firms to evaluate the increased opportunities and competition in their market segments. The author states that in planning a common market program, marketers should be aware of certain factors emerging from EC directives and from the marketing environment which could threaten their Pan-European strategies. The chapter discusses the problems likely to be encountered in relation to marketing mix strategies.

Riccardo Varaldo and Andrea Piccaluga present the challenge of a mix between global and local marketing strategies in Chapter 8. They claim that the competition of the European single market gives birth to a new competitive framework which will put European as well as non-European firms in front of new challenges. According to them, the single market will become more accessible but not more similar than before 1993. The most important decision for the marketers would be those of penetration and expansion strategies and global and local marketing activities.

In Section III, Chapter 9, "East and Central European Marketing: 1992 and Beyond" by Gabor Hovanyi, presents an Eastern European perspective from Hungary. The effects of the new economic condition of EC after 1992 on the marketing efforts of the East European countries are considered as risk factors. The chapter analyzes the present economic situation and suggests measures to reduce these risk factors. Finally the chapter also discusses the opportunities of EC companies in the East European market. The plans of the Hungarian government for 1992 are also discussed and analyzed.

Chapter 10 by Hisrich and Jones examines how the significant coverage of the dramatic events of the past few years in Eastern, Central Europe and the former Soviet Union has elevated interest in doing business in these areas on the part of business people, government officials, and consumers alike. The importance of this activity to both the once-controlled economies and to Western companies cannot be overstated. One mechanism for achieving this business activity–joint ventures–is the focus of this chapter. All aspects of U.S. joint venture activity in Hungary are examined as a potentially good mechanism for entering into former Socialist countries.

Chapter 11 by Arch Woodside and József Kandikó, "Decision Processes in Strategic Alliances: Designing and Implementing International Joint Ventures in Eastern Europe," addresses the use of a micro-analytical data collection method: decision systems analysis. It is used for mapping decision processes in designing and implementing two international joint ventures. Theoretical propositions for explaining international joint ventures and motivations are suggested based on the reported observations of the decision processes and the work of Kogut (1988), Ohmae (1989) and others.

In the final section, Chapter 12, "Fortress Europe: Which Industries Are Most Vulnerable?" by Trina L. Larsen and Robert T. Green, presents a very useful analysis on the industry level. This chapter is particularly important as it deals with a level not normally addressed by business people and researchers. Most other studies, in this volume and elsewhere, deal either with the company or with the country policies and strategies towards European integration. Here the most vulnerable industries are ranked with viable arguments and reasoning.

In Chapter 13, "A Normative Framework for Assessing Marketing Strategy Implications of Europe 1992" by Subhash C. Jain and John K. Ryans Jr., implications of a single European market are considered to change marketing dramatically in Western Europe. The chapter discusses the implication from the viewpoint of non-EC companies. A framework identifying the underlying variables is developed. Moreover, an agenda for future research on regional market integration is proposed.

Finally, in Chapter 14 the coeditors synthesize the existing body of knowledge relating to the current state of affairs on Euro-marketing. They further prognose likely occurrences and developments which are expected to take place in Europe beyond 1992. In particular, they present the forthcoming threats and opportunities for EC-member as well as non-member companies. In the final section of this chapter some managerial implications for the companies and managers are also presented. They claim that although it is difficult to forecast the patterns of competition which would finally emerge, the managers cannot just sit and wait for these new realities to emerge. This chapter also provides a number of examples of EC-member as well as non-EC-member companies and their strategies to cope with the post 1992 market. It is concluded that speed as regards to innovations and new product development is going to be very crucial. Moreover, it is claimed that a need for a new type of manager–"Euro manager" or "global manager"–is becoming apparent. This new manager would not have any nationality, would be internationally educated, would have lived in diverse environments and would speak at least 2-3 languages.

BIBLIOGRAPHY

Dudley, James W. 1989. 1992 Strategies for the Single Market. Kogan Page, London.

Kogut, Bruce. 1988. Joint Ventures: Theoretical and Empirical Perspectives. *Strategic Management Journal*, (9): 319-332.

Milmo, Sean. 1990. EFTA/EC Negotiations May Expand Europe's '92 Plans. *Business Marketing* (February): 22.

Ohmae, Kenichi. 1989. Managing in a Borderless World. *Harvard Business Review*, 67 (May-June): 152-161.

Rowley, Anthony. 1989. On to the Drawbridge. *Far Eastern Economic Review* (May 18): 68.

Thuermer, Karen E. 1992. Ready, Set, Go Pan-European. *Global Trade*, 112(1): 30-32.

Tully, Shawn. 1991. Now The New Europe. *Fortune*, 122(13): 136-137.

Wills, Gordon. 1991. Does the Single Market Influence National Marketing Thinking? *European Business Review*, 91(1): 5-10.

Chapter 2

The Challenges of the European Community (EC) Industrial Policy

Cecilia Andersen

INTRODUCTION

In the context of the realization of the European Community 1992 initiatives outlined in the Commission White Paper of 1985, the Commission is also taking important steps with respect to industrial policy. These initiatives can be expected to have an impact upon the global competitive position of European business and may even affect the business activities of companies located outside the European Community.

This chapter deals with:

- The content of the 1990 Commission Communication on the industrial policy in an open and competitive environment;
- The application of these guidelines by the Commission to the Electronics and Information Technology industry;[1]
- The effects of the guidelines on the content of the Treaty on European Union;
- Expectations for the industrial policy of the Community.

The purpose is to make business executives understand what they can expect of the Community and to provide them with the information necessary to take advantage of EC measures that support the development of business activities.

---

1. The chapter uses information contained in: Andersen, C. (1992). *Influencing the EC: Guidelines for a Successful Business Strategy.* Kogan Page. London.

THE COMMUNITY INDUSTRIAL POLICY
FOR THE NINETIES

In advance of the achievement of the 1992 objectives, the Community had already laid the foundations for the further development of the European business environment by determining the outline of the Community industrial policy for the nineties. The framework described applies to European as well as foreign companies doing business in the EC and may, on occasion, affect non-EC markets. Industrial policy involves all policies of the state in relation to industry. These may include both policies that intervene in industry or those that seek to minimize intervention. Both approaches can be simultaneously pursued. The European Round Table of Industrialists defines industrial policy as: "a set of measures designed to ensure that industry has the environment it requires to develop in an orderly fashion in the face of competition."[2]

The Commission document is a balance of interventionist and non-interventionist proposals that represent a compromise between the supporters of each approach. It was debated by the European Parliament and adopted by the Council of Ministers. As such it is not Community Legislation but a declaration of intent with regard to future actions.[3]

The Commission document outlines very precisely its role in the European business environment.

1. An open and competitive environment is necessary for business to operate in.
2. It is the responsibility of business to be sensitive to the market and to react to its signals.
3. As such the Community is eager to help industry but will not take measures in any sector which might hinder market led structural adjustment.
4. The Community will try to eradicate superfluous bureaucratic regulation.

---

2. European Round Table of Industrialists, Reshaping Europe. Brussels, 1991.
3. Commission of the European Communities, "Industrial Policy in an Open and Competitive Environment." COM (90) 556-final.

5. The Community will consult with representatives of industry at the earliest stages of future proposals. These will include representatives of SMEs as well as those of large firms in special sectors.
6. These consultations should help European policy makers to address issues important to industry correctly.
7. Consumer groups and employees' representatives will also be consulted.

The Commission has selected a set of macro-economic objectives:

a. The continued growth of world and Community-wide competition;
b. A more stable international trade environment;
c. Greater exploitation by firms of the market potential of developing countries;
d. Heightened environmental concern;
e. The development of Central and Eastern Europe;
f. Dealing with the social difficulties posed by the aging of the European population.

To achieve these aims European industry must develop:

a. Global corporate strategies;
b. An ability to keep abreast of international industrial competition. This will require investment in human capital and the adoption of high-paced structural change;
c. The ability to generate sufficient financial resources by maintaining levels of profitability;
d. Wide innovative capacities in business;
e. A better balance between supply and demand for goods and services to facilitate the diffusion of technological innovations;
f. A capacity to foresee and develop the human resources skills needed to meet technological advances and their related new ways of organizing work.

The Community means its measures to have a stimulatory and coherent effect on the business environment. The paper recognizes five prerequisites for structural adjustment and outlines two catalysts and four accelerators to help achieve it.

The Five Prerequisites for Change

1. A strict competition policy;
2. A stable economic environment and fiscal policies favorable to business;
3. A continued high level of education;
4. Economic and social cohesion;
5. Strong environmental protection.

Competition Policy

Tight restraints on large monopolies and state aids are necessary. The negative effects of concentrations will be assessed relative to the particular market on which competition is to be maintained and this need not be limited to the community market. State aids will be closely monitored to ensure that they do not hinder structural adjustment. Currently the four largest member states account for 88% of all aid granted. The Commission hopes to reduce the concentration of aid in the more prosperous areas to allow aid in poorer regions to proportionately represent a significant contribution to regional development. Sectoral aids will also be strictly controlled. The Commission hopes that non-member states will follow its lead away from state subsidies.

A Stable Economic Environment

The establishment of a stable economic environment has allowed for industrial recovery and for prices to reflect the markets more clearly. But fiscal policies should now try both to lower the cost of funds for investment and increase their availability. Special measures are required by member states with respect to the fiscal treatment of depreciation and retained earnings.

High Levels of Education

To remain an advanced economy and to cope with its cultural diversity, the EC needs the human resources to develop and assimilate new technologies and organizational methods. The Community and member states must promote the necessary lifelong market-oriented research and training.

Economic and Social Cohesion

This will be encouraged by:

a. Supporting the adjustment of less favored regions to the single market through the Community's structural funds;
b. Consulting and informing employees at all levels of responsibility within enterprises so as to stimulate receptiveness to change;
c. Providing sufficient social protection to soften the effects of changes;
d. Supporting innovative working habits (such as flexible working hours) that facilitate adjustment to changing market conditions and improvements in working conditions.

Strong Environmental Protection

As the current market becomes increasingly environmentally sensitive, a competitive edge is to be had by holding a leading position in the field of environmental protection. The Commission will help European industry obtain this competitive advantage by proposing standards of protection that are both predictable and stable. These standards, however, should permit that:

a. European firms be still able to compete with their international competitors after having complied with strict EC environmental standards;
b. Competitive conditions in the internal market be maintained by raising EC standards to equal the most stringent found in any member state;

c. Industry be still able to produce on a sufficient scale to be viable and amortise the required investments.

The Catalysts

The two principal catalysts for adjustment are the internal market and the commercial policy of the Community.

The Internal Market

This program amounts to an industrial policy in its own right because it aims to establish a home market of the size and quality required by European industry. The Community hopes to achieve this mainly through its activities in respect of:

a. Standards and product quality
b. Public procurement
c. The abolition of national quotas
d. The legal framework for business
e. Trans-European networks

Standards and Product Quality

The Community must set standards of a high technical nature that are compatible with international standards. But the objective of an open internal market is served by technical harmonization which confines legislation to the essential requirements to which products must comply so as to protect public health, safety, the environment, and the consumer. This limitation and standardization will serve to evade the erection of technical barriers.

Voluntary European standards, worked out by the European standard setting bodies in collaboration with business now provide manufacturers with a set of technical specifications recognized in each directive as giving a presumption of conformity to the essential requirements. Well worked out standards lead to greater competitiveness. They lower costs for producers, make customers more familiar with particular products and open new markets, especially for developing new technologies. But to achieve these benefits the standards must be implemented at the national level and inspection and testing be done as much as possible before or during production.

Public Procurement

The Commission will monitor the public procurement policies of member states more closely. This is vital as total public procurement is estimated at ECU 600 billion, that is, 16% of GDP in 1987. It accounts for 30% of all sales of power generation equipment, computers and office machinery, 50% of sales of aerospace equipment and 90% of sales of railway rolling stock and telecommunications equipment.

However, despite its importance, public procurement remains very closed. For the larger member states, average market penetration by imports is around 20%. In certain sectors this can be as low as 4% or even 1% in some cases. Community rules dictating that certain public supply contracts be awarded on a non-discriminatory basis have clearly not been effective, as only about 2% of contracts have been awarded to companies from other member states.

The Community has therefore amended the 1977 Directive which applies to all public supply contracts above certain thresholds. The main threshold of the amended Directive is ECU 200,000. The Directive provides for three procedures in descending order of openness:

a. The open procedure: tenders are open to all interested parties;
b. The restricted procedure: suppliers are invited to tender;
c. The negotiated procedure: contracting authorities contact suppliers of their choice and negotiate with them.

The open procedure must become the norm.

The council has further adopted an Enforcement Directive in 1989. Member states must create review procedures for the speedy examination of alleged infringements before the award of the contract. The commission can call for such a review before the award of the contract if it feels that there has been a "clear and manifest infringement" of the rules.

The Council of Ministers has reached a common position on the extension of the public procurement rules to the previously excluded sectors of water, energy, transport and telecommunications, but only for contracts above certain higher thresholds. The Directive to follow will apply not only to contracting entities which are public authorities or public undertakings, but also to private sector firms which have been granted special or exclusive rights. The Directive will be complemented with an enforcement Directive.

National Quotas

Member states still operate over two thousand national quotas on imports from third countries and use bilateral "voluntary export restrictions" to shield their industry from third country imports. This is particularly so in the automobile, textile, toy, porcelain and chemical sectors. To complete the internal market it is necessary that such measures are removed. This may lead to horizontal support measures but not to protective strategies and subsidies.

The Legal Framework for Business

The Commission will take the necessary steps to ensure:

a. Harmonization and reform of taxation legislation to eliminate the main obstacles to cooperation and restructuring of enterprises across frontiers posed by diverse tax systems;
b. The development of European legal instruments for firms so that they can choose the most appropriate legal form given their size and need. Firms can then avoid the legal and practical constraints of twelve different legal systems;
c. The protection of intellectual property by the provision of a Community patent system and adequate rules for the protection of intellectual property and data protection.

Trans-European Networks

The Commission urges the development of greater trans-European networking to create the missing links between existing national systems and permit the free movement of goods and people in a European economic area. Railroad systems, national energy distribution systems, and telecommunications networks need to become more integrated. Pre-normative research work on system integration should lead to common methodological and standards bases. Training networks between universities, firms and research centers should give rise to an international system of training.

The Commercial Policy of the Community

The Community trade policy will seek to ensure openness through vigilance. Agreed international rules will be rigorously enforced. But such an approach by the Community requires the equal compliance of its trading competitors. A successful completion of the GATT Uruguay Round should lead to better international trade rules and improved international trade relations. The rules of anti-dumping need to be clear and exacting. The Community has vowed to consistently apply them.

The Accelerators

The Commission will aim to accelerate adjustment by measures that:

1. Develop the technological capacity of the Community;
2. Promote small and medium size enterprises;
3. Improve the use of human resources;
4. Support the development of a lively and competitive business services sector.

THE TECHNOLOGICAL CAPACITY OF THE COMMUNITY

The Commission support is to entail integrated measures to:

a. Promote precompetitive projects;
b. Make available basic research results to small and medium sized enterprises;
c. Allow the full enjoyment of the benefits flowing from an open market;

d. Heighten the level of training especially through specialized centers of education.

Support for Small and Medium Enterprises (SMEs)

The Community supports the creation and survival of SMEs. The Community promotes their operation by providing tailored information and business services. It further stimulates cooperation between firms through various schemes.

Human Resources

The looming skills shortages and the much faster rate of innovation make the versatility and quality of human capital a key determinant of industrial competitiveness. Vocational training and more efficient redeployment through retraining should allow for a better use of the Community workforce. It is the responsibility of business to respond to this need by systems of continuous training and the Community shall support such endeavors.

Business Services

The Commission aims to complete an open Community-wide market for the business services sector to allow for competition and dynamism. Such an internal market for the financial services sector will result in cost savings to industry.

Ensuring Coherence and Effectiveness

Coordinator. The Community can be relied upon by business to take the initiative when it feels that action on a Community level would be the most efficient approach. With the completion of the internal market, many markets relevant to firms will no longer correspond to national boundaries. The Commission will seek to identify very carefully the correct mix of Community, national, or regional initiatives to meet these ever-changing market circumstances. In this way the Community may coordinate a varied and flexible policy.

Alignment of Policies with the Community Industrial Policy. The Commission will oppose strongly any sectoral policies of an interventionist kind. They are not considered to promote structural adaptation. However, the Commission will countenance policies for specific sectors such as telecommunications, IT, aeronautics, and the maritime industry, as long as they conform to the spirit of the industrial policy of the Community. Special policies may also be acceptable in the areas of joint research and training as they tend to support rather than hinder industrial competitiveness.

Inspire Coherent Global Strategies. The intention is that the industrial policy will inspire European companies to develop coherent global strategies and strengthen their internal and external competitiveness. This, it is expected, will lead to international investment, especially in Central and Eastern Europe. Business must also use the regional diversity of the Community. A competitive advantage is to be gained by the exploitation of under-utilized regional resources through appropriate specialization.

The Application of the Guidelines to the European Electronics and Information Technology Industry

The Commission document has been followed by a series of specific sectoral papers on the European electronics and IT industry, biotechnology, maritime industries, and telecommunications.[4] These progressively develop a body of rules for relations between the Community and business. These rules apply equally to foreign companies operating in the Community.[5]

The Requirements of the European Electronics and IT Industries

A special Commission Communication is provided on the electronics and IT industries in recognition of their importance. This importance derives both from their size (world-wide turnover of

---

4. Commission of the European Communities. "The European Electronics and Information Technology Industry: State of Play, The Issues at Stake and Proposals for Actions." SEC (91) 565-final.
5. Ibid.

ECU 700 billion in 1990 and Community wide turnover of ECU 175 million) and their role as enabling industries, providing other sectors with the now vital resource, "information." We may divide IT products and services into three main categories:

1. Components which are the basis of any electronic equipment or system;
2. Computers, consisting of hardware, peripherals (discs, printers, screens, etc.), and software;
3. Office and industrial automation applications; consumer electronics.

Demand in Europe for electronics and IT products is growing apace. It stood for a quarter of world demand in 1984, rising to a third in 1989. Forecasts for the year 2000 are for sustained growth in demand of 11% for active components, 11% for computers, and 4% for consumer electronics. The European electronics and IT industry has reached an annual growth rate of approximately 15%. Turnover jumped from ECU 55 billion in 1984 to ECU 150 billion in 1989. It now represents nearly 5% of GDP in Europe. This compares with 5.5% in Japan and 6.2% in the United States.[6]

However, European demand outstrips European supply. This is largely due to Japanese and American domination of the world production in key sectors. In the area of semiconductors Japan has 49.5% of the share of production, the U.S. 36.5% and Europe only 10%. In computer peripherals Japan has 40% of world production and Europe 15%. In consumer electronics American firms control 60% of world production and European firms merely 20%. Computer production in Europe only satisfies 2/3 of the home market demand and 60% is produced by American based firms.

The consequence is a trade deficit which has widened since 1980. The deficit was ECU 31 billion for electronics as a whole, due chiefly to the need for components. The deficit for computers was ECU 15.5 billion, and for consumer electronics, ECU 9.6 billion.

The Commission considers that European firms must:

---

6. Ibid.

a. Overcome traditional limitations in the European Market;
b. Spend more on research and development;
c. Implement global strategies.

The Segmentation of the European Markets

The absence of an open European market leaves business with badly fragmented markets. These limit the economies of scale causing European firms to have higher production costs than their competitors. The affect is both current and cumulative. Small networks, few users and differing proprietary standards and systems give rise to captive national demand, thus curtailing the exploitation of network externality benefits. This reduces the ability of firms to meet the costs of developing new products and services to meet the markets' demands. However, the opening of standards and systems means more competition and therefore a fall in profits. Simultaneously there is a rise in costs because old and new generation equipment need to be serviced at the same time.

Research and Development Difficulties

Slow Market Reactions

European consumers are cautious and prefer to see new technologies accepted elsewhere in the world before investing in them. The lack of sufficient innovative users relative to the U.S. or Japan has meant that European firms are seldom the first to come on the market with new products. They thus fail to enjoy the profits generated by the high prices put on new successful products that can fund research towards the next generation of products.

Capital

The European financial markets are also more cautious than the American or Japanese. The financial institutions do not easily invest in high-risk operations or start-ups. Capital is therefore more expensive and harder to come by for European firms than for their competitors and this is reflected by the figures. European firms now equal the spending of Japanese and American firms in relation to their turnover, but it is significant that the ECU 14 billion (1989) total investment expenditure of the seven largest European firms was much lower than that of the six largest Japanese firms (ECU 22 billion) and the seven largest American firms (ECU 20 billion).

Human Resources

Europe lacks engineers and researchers with up-to-date training in the production, adaptation, or even use of leading-edge technologies. Firms cannot find enough qualified personnel to develop new products, nor sufficiently qualified users to buy them.

Industrial Diversity

Large American and Japanese firms maintain low costs and inspire diversity of approach by purchasing many of the components from other smaller firms. By contrast, European firms have produced all their components themselves at the cost of efficiency–the internal demand of a firm never equalling that of the whole market. Japanese groups such as Toshiba, Hitachi, NEC and Fujitsu are simultaneously amongst the top ten world producers of two or even three segments of the components-IT-consumer electronics chain.

Global Strategies

Japanese and American companies take from the global market to fill gaps in basic expertise, financing for research or technological innovation. By contrast, European firms face greater competition at home and lack the resources for similar aggressive global acquisition strategies. They are consequently faced with grave difficulties.

The Proposals of the Commission

The Commission considers that it is for business to take the initiative to adapt new corporate strategies, pool resources, become complementary and form alliances while respecting Community rules. The Commission in its sector paper states that it will support such efforts and, if necessary, will ask member states for a further extension of Community powers to permit effective action.

The outline given of actions to be taken by the Commission is still very vague and in need of elucidation. They deal with:

a. Demand stimulation through trans-European networks–The proper functioning of the internal market requires the linkage of various national networks. Member states, it is suggested, could invest in computerized links between their administrations with high levels of operative integration. Modern networks could arise in the areas of computerized telecommunications, infrastructures for distance learning, transport, public health and the protection of the environment. The Commission can help with planning but the financing will have to be found by the parties concerned.

b. Research and technological development (R&TD)–Research expenditure is lower in Europe than in the U.S. or Japan and such research as does occur suffers from a lack of coordination causing reduplication. The Community can help industry by targeting its support to obtain European improvement with respect to software, computer integrated manufacturing (CIM) and engineering, microelectronics, high performance computing and telecommunications.

c. European managers need to acquire multi-disciplinary technological and information technology skills. To this end, the Commission will augment programs such as COMETT (Community Action Programme in Education for Technology) and DELTA (Developing European Learning through Technological Advance). The best possible use of the 450, 000 research workers in Europe must be stimulated by (1) Networking research centers, laboratories and institutions. (2) Placing emphasis on basic research in the fields of pure science and its technological application, and social and human sciences which will impact most upon European competitiveness.

d. External relations–The Community must have (1) an open multilateral trade system, (2) Access to the markets of main trading partners, (3) Fair competition in international markets, (4) International co-operation on standardization and on new topics such as intelligent manufacturing systems (IMS).

The Community must realize and business exploit the opportunities resulting from (1) the integration of European markets with the

EFTA and East European markets and (2) restructuring aid for Central and Eastern European countries.

The competition powers of the Commission can help protect the global interests of European firms. It is the opinion of the Commission that equal competitive conditions do not exist for all companies operating in the world market. For example, the Japanese economic and political systems structurally protect their consumer electronics industry by ensuring close cooperation between public authorities and industry. There also is strong horizontal and vertical integration of industrial groups, banks and distribution networks. The Commission views also the massive orders for high tech equipment, expensive R&D programs and discrimination against foreign firms effected by the U.S. government as amounting to protection of its national industry.

Foreign companies may also be using dominant positions to breach EC rules. For example, very large companies may use their wide range of activities in the electronics sector to cross-subsidize certain products and activities so as to undercut competitors and gain market shares. The Commission plans to investigate the activities of main competitors of Community firms and if necessary put pressure on the national authorities of such firms to curb their practices. The anti-dumping procedure, although seen as a last resort, has been used for several electronics and IT products such as semiconductors, photocopiers, printers, video recorders and television receivers.

The Business Environment

The business environment ought to be improved by (1) talks between public authorities, banks and financial institutions to diversify European systems of financing, (2) more rapid European standardization and the integration of these standards into products, (3) greater development of electronics and IT through the structural policies used for the development of less prosperous regions. This could allow new markets to emerge and improve the competitive performance of industrial centers in countries such as Portugal.

European industry reacted positively, but cautiously to the Commission paper. It was generally felt that such a paper was encouraging but clearly of no use unless it led to concrete action. Their wariness seems well founded given the ensuing strong disagreement as to what actions were appropriate between the Commission, member states and industry. For example, France does not support the official non-interventionist stance of the Commission but instead favors a policy of positive intervention on the part of the Community to bolster the flagging European electronics industry. The decisions of the Maastricht Conference will no doubt affect the ongoing debate.

The Content of the Treaty on European Union (Maastricht)

The intentions of the Commission are now reinforced by certain important innovations agreed upon under the Treaty on European Union at Maastricht by the representatives of the member states. The relevant innovations are those on (1) industrial policy, (2) trans-European networks, (3) research and technological development and (4) education and training.

Industrial Policy

The new Title XIV (industry) of the Treaty stipulates that the Community will ensure that necessary competitive conditions exist for industry within the Community. The Community will concentrate its action upon:

a. Hastening industry's adjustment to structural changes;
b. Encouraging a favorable environment to initiative and the development of undertakings throughout the Community, particularly of SMEs;
c. Obtaining the improvement of current innovation research and technological development policies in industry.

The member states and the Commission shall consult each other and collaborate. The Commission may take all the appropriate initiatives to promote this coordinated effort. The Community must support the stated objectives by the policies and activities pursued under other provisions of the Treaty but the Council of Ministers can, acting unanimously, on a proposal of the Commission, after consulting the European Parliament and the Economic and Social

Committee, decide on certain specific measures in support of action taken in member states.

Due to strong differences it was not easy to have this Title included in the Treaty. To assuage non-interventionists a compromise was obtained whereby the Title ends with the statement that the Title does not provide a basis for the introduction by the Community of any measure likely to distort competition. A strict interpretation of this could severely limit the effect of the Title.

Trans-European Networks

The Union Treaty states that the Community shall aid the establishment and development of trans-European networks in the areas of transport, telecommunications and energy infrastructures. Within an open internal market, action by the Community will aim to promote the linkage and interoperability of national networks and access to those networks. Special attention shall be paid to the need to connect island, landlocked and peripheral regions with the central regions of the Community.

The Community must clearly elucidate the objectives, priorities and broad lines of the measures envisaged. These guidelines must identify projects of common interest. The Community must also implement any measures which may be necessary to ensure the inter-operability of the networks, particularly in the field of technical standardization.

These projects of common interest identified in the guidelines can be supported by the Community but financed by the member states. This may involve financing for feasibility studies, loan guarantees or interest rate subsidies. The new Cohesion Fund (to be established no later than December 31, 1993) is to support projects in the field of the environment and trans-European networks and can also help finance projects in the area of transport infrastructure. The Community must in such cases judge the economic viability of the proposed projects.

It is the task of member states to coordinate policies affecting the promotion of trans-European networks and the Commission may actively ensure that this occurs. The Community may also choose to work with third countries to promote mutually beneficial projects or to secure the operational integration of the networks when appropriate.

Research and Technological Development

The policy of the EC is to encourage firms, research centers and universities in their work and to help firms fully exploit the internal market, especially by opening national public contracts, harmonizing standards and clearing away legal and fiscal obstacles to cooperation. The main innovation of the Union Treaty is that the multiannual framework programs used for this purpose shall be adopted through the new co-decision procedure but based upon unanimous agreement of member states. This procedure places greater importance upon the European Parliament. The program is carried out by such instruments as ESPRIT (European Strategic Programme for Research and Development in IT) and RACE (Research and Development in Advanced Communications Technologies for Europe). These two programs benefit from large EC funding. In the future, the procedure for adoption of such programs will require a qualified majority in the Council of Ministers (54 votes out of 76) in consultation with the European Parliament. The Community may also, by unanimous vote and in consultation with the European Parliament, set up joint companies or any other structure needed for Community research, technological development and demonstration programs. The Commission shall report each year to the European Parliament and the Council of Ministers on its progress with respect to research and development.

Education and Training

The Community is to develop quality education by urging cooperation between the member states and supporting this action. However, it must respect both the responsibility of Member States for the content of teaching and "their cultural and linguistic diversity." The Community action shall aim at:

a. Developing a European aspect to education (in particular through language teaching);

b. encouraging the mobility of students and teachers;
c. promoting cooperation between educational institutions;
d. organizing exchanges of information on educational experience;
e. encouraging educational exchanges;
f. supporting distance education;
g. cooperating with third countries;
h. adopting incentive measures.

The Community will also take action in the field of vocational training to bolster the action of the member states while still respecting their autonomy with regard to content. The idea is to:

a. Facilitate adaptation to industrial change;
b. Allow access to vocational training and encourage mobility;
c. Inspire cooperation between training establishments and firms and to develop information exchanges.

CONCLUSION

The need for an effective Community industrial policy is a natural consequence of the 1992 European Community thrust. European industry is increasingly aware of not only the challenges but also the dangers that face their operations as a result of the realization of the internal market. The changes of the European Union Treaty show a recognition by the member states of the perils. Private industry must make its own painful adjustment to the single market within a competitive and dynamic environment. It must face the dangers and not be protected by interventionist policies which will merely foster weakness. The Community can contribute to this by making sure that its R&D expenditures, while remaining focused on pre-competitive research, pursue further the development of new technologies which all industry can exploit. Its funding of vocational training can also be guided more towards the retraining of workers in industrys in need of restructuring. The Community will at the same time need to ensure that the openness enjoyed on the European markets by foreign firms is matched by equal freedom of access to foreign markets so that the global trade environment may be free, competitive, and fair.

Chapter 3

The European Internal Market: Between Scylla and Charybdis?

Bert Piëst
Henk Ritsema

INTRODUCTION

Presently, companies in the European Community may still have to forgo certain market opportunities. Technical standards and products norms, for instance, may vary considerably between the member states. The consequence for companies is that they have to adjust their products and practices to the legal requirements of each of the countries involved. This in turn may result in relatively high costs for research and development (R&D) and a diminishing potential for taking advantage of large scale production.

At the end of 1992 there were no longer supposed to be any trade barriers between the member states of the European Community. According to the "White Paper" of the European Commission (1985), this internal market would have to be accomplished by the end of 1992. Some 280 measures proposed by the Commission would have to result in a free European Community market. It is frequently assumed that the completion of the internal market will change the structure of competition in industries and will urge companies to reconsider their strategies (Daems, 1990; Franko, 1989; Hunsicker, 1989; Kaikati, 1989; Mitchell, 1989; Quelch, Buzzel and Salama, 1990; Vandermerwe, 1989).

Discussions with regard to the internal market seem to point in the direction of a specific type of strategy to be pursued in this "new" market: exploiting the benefits of large-scale production and offering products at a lower price than competitors (Calingaert, 1989; Cecchini, 1988; Emerson, 1988; Higgins and Santalainen, 1989). Although such a strategy might make sense, there is also reason to believe that alternative courses of action should be taken into consideration as well. Without doubt there are a significant number of changes materializing within the European Community. Companies are actually in a process of reviewing their strategies. It is, however, a misunderstanding to believe that all or most of the changes that are taking place can be directly related to the completion of the internal market. Many of the changes have little or nothing to do with Europe 1992, as the internal market is generally referred to.

In this paper it is suggested that Europe 1992 is of minor significance for the majority of companies. This is not to say that companies do not have to reconsider their strategies. Companies have to adapt their strategies to new circumstances. It is only meant to say that many of the strategic changes are not a direct result of the completion of the internal market. A framework is presented which allows management to identify whether or not competition in their industry will substantially increase in Europe 1992. Promising strategies and their vulnerability for the completion of the internal market are presented.

THE EFFECTS OF MARKET INTEGRATION

It is often suggested that the completion of the internal market will induce a series of integration effects which will promote the efficiency of Community firms and will force firms to compete on prices. The line of reasoning is as follows (Emerson, 1988; Cecchini, 1988). The removal of non-tariff barriers results directly in the reduction of initial costs (costs related to, for instance, completing documents at the borders). But additional mechanisms are set in motion by the barriers being removed: the constraints imposed on economic activity by the small size of markets are removed and at the same time, the spur for competition is increased. The mechanism by which the removal of barriers influences the economy, as developed by Emerson, (1988) is shown in Figure 3.1. The economic effects can be divided into at least two categories:

- lower costs resulting from economies of scale, made possible by the larger volume of output and by restructuring processes;
- the pressure of competition on prices should lead to a reduction in price cost margin and to incentives for firms to increase their technical efficiency by minimizing their costs so as to maintain their margins.

In other words, it is assumed that the completion of the internal market will force companies to exploit the potentials for cost reduction as a result of the economies of scale that are made possible by the opening of markets. It is also assumed that international exposure means increased international competition and that the consequences of increased competition will first show up in prices. Price levels vary considerably between member states (cars sold in the Netherlands, for instance, are considerably more expensive than in Germany). It is therefore assumed that firms will be encouraged to reduce their margins to the levels imposed by competition and do something about their costs.

CHALLENGING THE ASSUMPTIONS BEHIND EUROPE 1992

Without doubt firms will face severe competition as a consequence of the completion of the internal market. The assumption that firms will be induced to exploit economies of scale and will focus on cost reduction in order to stay cost- and price-competitive is also true. It is, however, also without doubt that the line of reasoning will not hold for all firms. As a matter of fact, it will only hold for the minority of companies. The assumptions underlying the line of reasoning are somewhat shallow because they tend to ignore the different circumstances companies have to operate in. The wish that the completion of the internal market will lead to intensified competition and lower prices makes the assumption appear biased. There are at least four assumptions underlying the premise that firms will be focused on a low-cost strategy in Europe 1992 which will be reviewed hereafter. The four assumptions are:

- Firms are presently affected by the presence of non-tariff barriers.

- The scale on which companies presently produce is not efficient due to the relatively small size of the markets within the European Community.
- Consumer preferences are more or less alike between the member states.
- A low-cost strategy is the one best strategy for companies in the internal market.

The Number of Trade Barriers that Presently Exists

Not all companies are equally affected by the presence of technical barriers. In the area of mechanical engineering, numerous technical barriers exist at present. The electrical engineering sector suffers from differences in standards in telecommunications equipment. Companies trading transport goods are also strongly affected by technical obstacles, with motor vehicles and other transport equipment the outstanding examples in this context. On the other hand, consumer electrical appliances no longer experience significant trade barriers as a result of the low-voltage directive of 1973. Companies in the industries "paper and printing" and "artificial fibers" are also not substantially affected by the existence of technical barriers. It is then to be expected that the structure of competition in these industries will not be substantially influenced by the completion of the internal market.

Economies of Scale

Economies of scale arise if an increase in input results in a more than proportionate increase in output, and hence in a fall in unit costs. Although many sectors of activity have scope for economies of scale, some industries can gain greater benefits than others. The minimum efficient technical scale (METS) that is required in, for instance, the "motor vehicles industry" and "chemical industry" is substantial. In the "footwear and clothing industry" and the "leather and leather goods industry" the required METS of operations is considerably lower (Pratten, 1987).

Industries are also not equally sensitive to deviations from the required METS. Companies in the "motor vehicles industry," for

FIGURE 3.1. Effects of the elimination of non-tariff barriers

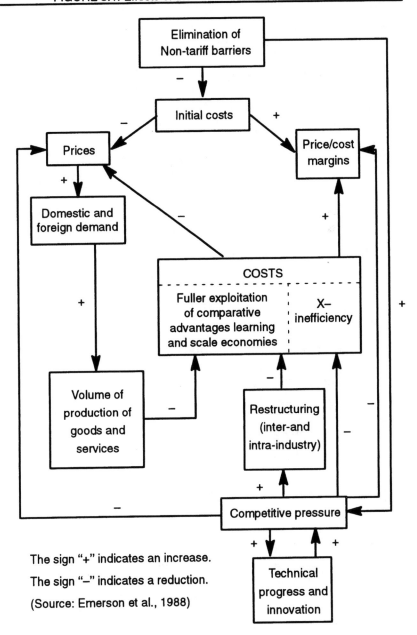

The sign "+" indicates an increase.
The sign "–" indicates a reduction.
(Source: Emerson et al., 1988)

instance, are more sensitive than industries in the "footwear and clothing industry." Companies in the "motor vehicles industry" face an increase in costs of between 6-9% if they operate at a level that is half the required METS. Companies in the industry "other means of transport" may even face an upswing in costs of between 8-20% if they manufacture their products at a scale that is 50% of the required METS. Companies in the "footwear and leather industry" are confronted with a minor increase in costs of about 1% and companies in the "drink and tobacco industry" of about 1.5% (Pratten, 1987).

From this the following conclusions can be drawn.

- The required scale on which companies can efficiently produce varies from industry to industry. In some industries the required METS is quite small. This means that the opening-up of the European market due to the abolishment of technical barriers will not have a substantial influence on the scale on which the companies in these industries operate.
- For companies in some industries it is more important to operate at the required METS than for companies in other industries.
- Combining the first two conclusions results in the third conclusion that a fall in costs due to economies in scale will be apparent only in industries that presently cannot operate at the required METS and that face a substantial increase in costs if they do not operate at that scale.

Uniform Consumer Preferences

Only in the case that consumer preferences across the member states are more or less alike, can companies benefit from producing standardized products at a large volume. The belief that consumer segments are united across national boundaries by the same attitude and lifestyles is indeed gaining currency. Coca Cola and McDonald's hamburgers usually serve as an example in this context. These standardized products are distributed throughout the member states. Since the same product features may appeal to consumers throughout various member states, companies may indeed consider the scope for marketing a product or a service in as many countries as possible. It cannot be denied that this strategy can be employed with success in the internal market. United Distillers (UD), for example, has reviewed the way its brands are marketed in European Community countries with this strategy in mind. Johnnie Walker, a UD product, has been marketed in somewhat different ways in each of the European countries. UD investigated to establish whether there is greater communality between the markets. The emphasis of such a strategy is to produce at low costs while maintaining the features that appeal to an international public.

Although focusing on similarities rather than on dissimilarities between the customer preferences of the member states can be a fruitful strategy, it is also evident that firms seasoned in international business activities have committed colossal blunders because of their insensitivity to different attitudes and lifestyles of consumers. Indeed it has to be recognized that the culture to which consumers belong plays a major role in the way they respond to a company's marketing mix. Hofstede (1983) investigated the culture of seventeen European countries. His conclusion was that all societies are unequal, but some are more unequal than others. He found that based on four cultural dimensions, the seventeen European countries could be classified into six culture-driven segments. These six different segments may require quite different marketing approaches. Therefore, a company may be well advised to adapt its products and/or services to the prevailing cultural circumstances. For the time being companies will most likely have to take into account that there will "only" be clusters of Euro-Consumers (Vandermerwe and L'Huillier, 1989). Since cultures change slowly, European-wide and even world-wide strategies advocated by, for instance, Levitt (1984) and Ohmae (1985) are somewhat premature.

A Low Cost Strategy

Closely related to the assumption that companies will focus on consumer similarities between the member states is the assumption that companies might pursue a low-cost strategy. The preferred strategy, so it is assumed, is producing and distributing a large volume of standardized products throughout the member states. It is assumed that the existence of technical barriers and the discriminating practices of public procurement hamper companies from exploiting the potential of economies of scale. If, in the internal market, technical barriers and discriminating practices of government procurement have been abolished, it is assumed that nothing stands in the way of efficient, large-scale production.

This line of reasoning tends to neglect the benefits of a differentiation strategy. A strategy of differentiation rests on the premise that consumers are willing to pay a premium price for differentiated products. Through differentiation, companies are able to create brand awareness and customer loyalty. This means that companies can develop and preserve their own market niche and thus are able to develop a competitive advantage that is better sustained than an advantage solely based on price (Porter, 1980). Accordingly, it is to be expected that the increase in competition will be moderate in industries in which there are many possibilities to differentiate the products from competitors.

A FRAMEWORK

In regard to the arguments mentioned above, there are reasons to believe that not all companies are equally affected by increased competition. The question to be addressed is under which conditions can an increase in competition be expected? In the framework that will be presented the starting point for analyzing the possibilities for increased competition are the strategies that companies presently might pursue within the European Community.

Basically, companies can pursue strategies along two dimensions: the geographic scope they operate in and the possibilities to differentiate their products from competitors (Gogel and Larréché, 1989). Companies can service a domestic market or can operate on an international scale. In the first case the geographic scope of the company is narrow. In the second case the scope is broad. In the case of a broad geographic scope the company can service the market from a large scale production plant or from more and smaller production plants that are located in different member states.

Companies can either have few or many possibilities to differentiate their products from those of their competitors. If the possibilities for differentiation are slight, companies offer standardized products. They are said to follow a low-cost strategy and try to compete on the basis of price. A pure differentiation strategy means that competition can take place on many elements other than price, such as design, brand image, technology and service. Relating these two dimensions to each other results in the matrix shown in Figure 3.2. From this figure it can be seen that companies can employ at least four different strategies:

- a low-cost strategy combined with a narrow geographic scope (cell I);
- a low-cost strategy combined with a broad geographic scope (cell II);
- a differentiation strategy combined with a broad geographic scope (cell III);
- a differentiation strategy combined with a narrow geographic scope (cell IV).

When attempting to estimate the changes in competition, the four factors mentioned cannot be dealt with on an individual basis. Eventually, it is the combination of these factors that will or will not substantially influence the structure of competition in industries. A way to get insight into whether or not competition will increase is to analyze the different situations that may prevail in the four cells of Figure 3.2.

Low-Cost Strategy Combined with a Narrow Geographic Scope (Cell I)

In this cell competition is likely to be very tough. Companies in this quadrant have few possibilities to differentiate their products from those of their competitors and produce largely for the domestic market. What will happen once the trade barriers have been abolished? Since there appears to be no reason why the possibilities for differentiation should increase, the companies in cell I will try to broaden their geographic scope *provided* that operating on a European scale will result in economies of scale. If the companies in cell I do not enlarge their scale of operations, they will face a cost disadvantage with respect to companies that have rationalized their production. If, however, the companies in cell I already produce at the required METS (the required METS is relatively small) the

FIGURE 3.2. Strategies in the internal market

geographic scope

		narrow	broad
possibilities for differentiation	small	I	II
	large	IV	III

influence of the completion of the internal market will be relatively small.

Low-Cost Strategy Combined with a Broad Geographic Scope (Cell II)

The companies in cell II are companies that:

- operate in industries in which few trade barriers to intra-Community trade are present; or
- have production plants in several member states in order to easily adapt their products to the different national technical standards or in order to avoid customs procedures.

In the first case effects of the completion of the internal market will be slight since companies in this situation have already rationalized their production. To put it differently, they probably already operate at the required METS. In the second case companies can rationalize their production by reducing the number of production plants provided that each of the plants does not meet the required METS. The production can then be organized more efficiently. In this case an increase in competition may be the result. Companies which can best rationalize their production may translate this advantage in lower prices and consequently may be able to attack the less efficient competitors with success.

Differentiation Combined with a Broad Geographic Scope
(Cell III)

In this cell, there appear to be three different situations:

- there are few trade barriers, yet companies have production plants in several member states to adapt their products to national consumer preferences;
- there are few trade barriers and the companies distribute their standardized products from a large scale production plant;
- there are many trade barriers because of which companies have been urged to have production plants in several member states.

In the first case the companies have a defendable position because they produce tailor-made products and have been able to create consumer loyalty. In the second case the companies produce products that appeal to a large international public. Since there are few trade barriers at present, production has already been rationalized. Consequently the effects of the completion of the internal market on competition will be slight. In the third case the abolishment of trade barriers may evoke two different responses. First, if the preferences of the consumers are more or less alike between the member states, companies may rationalize their processes and become more efficient producers provided that at this moment a situation prevails in which the respective production plants do not produce at the required METS and the sensitivity to deviations from the required METS is large. Yet, compared to the situation in cell II, the increase in competition may be modest. This is so because just like the first case there is not a unilateral relation between competition and price and thus efficiency. If in this situation the respective production plants already produce at the required METS or the sensitivity to deviations from this scale are small, there appears to be no reason to expect that competition will increase dramatically. Second, if the consumer preferences are divergent between the member states, there appears to be no reason why competition should increase. In this situation, companies can follow a strategy of consolidation.

Differentiation in a Domestic Market (Cell IV)

In the case of a large number of possibilities for differentiation and a narrow geographic scope it is not to be expected that competition will become very tough in the internal market. Several situations can be distinguished in this quadrant.

- The companies already produce at the required METS or the sensitivity to deviations from the required METS is slight. In this case the effects of the abolishment of trade barriers on competition will be insignificant.
- The companies do not operate on a broader geographic scale due to the existence of various trade barriers. When the trade barriers have been removed these companies may then decide to expand their operations in order to achieve economies of scale. Since the possibilities for differentiation are high the companies can develop their own niche. Accordingly, there will only be a modest increase in competition. This strategy is only to be expected when they can produce products that appeal to a large international public and when the companies do not yet operate at the required METS.
- The companies do not operate on a broader geographic scale due to the fact that customer preferences differ substantially between the member states. In this case there will hardly be an increase in competition since producing and distributing products on an international scale is not required.

In Table 3.1 the relevant scenarios are described and the consequences for the level of competition that is to be expected are summarized. It can be seen from this table that only in two of the twelve relevant scenarios is competition expected to increase substantially. In other words, there is reason to expect that the assumption that *the* competition in the internal market will increase is an exaggeration at least.

VULNERABILITY OF THE STRATEGIES

The strategy to be preferred is not only dependent on the expected increase in competition, it is also dependent on the vulner-

Table 3.1. Preferred strategies in the internal market			
Present strategy	present circumstances	increase in competition	preferred strategy
Low-cost, narrow geographic scope	companies produce at required METS or sensitivity to deviations from required METS is small	low	consolidation
	companies do not produce at required METS and sensitivity to deviations from required METS is large	high	expansion of activities on an international level
Low-cost, broad geographic scope	few trade barriers	low	consolidation
	many trade barriers, the required METS and the sensitivity to deviations from the required METS are large	high	rationalize production
Differentiation, broad geographic scope	many trade barriers, convergent consumer preferences between the Member States, companies already produce at required METS or sensitivity to deviations from required METS is small	low	consolidation
	many trade barriers, convergent consumer preferences between the Member States, companies do not produce at required METS and sensitivity	moderate	rationalize production

Table 3.1. (continued)			
Present strategy	present circumstances	increase in competition	preferred strategy
	to deviations from required METS are high		
	many trade barriers, divergent consumer preferences between the Member States, companies produce at required METS or sensitivity to deviations from required METS is small	low	consolidation
	few trade barriers, divergent consumer preferences between the Member States	low	consolidation
	few trade barriers, convergent consumer preferences between the Member States	low	consolidation
Differentiation, narrow geographic scope	many trade barriers, convergent consumer preferences between the Member States, companies produce at METS or sensitivity to deviations from required METS is low	low	consolidation
	many trade barriers, convergent consumer preferences, companies do not produce at required METS and sensitivity to deviations from required METS is small	moderate	rationalize production

Present strategy	present circumstances	increase in competition	preferred strategy
	few trade barriers, divergent consumer preferences between the Member States	low	consolidation

ability of the strategy. The strategy in cell I (low-cost strategy combined with a narrow geographic scope) can be successful if the required METS is quite low or if the sensitivity to deviations from the required METS is slight. If the required METS is quite small, the scale of operations which is required for servicing a domestic market may be large enough. If, however, the required METS is rather large and if sensitivity to deviations from the required METS is high, companies in this situation are vulnerable to actions of companies that sell the same undifferentiated products to an international public (cell II). In that case companies in cell I produce at a scale that may be too small to achieve economies of scale. The companies in cell II which sell the same products throughout the member states will have better opportunities to achieve economies of scale and thus offer products at lower prices.

Under the circumstances, the strategy which is pursued by the companies in cell II may have advantages in comparison to the strategy followed by the companies in cell I. This is not to say, however, that the strategy in cell II is not a vulnerable one. The companies in cell II offer standardized products and services to an international public. Since there are only a few possibilities for differentiation, the companies focus on similarities in consumer preferences between the member states and can achieve economies of scale through large-scale production. This strategy is vulnerable to the extent that the required METS or the sensitivity to deviations from the required METS decrease. In that case the companies in this cell will face the competition by the domestic producers of cell I.

The strategies followed by the companies in cell III and IV are less vulnerable than those pursued by the companies in cell I and II. Since there are many possibilities to differentiate products from competitors, companies in cell III and IV are able to find their own specific niche. Strategies based on differentiation cannot be copied easily since these kinds of strategies are usually accompanied by a high level of brand awareness and customer loyalty.

In a way, however, the strategies pursued by the companies in cell III and IV are vulnerable. The strategy followed by the companies in cell III can be based on two different organizational forms. First, the companies can service an international public from a large-scale production plant. In this case the companies offer standardized products and focus on similarities in consumer preferences between the member states. This strategy is vulnerable to the extent that consumer preferences become more divergent. Having production plants in several member states may then be the strategy to be preferred. Consequently, the companies in cell III have to meet the competition from the companies which produce more or less the same products for a domestic market. However, the trend towards more divergent consumer preferences is not likely to occur. The strategy is also vulnerable if the required METS or the sensitivity to deviations from this scale decrease. In that case the companies in cell III have to face an increased competition from the companies that produce more or less the same products for a domestic scale.

The strategy followed by the companies in cell IV is vulnerable if the consumer preferences between the member states become more alike. In that case an international scope is to be preferred in order to achieve economies of scale. The strategies followed by the companies in the four different cells and their vulnerabilities are summarized in Table 3.2.

The arguments made above lead to the conclusion that several strategies in the internal market can be pursued. Each of the strategies can be successful depending on the circumstances that prevail. Each of the strategies has its own vulnerability. Therefore, the assumption behind Europe 1992 that a low cost strategy is to be preferred in the internal market needs to be modified. Since the circumstances prevailing in industries can vary considerably, companies are well advised to analyze the conditions in their industry thoroughly and act accordingly.

Table 3.2. Vulnerability of strategies in the internal market		
Strategy	When preferred?	When vulnerable?
Low-cost strategy combined with a narrow geographic scope	If the possibilities for differentiation are slight If the required METS or the sensitivity to deviations from the METS are small	If the required Mets or the sensitivity to deviations from the required METS increase
Low-cost strategy combined with a broad geographic scope	If the possibilities for differentiation are slight If the required METS or the sensitivity to deviations from the METS are large	If the possibilities for differentiation increase If customer preferences between the Member States diverge
Differentiation strategy combined with a narrow geographic scope	If the possibilities for differentiation are high If the customer preferences between the Member States are divergent	If the customer preferences between the Member States converge
Differentiation strategy combined with a broad geographic scope	If the possibilities for differentiation are high If the customer preferences throughout the Member States are uniform If the required METS or the sensitivity to deviations from the METS are large	If the customer preferences between the Member States diverge If the METS or the sensitivity from deviations from METS decrease

CONCLUDING REMARKS

Will the completion of the European Community result in increased competition and will it force companies to follow a low-cost strategy? It appears that these questions cannot be answered by a straight yes or no. Without doubt the implementation of the measure taken by the European Commission will have its impact on certain sectors of industry. Especially those companies that, due to the existence of trade barriers, do not produce at METS and which as a result cannot produce efficiently may have to reconsider their strategy. If they can offer products that appeal to a large international public they indeed may be able to achieve economies of scale and may attack the less efficient producers with success.

The anxiety of many companies, however, appears not to be justified by the prevailing circumstances. One has to remember that the accomplishment of European internal market is not a completely new phenomenon. Since the Community's foundation in 1958 the abolishment of trade barriers between the member states has been one of the main objectives. Therefore, the merger mania in Europe that is often described as one of the consequences of the completion of the internal market is surprising at least. More than once the arguments for a takeover are based on subjective perceptions of what is going to happen. The truth about Europe 1992, however, is that companies in several industries will discover that the consequences of the "White Paper" are more or less insignificant.

There is no such thing as *the* effects of Europe 1992. In this paper it has been argued that the impact of the completion of the internal market will be dependent on factors such as:

- the possibilities to differentiate the product on elements other than price;
- the minimum efficient technical scale on which companies have to operate or the sensitivity to deviations from this scale;
- the convergence or divergence of consumer preferences between the member states;
- the number of trade barriers that are existent at present.

Companies preparing themselves for Europe 1992 have to analyze thoroughly what kind of situation they are in at present. It is likely that they will discover that regardless of the prevailing (industry) circumstances and their own internal strength, Europe 1992 will position them between Scylla and Charybdis!

BIBLIOGRAPHY

Calingaert, Michael. (1989). *The 1992 Challenge: Development of the European Community's Internal Market.* National Planning Association: Washington, DC.

Cecchini, P. (1988). *The European Challenge 1992: The Benefits of a Single Market.* Gower: Aldershot.

Commission of the European Communities. (1985). *Completing the Internal Market.* White Paper: Brussels/Luxembourg.

Daems, Herman. (1990). "The Strategic Implications of Europe 1992." *Long Range Planning,* Vol. 23, No. 3.

Emerson, M. (1988). "The Economics of 1992, An Assessment of the Potential Economic Effects of Completing the Internal Market of the European Community." *Directorate-General for Economic and Financial Affairs,* No. 35.

Franko, Lawrence G. (1989). "Europe 1992: The Impact on Global Corporate Competition and Multinational Corporate Strategy." *European Business Journal,* Vol. 1, No. 3.

Gogel, Robert and Jean-Claude Larréché. (1989). "The Battlefield for 1992: Product Strength and Geographic Coverage." *European Management Journal,* Vol. 7, No. 3.

Higgins, James M. and Timo Santalainen. (1989). "Strategies for Europe 1992." *Business Horizons,* July/August.

Hofstede, G. (1983). "The Cultural Relativity of Organizational Practices and Theories." *Journal of International Business Studies,* Fall.

Hunsicker, J. Quincy. (1989). "Strategies for European Survival." *The McKinsey Quarterly,* Summer.

Kaikati, Jack G. (1989)."Europe 1992–Mind Your Strategic P's and Q's." *Sloan Management Review,* Fall.

Levitt, T. (1984). "The Globalization of Markets." *The McKinsey Quarterly,* Summer.

Mitchell, David. (1989). "1992: The Implications for Management." *Long Range Planning,* Vol. 22, No. 1.

Ohmae, K. (1985). "Becoming a Triad Power: The New Global Corporation." *The McKinsey Quarterly,* Spring.

Porter, M.E. (1980). *Competitive Strategy, Techniques for Analyzing Industries and Competitors,* The Free Press.

Pratten, C. (1987). *A Survey of the Economies of Scale.* Report prepared for the EC-Commission, Brussels.

Quelch, John A., Robert D. Buzzel, and Eric R. Salama. (1990). *The Marketing Challenge of 1992,* Addison-Wesley Publishing Company: Reading, MA.

Vandermerwe, Sandra. (1989). "Strategies for a Pan European Market." *Long Range Planning,* Vol. 22, No. 3.

Vandermerwe, Sandra and Marc-André L'Huillier. (1989). "Euro-Consumers in 1992," *Business Horizons,* January/February.

SECTION II.
EUROMARKETING STRATEGIES:
WESTERN EUROPE

Chapter 4

Consumer Behavior and Marketing Issues in the Europe of Post-1992

Erdener Kaynak
Pervez N. Ghauri

INTRODUCTION

In 1985, the European Community Commission issued its White Paper, *Completing the Internal Market*, in which it declared its intention to enact by the end of 1992 all legislation needed to create a unified European Market. On July 1, 1987 the single European Act came into force and provided a legal framework for the activities necessary to create a single internal market. It provided a time scale for 300 pieces of legislation to be enacted by December 31, 1992 (Dudley, 1989).

Three years later, in February 1988, the accounting firm, Ernst and Whinney, disclosed the findings of its study of European businessmen, which indicated low levels of awareness, with the possible exception of France, of 1992 as a significant date and correspondingly low levels of preparation for the attendant changes that date will entail (Ogilvy and Mather, 1988).

The Europe of 1992 is one of the most relevant and widely published topics in today's business journals and newspapers. Europe as a single market and economic superpower is finally becoming a reality and, as a result, Europe is rapidly becoming a battleground for a higher market share for the world's major corporations from North America, Europe and Asia. By restructuring their corporate hierarchies and organizations, widening their product lines and by creating internal-European acquisitions, these corporations

57

are hoping to exploit a market that buys $600 billion worth of goods and services (Melcher, 1988). With 342 million customers, the United States of Europe would be the largest internal market in the developed world, some 92 million larger than the United States of America. This expanding internal market will be a test ground for U.S.-based corporations' strengths as strategic planners and as global marketers for many years to come.

THE ENVIRONMENT

One of the first steps necessary to understand the European Community (EC) is to study its composition and its development process from the beginning. This will be accomplished by addressing the following five interrelated questions:

1. What countries belong to the EC?
2. How did the EC develop?
3. How is it organized?
4. Is a successful unification of Europe possible by 1992?
5. What are the marketing implications of this forthcoming unification?

Composition

What countries belong to the EC? The EC was founded by six countries in 1957 through the Treaty of Rome. The member states were Belgium, France, Germany, Italy, Luxembourg, and the Netherlands. In 1973 three more countries joined the community, Great Britain, Ireland, and Denmark. Greece joined in 1981 and Spain and Portugal in 1986. The European Economic Community is today composed of 12 European countries whose people speak nine major languages. Specifically, the member countries are Germany, France, Greece, Spain, Italy, United Kingdom, Belgium, Portugal, The Netherlands, Denmark, Ireland, and Luxembourg. As mentioned previously, with 342 million consumers the union of these countries into a single trade market will make it bigger in population than either the United States or Japan plus its capitalist neighbors. Table 4.1 shows EC's socio-economic indicators in a comparative manner.

It has been observed that, while, Norway and Switzerland for different reasons of their own may not be immediately joining the EC, Sweden, Austria and even Finland have recently asked to be let into the union. This would make the market even larger. Today, half the world trade is conducted in the European Community. The combined gross domestic product (GDP) of its members make it the second largest economic block in the world, after North America. It has 228 of the top 1000 companies in the world. The member states range from Luxembourg with a population of 0.4 million, to Germany with more than 80 million people. The significance of this market to U.S.-based companies is demonstrated by the fact that in 1990 United States exports to countries belonging to the EC ex-

TABLE 4.1. Major Socio-Economic Indicators for the EC in 1990.

Country	Population (m.)	Density (persons per km2)	Share of World GNP	GDP Total ECU m.	ECUs Per Head	Real Growth (% pa)
Denmark	5.1	119	4.0%	47	9,200	2.7
Luxembourg	0.4	142	5.9%	3	7,800	1.9
Germany	80.0	245	4.8%	514	8,400	2.5
Netherlands	16.5	427	1.3%	103	7,100	2.0
France	55.1	101	4.2%	422	7,700	1.3
Belgium	9.9	325	6.7%	66	6,700	0.2
U.K.	56.5	232	4.1%	374	6,600	3.0
Italy	57.1	190	4.1%	296	5,200	2.3
Ireland	3.5	51	2.5%	15	4,300	2.0
Spain	38.6	77	10.7%	140	3,600	2.1
Greece	9.9	75	2.1%	27	2,700	2.1
Portugal	10.2	111	6.5%	17	1,700	3.3
Total	342.0	143	3.6%	2.024	6,300	2.1

Source: Various Euromonitor and *The Wall Street Journal* issues in 1991 and European Economy, Annual Economic Report 1991-1992, Brussels, December 1991, p. 24.

ceeded $53 billion. This is more than double the value of U.S. goods exported to Japan (*Economist,* 1988).

In general terms, among the member countries, enthusiasm for the unification is varied. France is said to be the most enthusiastic supporter with 70% of its companies viewing the venture as an opportunity. Italy and The Netherlands also support the move enthusiastically. Evidence shows that Italian large business preparation for the union is reflected in the fact that in the recent past, Italian businesses have dominated about 41% of the major European takeover/merger transactions (*Economist,* 1988).

Less positive attitudes towards union are reportedly shared by Germany, Spain, Belgium, Denmark, and the United Kingdom. In recent months, France also started experiencing difficulties in its relationship within the community. With a healthy economy of its own, Germany has little need for the union to prosper, but three of its major companies, Bayer, Hoechst, and BASF, conceded that they "can hardly wait because they can't be beaten in a free market" (Ogilvy and Mather, 1988, p. 12). Spain, on the other hand, has little experience in marketing products abroad and is encouraging its businesses to acquire large foreign partners and its banks to merge in preparation for the unified market. Belgium can best be described as "unsettled" after the international scramble for control of Societe Generale de Belgique, the company that dominates its economy. A Scandinavian member, Denmark is said to be coolly resigned to the forthcoming unification. As for the United Kingdom, even though it would gain enormously in the finance and insurance sectors, this country is reported to be wary of the union because of the potential threat to its sovereignty and fragile economy.

Greece, Portugal, Ireland, and Luxembourg, under projected circumstances, should prosper as a result of the union; but even in these countries, the desire for and the sense of separate nationality is strong. Despite tremendous economic and financial benefits in sight, these countries too look at the European unification efforts in non-economic and non-financial terms.

Development of the European Community and Its Organization

The European Community includes three communities: (1) The European Coal and Steel Community (ECSC), established by The

Treaty of Paris in 1951 but was fully implemented in 1985; (2) The European Atomic Energy Community (EAEC); and (3) The European Economic Community (EEC). The last two were established in Rome in 1957 and came into force in January of 1958. In 1965 a "Merger Treaty" was signed in Brussels that stated the three communities would create a single "Council of the European Communities," a "Commission of the European Communities" and an "Audit Board." On July 1, 1967 these organizations started to operate. Moreover, the three communities together were given the name of "The European Community (EC)" by the European parliament in 1978. It was also decided that any European state could apply to become a member provided: (a) the applicant is a European state, (b) it is a democratic state, and (c) it accepts the political and economic objectives of the European Community.

The operations of the EC are organized under four major bodies: (1) The Council of Ministers, (2) The Commission, (3) The Court of Justice, and (4) The Assembly of European Parliament. Moreover, there are some supporting institutions such as: The Court of Auditors, The Economic and Social Committee and The European Investment Bank.

Each member country has one representative in the Council of Ministers which is the main decision-making body. Based on the proposals from the Commission and advice from the European Parliament and Social and Economic Committee, the Council makes the final decisions. The process of decision making is explained in Figure 4.1. The office of the President of the council is held by each member state in alphabetical order for a period of six months. Decisions are taken on simple or qualified majority and different states have different weight to their votes: ten votes each for Germany, France, Italy, and UK; eight votes for Spain; five votes each for Belgium, The Netherlands, Greece, and Portugal; three votes each for Ireland and Denmark; and two votes for Luxembourg. There is a total of 76 votes, of which 54 votes are required for a qualified majority. The council normally works on the basis of unanimity.

By the end of the 1970s the result was a series of draft directives, some of which were helpful and many of which were restrictive and insensitive to the way commerce works. They provided little benefit to either the consumers or the producers (Ogilvy and Mather, 1988,

FIGURE 4.1. The Decision-Making Process in EC

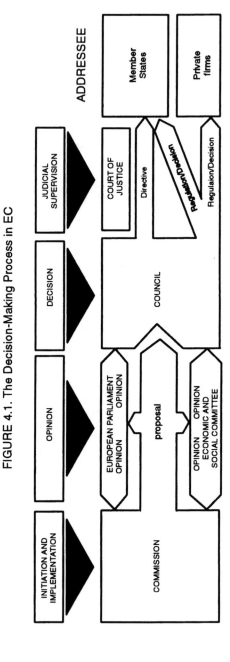

Source: Goodman, 1992. p. 50

p. 15). In defense, the international business community put together a lobby to protect its interests. Accordingly, during the 1970s and 1980s, new directives took an average of five years to pass from introduction to implementation, even if they were relatively non-controversial.

The first break in this cycle occurred in 1978 with the European Court of Justice's "Cassis de Dijon" judgement against the West German government and in favor of a company which wished to import a French liquor. The decision was based on the grounds that "any goods legally manufactured and marketed in a member state should be able to be sold in another member state without any interference" and could be blocked only to satisfy a limited range of issues such as health, safety, or consumer protection in the public interest as determined by the Community Law (Ogilvy and Mather, 1988, p. 17).

Then, in 1985, the European Commission published the White Paper, *Completing the Internal Market*, which called for more than 300 legislative actions to be taken to open the European market by the end of 1992. All 300 of those proposals were bundled into a piece of Pan-European legislation called the Single European Act of 1987 (Hoop, 1988). By the end of 1988, however, only about 25% of these proposals had been enacted by the 12 EC countries.

Plausibility of Unification of Europe

Is a successful and real unification of Europe possible? The intent of creating a single trade market is to allow goods, services, people, and money to move freely among the member countries. Reduction of inefficiencies caused by fragmented, nationalistic economies and bureaucratic systems should result in gains in economies of scale and in productivity and efficiency. Official estimates of the total savings from abolishing all trade barriers and from establishing free market integration may amount to over 200 billion ECU savings or five percent of Gross Domestic Product of the EC economies (Hoop, 1988, p. 40). Table 4.2 shows the efficiencies and benefits to be achieved by unification of Europe.

With unification of Europe, more competition at all levels should result, creating a greater selection of attractively priced goods and services for European consumers with guarantees and warranties being valid throughout the EC. In addition, honoring educational

TABLE 4.2. Macro-Economic Consequences of EC Market Integration for the Community in the Medium Term

Relative Changes %

	Customs Formalities	Public Procurement	Financial Services	Supply Side Effects	Average Value	Total Spread
GNP	0.4	0.5	1.5	2.1	4.5	3.2 – 5.7
Consumer Prices	(1.0)	(1.4)	(1.4)	(2.3)	(6.1)	(4.5) – (7.7)
Absolute Changes Employment (000's)	200.0	350.0	400.0	850.0	1,800.0	1300 – 2300
Budgetary Balance (% Point of GNP)	0.2	0.3	1.1	0.6	2.2	1.5 – 3.0
External Balance (% Point of GNP)	0.2	0.1	0.3	0.4	1.0	0.7 – 1.3

and professional standards across the Community will provide greater employment flexibility and mobility to students and professionals alike.

Since there are no national tariffs or import quotas among EC members, the Community is already a single market as far as tariff barriers are concerned. Accordingly, non-tariff barriers will provide the greatest challenge to the Europe of 1992. These barriers can be described as (Hoop, 1988, p.40):

	Billion ECU	% of GDP
Gains from removal of barriers affecting trade:	8 – 9	0.2 – 0.3
Gains from removal of barriers affecting overall production:	57 – 71	2.1 – 2.4
Gains from removing barriers (sub-total):	65 – 80	2.2 – 2.7
Gains from exploiting economies of scale more fully:	61	2.1
Gains from intensified competition reducing business inefficiencies and monopoly profits:	46	1.6
Gains from market integration (sub-total):	62 – 107	2.1 – 3.7
Total For 12 Member States at 1988 Prices	174 – 258	4.3 – 6.4
Mid-point of above	216	5.3

Source: Commission of EC, study of Directorate-General for Economic Affairs, Brussels 1990.

1. *Physical Barriers:* These include border and customs controls and their attendant administrations. United Kingdom, France and The Netherlands are the three communities which most strenuously oppose the abolition of these physical barriers because of their concern over terrorism and drug trafficking.
2. *Technical Barriers:* Technical and environmental regulations, divergent national standards, conflicting business laws, and

nationally protected procurement markets are included in this category.

3. *Fiscal Barriers:* These barriers consist of differing tax rates and structures in member countries, with treatment of the value-added tax (VAT) being a major source of disagreement.

4. *Cultural and Consumer Related Barriers:* These barriers, which include language barriers, climate, race, topography, nationality, and education among others, are probably the most insidious of the barriers to be overcome while creating a unified Europe.

Notwithstanding the importance of these obvious barriers to unification, there is even further room for speculation on the plausibility of successful implementation. There are two types of factors, namely supply and demand factors, affecting a unified European market by the end of 1992, although on January 1, 1993, at least on the paper, barriers to trade will have been lifted. But whatever changes take place will have been implemented on the supply side involving creation of physical, technical and fiscal changes through the help of 300 specific measures. Most of the influencing factors on the demand side will remain unchanged for many years to come (Table 4.3).

First, Europe of 1992 is a political initiative. The situation seems to offer excellent opportunities to multinational corporations, with the general consensus being the United States and Japan will be the clear winners (Riemer, Heard, and Peterson, 1988, p. 40). In addition, there has been no attempt to repeal Clause 115 of the Treaty of Rome, which permits governments to take protective action in case of economic difficulty of their own. Will the losers withdraw? How long will the winners subsidize the losers? What will be the reunifications of these types of initiatives by member states?

A second concern is the EC's "track record." The 1985 White Paper is a very good working document, but is it truly possible for countries who compete and who have been historical enemies to cooperate to the extent that will be required by Europe of 1992? The President of the Council of Ministers has suggested that eventually 80% of European social and economic legislation will be initiated by the Community, not by national governments (Ogilvy and Math-

TABLE 4.3. Forces in Favor of and Against European Unification

January 1, 1993

Barriers to Trade Have Been Lifted

Supply Factors		Demand Factors
Uniformity	How to Create Commonalities?	Divergence
Physical		Country
Technical		Regional
Fiscal		Consumer

* Trade Liberalization	* Regional Preferences
* Liberalized Transportation	* Income
* Mutual Recognition	* Habits/Traditions
	* Language
	* Cultural
	* Climate

300 specific measures needing
to be implemented in order
to dismantle internal trade
barriers and create a single
market.

er, 1988). Will the United Kingdom and France agree to this loss of sovereignty? How will member countries find common grounds for mutual understanding?

Another potential stumbling block is the time table itself. In 1985 the White Paper set forth 300 pieces of legislation to be drafted, debated, and adopted in seven years. By 1988, 30 of those actions were dropped and less than 100 more were adopted. Many of the remaining issues, some of which are highly controversial, have not yet even reached the first draft stage. Historical evidence shows that, generally, at least four years are necessary to adoption of

Directives. A longer period is usually required for controversial or complex issues. Students of 1992 have viewed December 31, 1992, as a keystone when all relevant legislation will be in draft, but final adoption will probably come some what after.

A final consideration about a united Europe regards enforcement of the new Directives. With two-thirds of the EC's current budget going to support the Common Agricultural Policy, it is obvious that the EC authorities are counting on aggrieved companies to turn in transgressors. This environment has already provided organized crime with fertile ground to harvest and it promises to get even worse. It is already estimated that up to 20% of the EC budget goes astray to various frauds and this may only be the proverbial tip of the iceberg (Ogilvy and Mather, 1988, p. 20).

In summary, Europe as a single trade market has not been operational by the end of 1992. However, development toward that goal is in progress, and product developers and marketing planners should plan now to actively meet the market's needs and to avoid "catch-up" competitive strategies.

Marketing Implications of the European Community

In most cases, the consumer of post-1992 is similar to the consumer before the 1992 era. This is true because, generally, the legislative program for 1992 is not meant to directly affect the consumer at large. The consumer will benefit, however, from a wider choice of brands, lower prices, and greater freedom of movement. In addition, mutual recognition of professional and educational credentials will promote greater flexibility and mobility and will hopefully result in higher disposable income for individuals in these positions.

Although unrelated to the market changes taking place in Europe, several other characteristics of the consumer of post-1992 are of significance to the marketer. First, language barriers continue to be a problem despite greater freedom of movement among countries. The variety of foreign languages spoken in Europe are summarized in Table 4.4. Even among business people, less than one in two people speak a second language fluently. Among the general populace, a fair estimate is one in Table 4.4.

Almost certainly the second language of Europe will be English.

Instruction manuals, directions, and product packaging will need to be polyglot.

As in the other two trading blocks, namely North America and Asia, demographic and socioeconomic changes taking place in Europe will be of great significance to marketing planners in post-1992 Europe. These changes include a decline in the size of the average household as shown in Table 4.5; or described in the size of the young people's market (Table 4.6); the rise of the over-65, the single fastest growing group in Europe is the 50-54 age group; the slowing of population growth as a whole (Mazur, 1991) and increase in the size and the disposable income of the "empty nest" market, an increased prosperity overall, and an increased interest in health and leisure activities.

The EC is projected to grow in terms of population by only 4% by 2020, compared with 18% for Africa and 58% for Asia. The dramatic shift in age groups is underlined by the projections for

TABLE 4.4. Foreign Languages Spoken by European Business People (%)

	All	UK	France	Germany	Italy	Spain	Netherl.	Denmark
English	53	100	28	32	23	21	78	36
French	34	8	100	15	21	19	22	3
German	29	4	6	100	4	3	41	13
Italian	16	1	3	4	100	3	2	*
Spanish	12	2	3	3	2	100	3	1
Dutch	7	1	1	2	*	*	100	*
Danish	8	*	*	2	*	*	1	100
Any Foreign	46	12	39	50	35	43	100	40
No. of Lang.	1.3	1.3	1.1	1.2	1.3	1.2	1.5	1.3

(* denotes less than 1%)

Source: *Marketing to Europe,* Ogilvy and Mather, Brethlenholm Print, London 1988, p. 23 (Ogilvy and Mather 1988, p. 22).

TABLE 4.5. Population and Households (12 European Countries)

	1960	1970	1980	1990	1995*
Population (million)	280	299	317	342	360
Persons per household	3.3	3.1	2.8	2.6	2.3
Household (million)	85	96	113	130	165

* Estimated.

Source: Based on *Marketing to Europe,* Ogilvy and Mather, Brethlenholm Print, London 1988, p. 24.

Europe. For instance, the 1989 age pyramid for Europe looks very different from that of 1960. The 1960 pyramids shows both the baby boom years of 1946-1960 and the effect of two world wars. The 1989 pyramid highlights the sharp drop in the birth rate which began in the mid-1960s and speeded up in the mid-1970s and 1980s. What companies in Europe need to come to terms with is the effect of these age bulges on the demand for their goods and services. Older populations tend to have higher discretionary incomes, are mainly house owners, and are people who will not only have the freedom to spend, but the freedom to withhold that spending until they see what they want (Mazur, 1991, pp. 4-5). Hence, product strategies and marketing planners will need to adjust each aspect of their marketing mix variables in order to exploit the opportunities presented by these incumbent changes.

Identification of common needs across Europe will be fundamental for success in marketing the new Euro-brands, but so too will be identification of potential niche markets. It is expected that as "nationality" is limited, "regionality" will expand. This will present opportunities for local business people to satisfy regional consumer needs. It is, however, unwise to think that a unified Europe will support Europroducts. Beyond a certain number of products (Coca-Cola, Sony Walkmans) the number of truly universal products will drop off rapidly. Local preferences dictate that Fanta orange taste tart in Italy and sweet in Germany. The British prefer front loading

TABLE 4.6. The Aging Population (10 Countries)

	1950	1980	1990	1995*
65+ years	9%	13.3%	13.8%	14.2%
25 to 64 years	49.1%	48.7%	50.1%	52.7%
0 to 24 years	41.9%	38.0%	36.1%	33.1%

* Estimated.

Source: *Marketing to Europe,* Ogilvy and Mather, Brethlenholm Print, London 1988, p. 26.

washing machines while the French like their machines to load from the top.

Other unchanging influences on the 1992 consumer will be the effects of climate, culture, and national consumer characteristics. These factors influence every aspect of the consumer's life including the social, work, religious, and familial aspects. This is significant to the performance of businesses because "there is no hour during the working day during which a Head Office could telephone all its European branches and not find at least one out to lunch!" (Ogilvy and Mather, 1988, p. 22). The point is that there are simply some aspects of divergent lifestyles that cannot be legislated away and the business community will have to make adjustments for those aspects.

HOMOGENEOUS vs. HETEROGENEOUS MARKETPLACE

For companies developing marketing strategies to address, or exploit, the consumer markets of Europe at the end of 1992, marketers must ascertain whether the market place is homogeneous or heterogeneous in nature for its potential products/services. Identifying the market type will significantly influence market segmentation (subdividing of customers and products), target marketing, product positioning and the matching of products and customers.

According to *The Economist Intelligence Unit* report (Mazur,

1991), the EC consumer market, excluding the former East Germany, will be worth $4,730 billion by 1994. Including the contribution from the former East Germany, the total market will be almost as big as that of the U.S. (Table 4.7). But the European Consumer Market by 1994 will comprise an attitude of different segments in different product areas at different stages of market development (Mazur, 1991, p. 12).

It has been predicted that housing and leisure will be key areas of growth, while the decline of overall spending on food will be matched by rising demand for luxury and convenience goods. There will also be growing demand for products that are of high quality, are individualistic and reflect environmental concerns.

No one can say with certainty whether or not the marketplace associated with the Europe of 1992 will be homogeneous or heterogeneous in nature. It is believed that the economic deregulation previously identified associated with the Europe of post-1992 and its impact on the consumer market is far more of an evolutionary process than a revolutionary process. The consumer will inevitably benefit by greater freedom of action, a wider choice of brands and quite possibly lower prices. It is generally accepted that the consumer of post-1992 will resemble closely the consumer of pre-1992 in money respects. Some producers will be able to market the same product, to the same target market, for the same end use, promoting the same image and positioning against the same competitive environment in all of the 12 countries of Europe. But for every one of these products (e.g., carbonated drinks), there will be dozens of brands which face a much less homogeneous Europe. Tastes in food, clothing, cars, and leisure activity vary a great deal from the Nordic North to the Latin South for reasons of culture, consumer differences and climate, as well as tradition (Ogilvy and Mather, 1988, p. 22). Local modifications in formula, packaging, advertising, product design, and positioning will often justify their costs by higher customer loyalty and increased consumption rates. A vast heterogeneous market will continue to exist far beyond 1992 in Europe. Hence, European Consumers of the twenty-first century will not be drinking the same beer, driving the same cars, or eating the same cookies or chocolates.

The passing of Europe 1992 has not automatically erased lan-

TABLE 4.7. EC: Total Consumer Spending 1979-94 (ECU bn)

	1979	1984	1989	1990	1991	1992	1993	1994
Belgium	48.2	65.0	88.1	94.8	100.3	105.3	111.1	117.1
Denmark	25.6	37.2	49.4	51.9	53.9	56.3	58.8	60.9
France	234.1	382.8	515.7	551.0	575.0	608.4	642.8	676.4
(West) Germany	297.0	446.9	583.2	634.5	685.5	738.0	791.2	843.2
Greece	16.9	27.7	33.2	36.0	39.0	41.5	44.3	46.8
Ireland	7.3	13.2	17.3	18.9	20.3	21.7	23.0	24.6
Italy	158.3	326.9	486.4	526.8	557.1	599.1	651.8	696.0
Luxembourg	1.7	2.5	3.4	3.7	3.9	4.1	4.4	4.6
Netherlands	66.4	93.5	120.8	129.4	137.8	145.7	154.3	163.8
Portugal	9.5	17.2	26.3	28.9	32.1	35.2	38.5	41.8
Spain	88.9	129.0	215.0	235.2	255.5	269.0	289.9	308.4
UK	175.6	335.2	483.4	482.8	505.6	541.1	583.2	626.8
TOTAL	1,129.7	1,877.7	2,622.2	2,793.8	2,966.0	3,165.4	3,393.4	3,610.3

Source: Laura Mazur, "Marketing 2000 Critical Challenges for Corporate Survival," *The Economist* Intelligence Unit, 1991, London p. 12.

guage, behavioral and cultural differences concerning European countries. In fact, some advertising executives expect a backlash of nationalism as trade barriers collapse. The prospect of routinely advertising one brand with one campaign may be years away, if it ever happens (Belsky and O'Leary, 1988, p. 7). When transcending national borders, marketers and product development managers in most industries will face a host of constraints. Some of these, such as language barriers, rules and regulations, climate, economic conditions, race, topography, politics, stability, currency and occupations, are obvious. The most important source of constraints that face Europe is cultural differences rooted in history, education, economies, and legal systems (Mesdag, 1987, p. 73). Because of all these differences, the convertability of products among European countries varies enormously from one product category to another. The Europe of 1992 probably will remain dominated by heterogeneous markets well into the 1990s even beyond.

Language barriers will continue to dominate in the foreseeable future. Right now, even among businesspeople, less than one in two throughout Europe speaks a second language fluently (Kuttner, 1988). The ratio is even lower among the general population of the member countries. Consequently, instruction manuals, labels and advertising for multinational use will have to be polyglot, even in business-to-business contexts, and shortage of space will encourage the use of several alternative limited language packs.

Another factor contributing to a heterogeneous European market will be climate and the effects it has on such diversities as clothes, eating, drinking, leisure, travel, choice of car and even attitude toward work. This continues to reinforce traditional religious and racial traits.

Another factor contributing towards a more heterogeneous marketplace for many products and services is currency differences prevalent among member states (see Table 4.8).

Given the variety of currencies and varied exchange rates, the immediate development of a homogeneous marketplace in 1992 is very unlikely. Per capita income and disposable income also vary dramatically among European countries, creating different purchasing and consumption patterns (Table 4.9).

Industrial products, which tend not to be culturally bounded, include such products as steel, chemicals, electronics, computers

TABLE 4.8. Rates of Exchange (Mid-March 1992)

Country	Currency		US$
Germany	Deutche Mark	DM	1.8850
France	Franc	Fr	6.3670
Italy	Lira	L	1,381.25
Netherlands	Guilder	G	2.1275
Belgium	Franc	Bfr	39.47
United Kingdom	Pound	£	0.5918
Irish Republic	Punt	1£	0.7034
Denmark	Krone	Dkr	7.3285
Greece	Drachma	Dr	160.1
Portugal	Escudo	Esc	155.0
Spain	Peseta	Pla	116.9

Source: *The Wall Street Journal*–March 1992.

and agricultural equipment (Chan and Mauborgne, 1987, p. 31). Both product standardization and universal marketing strategy (global marketing) are appropriate for the majority of corporations producing such products. A homogeneous market for these products may exist in the Europe of 1992 as trade barriers are eliminated and regulations are eased. Industrial products have the advantage of economies of scale in production and marketing. In addition, the purchaser for industrial products is often a purchasing agent, as contrasted with a consumer for household goods. Purchasing agents use different types of evaluative criteria, are primarily interested in quality, and compare reputation of supplier and their price. These characteristics are for the most part independent of cultural differences. Industrial products are then less likely to have gains in market share resulting from product differentiation (Chan and Mauborgne, 1987, p. 32). While industrial products tend to be insensitive to cultural differences, minor adaptation and/or modification may be required by some of these products.

TABLE 4.9. National Income and Gross Domestic Product–1985

Country	National Income		GDP	
	Local Currency (bn)	$ bn	Local Currency (bn)	$ bn
Germany	1,709.60	787.3	1,937.00	713.4
France	3,140.70 (a)	477.9	5,018.80	724.6
Italy	609,823.00 (b)	319.4	894,346.00	599.9
Netherlands	385.47	157.3	429.57	175.3
Belgium	4,635.00 (b)	103.8	5,148.00	115.2
Luxembourg	189.96 (a)	4.2	238.96 (b)	4.0
United Kingdom	325.10	476.9	373.40	547.8
Irish Republic	14.40	19.3	18.20	24.5
Denmark	578.40	71.5	662.20	81.8
Greece	4,989.80	45.6	5.564.60	39.8
Portugal	——	——	3.524.80 (b)	20.7
Spain	28,069.00	200.4	32.085.00	229.1

(a) 1982
(b) 1985

Source: *Marketing in Europe*, Table #305, April 1988 *Economist* Intelligence Unit Ltd., London.

Unlike industrial products, though, consumer products such as food and beverages, cosmetics, pharmaceuticals, and health and beauty aids tend to be culturally centered, and therefore generally require both products and marketing adaption to the environment of specific countries; target market needs and subcultures are prevalent. For these products a very heterogeneous marketplace in Europe will continue to exist. Values, attitudes, education and religion all play a vital part in positioning products and identifying potential markets in the Europe of 1992 and beyond.

Marketing planners emphasize that nearly all businesses serve a multitude of market segments, and future market share gains will be materialized by those companies that target emerging segments appropriately and win them. The market place of Europe in 1992 is no exception (Cate, 1988).

The hope for Europe of 1992 is that people, products and services will be able to move among European nations with the same ease as they cross U.S. state borders. Health, safety and other technical requirements will be standardized, making it possible for a product approved for sale in one country to be accepted in another automatically without any impediments. The whole concept of 1992 will make the marketing management task a lot easier for many products; however, many market niches (sub-markets) will still continue to exist for reasons previously noted.

Multi-country market research into the triggers of buyer behavior will demonstrate not one but several Europes for the foreseeable future even though it may identify enough common needs to justify the launch of at least a few "Euro-brands" in major product categories. In the same way, producers will have an interesting choice of marketing approaches: identical campaigns in every country versus a common strategy with local executions versus a separately designed approach in each country (Ogilvy and Mather, 1988, p. 24). Neglecting marketing research will prove increasingly costly as cross-border competition increases within a unified European market starting on January 1, 1993.

SUPPLIERS IN 1992 EUROPE

There is no question that the changes in the European marketplace will have more effect on the supply side than the demand side. In the first place, competition will increase enormously. This will be the result of many member country companies not wishing to market their products outside of their home territory because of their size, product type, location or corporate goals/mission. Some other companies will adopt a wait and see attitude (Ogilvy and Mather, 1988, p. 29). On the other hand, the large multinational companies are already operating across Europe, and many companies with small home markets, such as the Netherlands, have exported for many years in order to survive. These companies will create immediate reduction in their present operating costs through faster distribution, elimination of minor technical variants, savings in logistics and materials handling, to fund an expansive posture. Other companies without such experience may attempt to create external sales drives for the first time as a result of market analysis or because they see attack as the best form of defence (Ogilvy and Mather, 1988, p. 29).

Competitive markets such as the ones that are going to emerge in United Europe sales tend to polarize between a small number of leading brands and a large number of relatively small specialized brands. Those markets not having such a structure tend to be unstable, with medium-size suppliers merging and their brands either growing to brand leader status, shrinking to minor size, or even being withdrawn from the market place. Therefore, it can be expected that the new brands entering during the initial years of the 1992 era will shake up sales. The new market leaders are highly likely to be giant Euro-Brands supplied by multinational corporations who have the resources of production and distribution, skills of selling and promotion, marketing muscle and financial strength needed to win a short-term competition. The other survivors would most likely be small market share, high-price, high-added-value "niche" products, supplied locally by producers with specific advantages or local knowledge and contacts. Suppliers not falling into any of these categories will likely be squeezed out by pressures coming from having advertising, sales promotions, predatory pricing, and distribution demands. Well-experienced multinationals will be the winners and will be able to create economies of scale mergers and acquisitions of middle-sized companies (Ogilvy and Mather, 1988, p. 30). The number of European mergers and acquisitions over the past two years has been quite high, showing a marked increase over the previous decade.

MARKETING TO EUROPE 1992–PROBLEMS AND OPPORTUNITIES

It should be accepted that sooner or later the main propositions of Europe 1992 will be implemented, and that most obvious administrative and technical barriers will be dismantled, even if it is evolutionary in nature. This will make the shipping of goods throughout the European countries easier and quicker, and consequently, cheaper (Hoop, 1988, p. 39). However, easier to ship does not imply easier to market. Consumers may be pleased at the prospect of wider choices, but as we have learned, they still will not buy goods which do not fit their current needs, or do not offer value for their money, or which they have not heard about, or which they cannot get in the shops they patronize. Each aspect of the consumer wheel (cognition, behavior and environment) must be thoroughly restudied in developing a marketing strategy for the concept of Europe 1992.

In Europe, the number of retail outlets is falling as consumers choose fewer but larger retailers. As a result of this, retailer power or its influence will increase substantially. Because of this, even the largest retail chains such as Aldi, Carrifaur, Dee, and Vendex seem to have little ambition to spread themselves throughout Europe. In the unified Europe, retailer power and domination will manifest itself in four ways:

1. Retailers will be free to use supplier sources wherever they see an advantage.
2. They are already beginning to forge formal alliances among retail chains who do not compete directly, to buy in common.
3. Retailers will have access to a much larger number of potential packers of private or own labels (Ogilvy and Mather, 1988, p. 32).
4. The retailers, both non-food and food–the latter of which has in the past been domestically oriented–are now moving rapidly along the path of internationalization, thereby employing a combination of investment, organic growth and buying alliances (see Table 4.10) (Mazur, 1991, p. 14).

Changes in product promotion as a result of all these proposed changes is more speculative in nature. Until issues of freedom of transmission of information are sorted out centrally, local media are likely to continue to require adherence to existing local laws and codes of conduct. However, the availability of super-national media will gradually extend throughout the 1990s. Media owners see Europe as an opportunity and are already investing heavily. In practice, they are likely to tailor television programming to local needs, with captions or dubbing for filmed material and multi-lingual audios for live broadcasts, justifying expensive technology (Reuzin, 1988). It is believed that new multinational consumer magazines are also a prospect for the future, to augment product promotion.

TABLE 4.10. Major European Food Retail Alliances, 1990

Group	Members	Country	Group	Members	Country
Sodei	GIB	Belgium	European Marketing Distribution	Markant	Germany
	Paridoc/Docs de France	France		Markant Food Marketing	Netherlands
Eurogroupe	GIB	Belgium		Selex Gruppo	Italy
	Rewe-Liebbrand	Germany		Selex Ibérico	Spain
	Vendex	Netherlands		Sodacip	France
European Retail Alliance	Ahold	Netherlands		Uniarme	Portugal
	Argyll	UK		Zev-Zentrale/ Julius Meini	Austria
	Casino	France	Di-Fra	Arland	France
incorporating:				Francap	France
Associated Marketing Services	Ahold	Netherlands		Louis Delhaize	Belgium
	Allkauf	Germany		Monoprix/SCA	France
	Casino	France		Montlaur	France
	Dansk Supermarked	Denmark	Deuro	Rallye	France
	ICA	Sweden		Asda	UK
	Kesko	Finland		Carrefour	France
	La Rinascente	Italy		Makro	Netherlands
	Mercadona	Spain		Metro	Germany/ Switzerland
	Migros	Switzerland	Nordisk Andelsforbund	Cooperative organizations	UK, Denmark, Finland, Iceland, Norway, Sweden

Source: Laura Mazur, "Marketing 2000 Critical Challenges for Corporate Survival," *The Economist* Intelligence Unit, Special Report 2126, London 1991, p. 15.

Advertisers will therefore have their choice of independent local campaigns, or a pan-European one through either local or multinational media or some combination.

Product pricing will be a critical subject. Once everyone has free access to goods and services across countries, consumers will have the right to buy wherever the price is lowest. Issues such as minimizing costs, maximizing profits and the European value added tax (VAT) will contribute greatly to pricing policies.

Designing products that match consumers' needs instead of the other way around will have eminence. The concept of Europe 1992 introduces several product design issues. Historically, most long-established products were designed for and launched into one country and, if later rolled out elsewhere, may have succeeded more by good fortune than by design (DiMingo, 1988, p. 36). Even consumer brand names in Europe frequently have local formulations, package design and promotional positioning. A key marketing task in Europe of 1992 will be to design product concepts that fit consumer needs equally in several countries.

A good approach will be to design products with stronger appeal tailored to more tightly-defined target groups who are willing to pay premium prices for recognizable and preferably unique added values over the competition.

The marketing strategy for Europe of 1992 should first and foremost be consumer oriented. In a great market like that presented by the Europe of post-1992 with heavy competition, the risks are too high to not consider the consumer first. Issues related to production, distribution and selling should also be integrated into the marketing strategy of making a specific type of customer happy.

In post-1992 Europe a thorough understanding of and relationship with the final consumer is very important. Understanding consumer behavior and expectations result in a decided advantage to the producer who thoroughly understands its target customers. This puts a premium on quality market research and advertising.

CONCLUSION

As previously stated, the concept of a single European marketplace in 1992 is much more of an evolutionary process than a revolutionary process. The starting point must be market research into the characteristics, behavior, conditions, wants, attitudes, and environments of Euro-consumers. From a managerial perspective, production and marketing will change considerably. Sourcing, order entry, diversified customer service levels, and communication will require much attention and will have a dramatic impact on consumer behavior and demands. Commonality of packaging, labels, and other items will need to be addressed in order to prepare appropriate marketing strategy.

Large European marketers such as Philips, Nestle, and Unilever have survived in Europe's snarl of trading regulations by nurturing strong, independent national companies (Cate, 1988, p. 46). When the barriers come down, smaller companies previously not organized for complex export trade will be able to move products across borders with the same ease as multinationals have done. That means previously unknown brands will suddenly be competing with established market leaders within the confines of new Europe.

To achieve economic unity, however, Europe and its member nations must go far. Political obstacles currently exist and will continue far into the 1990s. Europe also lacks a unified monetary system, one of the basic building blocks of a unified market. Its 12 nations use 11 different languages. Taxation structures and philosophies differ among the member nations. Finally, consumer social, economic, psychological, philosophical, cultural and value structures among the 12 nations are vast and diverse and are not likely to change dramatically in the next decade.

Post-1992 Europe poses some very real opportunities and challenges to the marketers supporting large European multinational companies, small single market European companies, as well as non-Europe global corporations, as these companies set out to capture market share in the new Europe.

BIBLIOGRAPHY

Alter, Stewart. "Why American Should Care." *AdWeek's Marketing Week*, June 6, 1988, p. 4.4+.
Belsky, Gail and Noreen O'Leary. "How '92 Will Change Things." *AdWeek's Marketing Week*, June 6, 1988, p. G.6+.

Cate, Kevin. "1992: Europe Becomes One," *Advertising Age*, July 11, 1988, pp. 46-56.
Chan, Kim W. and Mauborgne, R.A. "Cross Cultural Strategies." *The Journal of Business Strategies*, Spring 1987, pp. 28-35.
DiMingo, Edward. "The Fine Art of Positioning." *The Journal of Business Strategy*, March/April 1988, p. 36.
Dudley, James. *1992 Strategies for the Single Market*. Kogan: London, 1989.
Economist. "The Back Door Is Still Open." February 13, 1988, pp. 46-48.
Economist. "They've Designed the Future and It Might Just Work." February 13, 1988, pp. 45-46.
Economist. "Much Ado About 1992." March 26, 1988, pp. 65-66+.
Economist. "Everyman's Playground, What 1992 Should Mean for John Europe, His Wife and Children." February 13, 1988, pp. 48-49.
Economist. "So Hard to Make a Dream Come True." February 13, 1988, p. 47.
Hoop, Hans van der. "Europhobia or Europhoria?" *Distribution*, October 1988, p. 39.
House, Karen Elliott. "Europe's Global Clout Is Limited By Divisions 1992 Can't Paper Over." *The Wall Street Journal*, February 13, 1989, pp 12-18.
House, Karen Elliott. "For All Its Difficulties, U.S. Stands to Retain Its Global Leadership." *The Wall Street Journal*, January 23, 1989, pp. A1.
Kuttner, Robert. "The U.S. Should Applaud the Coming of Europe, Inc." *Business Week*, July 11, 1988, p. 16.
Lee, Susan. "An Impossible Dream?" *Forbes*, January 25, 1988, pp. 78-83.
Management Europe. "Marketing Research 1992: Keeping in Touch with European Customers." December 19, 1988, pp. 1-6.
Mazur, Laura. "Marketing 2000–Critical Challenges for Corporate Survival." *The Economist* Intelligence Unit: London, 1991.
McKenna, Regis. "Marketing in an Age of Diversity." *Harvard Business Review*, September-October 1988, pp. 88-95.
Melcher, Richard A. "Will the New Europe Cut U.S. Giants Down to Size?" *Business Week*, December 12, 1988, pp. 454-58.
Mesdag, Martin van. "Winging it in Foreign Markets." *Harvard Business Review*, January-February 1987, p. 73.
Northeast International Business. "1992 . . . Obstacles or Opportunities?" January 1989, p. 20+.
Ogilvy and Mather. 1988. *Marketing to Europe*. Brethlenholm Print, London, England.
Riemer, Blanca, Joyce Heard and Thane Peterson. "Laying the Foundation for a Great Wall of Europe." *Business Week*, August 1, 1988, p. 40.
Reuzin, Philip. "Europe Will Become Economic Superpower as Barriers Crumble." *The Wall Street Journal*, December 29, 1988, p. 1.
_____. "Reshaping Europe 1992 and Beyond." *Business Week*, December 12, 1988, p. 49.
Rosenbaum, Andrew. "Fortress–Or Facade?" *Industry Week*, February 6, 1989, pp. 54-55.

Studer, Margaret. "Swiss Go on a European Shopping Spree." *The Wall Street Journal*, August 31, 1988, p. 20.

Swenson, Chester A. "How to Sell to a Segmented Market." *The Journal of Business Strategy*, January/February 1988, pp. 18-22.

Wolf, Julie. "Help for Distribution in Europe." *Northeast International Business*, January 1989, p. 43.

Chapter 5

Marketing Planning and 1992: Observations and Expectations

Peter S. H. Leeflang
Charles P. de Mortanges

BACKGROUND

The development of economic blocks has played an important role in world affairs, particularly since World War II. Nations agreeing on the abolition of various forms of discrimination between their economies is generally referred to as "economic integration." It may take a variety of forms, from a very loose, incohesive arrangement, to an almost inseparable economic union. Examples of economic integration in increasing order of cohesion and intensity are: preferential tariffs; free trade associations; customs unions, common markets, economic unions; and full economic integration. Britain and its Commonwealth countries operate under a system of reciprocal tariff preferences, and the European Free Trade Association (EFTA) abolished tariffs among its member countries. A customs union imposes a common external tariff and has no internal tariffs. A common external tariff was introduced in the European Community (EC) in 1968.

A common market has the added feature of unrestricted factor mobility. On this point, it can be said that the EC is not a common market. According to a 1988 EC Council of Ministers' directive, no obstacles to the free flow of capital are allowed to exist as of July 1, 1990. However, it has been accomplished only in part. Countries like the Netherlands and Germany permit virtually unobstructed flows of capital, whereas in Greece and Spain such flows are either restricted, or free but subject to certain conditions. Even the free movement of goods and services within the EC is often impaired, primarily because of differences in tax rules.

Thus, the European Community has enjoyed common market status for 20 years only to a degree. Still, since a certain measure of harmonization of national economic policies has occurred, the EC has also moved considerably toward an economic union. It is the largest of the world's regional trading arrangements and currently consists of 12 full-member states. Geographic, ideological, and historical proximity are important factors in the process of economic integration (Balassa, 1960). This is evidenced by the EC itself, but also by trade agreements between the U.S. and Canada, between certain Latin American countries (LAFTA) and between certain Asian countries (ASEAN). Therefore, Poland may experience little difficulty in eventually joining the EC, as it meets both the community's geographical and historical requirements (as well as being on the road to meeting the ideological requirement). Turkey, on the other hand, has encountered nothing but postponement of action on its application to join the EC as a full member.

Balassa (1960) states that full economic integration. . . . "presupposes the unification of monetary, fiscal, social, and countercyclical policies and requires the setting up of a supra-national authority whose decisions are binding for the member states" (p. 2). The establishment of the European Parliament, the European Commission, and the European Court of Justice are examples of the serious intent to politically and legally unify Western Europe. Furthermore, the European Monetary System (EMS) and the European Currency Unit (ECU) are the beginnings of a European monetary union. Although they may serve as an example, the EC is still a long way off from full economic integration as exhibited by the cantons of the Swiss confederation, or the states of the United States of America. On this last point, *The Economist* (London) asserts in its July 9, 1988 issue that: "Incontestably, the vision of a great internal European market grew out of admiration for the American version" (p. 49).

"1992" is the euphemism for a number of guidelines presented in a White Paper which was approved in 1985. This proposal consisted of more than 300 directives designed to abolish virtually all remaining intra-EC trade barriers by the end of the year 1992. Project 1992 has since captivated politicians and business persons worldwide. In fact, it has been a very successful campaign, causing a flurry of renewed interest in an area previously plagued by perpetuated slow economic growth and high unemployment. This renewed interest came notably from the U.S. and Japan, and partly out of fear for being left outside the confines of an alleged "Fortress Europe." For the Europeans an important motive for starting project 1992 was to maintain economic and competitive parity with the other industrial super powers. Indeed, Lord Cockfield, EC Commissioner and principal author of the White Paper once said that, "we are definitely not less than the United States or Japan."

The key steps of the White Paper, designed to realize the objective of creating an undivided 320 million consumer market, are:

- Lifting border controls limiting intra-EC movement of goods and labor;
- Developing common EC industrial standards;
- Harmonizing various tax rates in the EC;
- Opening local and central government contracts to competition from within the EC;
- Allowing banks, insurance companies and other financial services firms to trade freely within the EC.

Currently, an ambivalent situation of euphoria (sometimes called "europhoria") and skepticism exists. As of this writing, with roughly 30 months to go before the deadline for completion of project 1992, significant progress has been made. The EC Council of Ministers has adopted over 70% of the single-market measures in the past four years. Yet, many obstacles on the road toward economic and political unity remain, especially in the area of taxation. Proposals to bring individual value-added tax (VAT) and excise rates more in line with each other are still facing lengthy negotiations. Some proposed tax measures failed to get any support at all, and no decisions have been made yet on the elimination of border checks because of alleged political lack-of-will by the individual member states.

Many of the proposed measures have a significant effect on the activities of the European business firm. The legal area is especially problematic. One difficulty is the very slow pace at which the member countries are translating EC legislation into their own national laws. This causes uncertainties and frustration among European companies since they do not have a direct voice in the EC legislative process. Yet these firms have to comply with their national laws which do, or do not yet, incorporate the EC legislation in question. Therefore, companies have concerns regarding the opportunities and threats of a single market, precisely because acceptance and speed of implementation of the new statutes vary from country to country. For instance, certainty about present and future legislation becomes particularly critical when entering into joint ventures, licensing agreements, mergers, and other cooperative arrangements between business entities.

The foregoing (hopefully) makes it clear that "1992" has, or will have, an effect on the marketing of goods and services. In this paper we will attempt to show the consequences of a single European market within the framework of the strategic marketing planning process. Under a single European market we assume that the five key steps of the White Paper, listed above, have been realized.

THE STRATEGIC MARKETING PLANNING PROCESS

In Figure 5.1, we present a flow chart of the steps of the strategic marketing planning process (Leeflang, 1987). The process consists of six steps namely:

I. An analysis of the external and internal environment and the gathering of information about the variables influencing those environments.

II. Based on the analysis and information will be determined with what, where, how, and when one positions himself in the market, in very general terms. This step can also be referred to as where the "mission," or "business" of the company is defined (Abell and Hammond, 1979). In addition, competitive strategies are formulated that are relevant for the entire organization. We call these "generic competitive strategies."

III.[1] Objectives and strategies are formulated for the functional areas on the basis of what has been established in step II. For the functional entity "Marketing" this means the determination of:

- *Strategic Marketing Objectives.* These objectives (e.g., market share, sales, contribution margins) are realized through the use of the marketing mix.
- *Marketing Mix Objectives.* These are objectives regarding, for example, product quality, and intensity of distribution and advertising.
- *Strategic Marketing Decisions.* Decisions made for the medium-term that affect the entire marketing mix, such as which segment(s) to serve.
- *Strategic Marketing Mix Decisions.* These affect only one or two elements of the marketing mix.

IV. The strategic marketing decisions and the strategic marketing mix decisions are translated, or operationalized, into the Annual Marketing Plan.
V. After the plan has been drawn up and approved it must be implemented.
VI. After implementation, the final step in the strategic marketing planning process is an evaluation of the plan.

Steps II, III, and IV are known, collectively, as the "three-cycle system," developed by Lorange and Vancil (1977). What takes place in steps I, II, and III is strategic marketing, whereas step IV refers to operational, or tactical marketing. In fact, steps IV, V, and VI do not really belong to the strategic marketing planning process. However, given the feed-back loops from IV to III, and from VI to I, we thought it necessary to include these steps. The feed-back loops from IV to III, as well as from III to II reflect our opinion that

---

1. As mentioned, this step is called "Functional Strategies." The strategic decisions made in other functional areas of the company (e.g., Finance, R&D, and Production) are, of course, not the primary task of Marketing. Still, through negotiation with other functional areas, or internal constituencies (Anderson, 1982), Marketing can influence their decision making.

FIGURE 5.1. Steps in the Strategic Marketing Planning Process

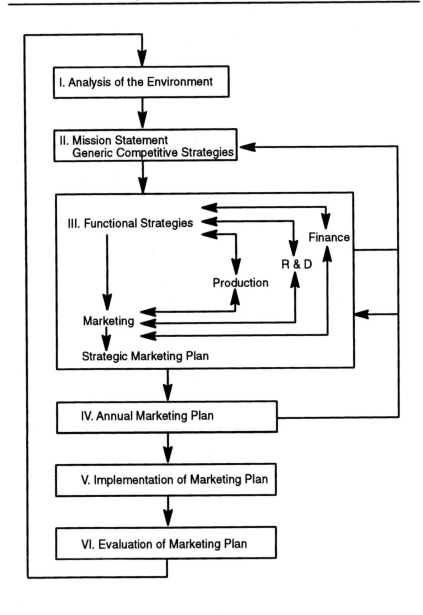

the three components of the "three cycle system" must be determined interactively.

THE POSSIBLE EFFECTS OF A SINGLE EUROPEAN MARKET

After describing, in some detail, the various steps of the strategic marketing planning process above, we will consider the possible effects of a single European market on that process.

Analysis of the Environment

The first step in the strategic marketing planning process consists of three parts: (1) external analysis, (2) internal analysis, and (3) the gathering of data to obtain information relevant to both analyses.

The directives of the White Paper are likely to have a strong effect on a firm's *external environment*. The adopted changes in the political environment will, undoubtedly, carry through into the legal and economic environments. The willingness by the individual countries to speed up the integration process is to a large extent dependent on their view of economic improvement as a result of the integration. We will limit our discussion to the expected changes in the values of the economic environmental variables.

Cecchini (1988) assessed a number of medium-term macroeconomic consequences of the single European market. A similar study was done in 1989 by the Netherlands' Central Planning Bureau (CPB), a Dutch government agency. Some key findings of these studies are presented in Table 5.1. It shows significant differences between the estimates of Cecchini (1988) and the Netherlands' Central Planning Bureau. One reason is that the Cecchini Report assumed adoption of all White Paper directives whereas the CPB did not. The CPB had taken a more cautious and, in our opinion, a more realistic approach. This approach is reflected in the estimates for the effects of integration on the level of employment, where the effects found by the CPB study are zero. This is based on the expectation that the increase in employment through the creation of new jobs will be canceled out by an increase in labor productivity.

Another important economic environmental variable is total con-

TABLE 5.1. Projected Changes in Selected Economic Variables

Variable	Cecchini 1988	CPB 1989	
	EC	EC	Netherlands
GDP (%)	3.2 – 5.7%	2.25%	3.25%
Employment	1.3–2.3 million	Nil	Nil
Consumption (%)	N.A.	2%	3.75%

sumption. It is expected that total consumption will rise in a single European market. However, this rise will not occur across the board, but will vary from industry to industry. Furthermore, developments in one industry will affect developments in another. In Table 5.2, we give an overview of some expected developments in various industries. It shows that "1992" will not have the same implications for all industries. For certain branches of manufacturing and tertiary services, we may expect positive effects of a single European market, but this is much less so for, say, mining and construction. A recent report by Euromonitor (London) also found that not all industries will benefit equally from a unified market. For instance, the report predicts an increase in car sales, a decrease in motorcycle sales, and a shift in sales of tobacco from northern countries to southern countries.[2]

Another expected effect of a single market in the area of consumption is greater standardization. This is the result of:

• Standardization of demand in general, and consumer expectations of product features and quality in particular;
• Internationalization of distribution;
• A greater internationalization of producers selling their products in more EC member states.

This standardization will apply mostly to durable goods such as household appliances, home furnishings, and clothing. Much less

2. See also *Marketing News*, April 24, 1989, pp. 2-5.

TABLE 5.2. Overview of Some Expected Developments in Various Industries

Industry	Production	Employment
Agriculture	(+)	0
Food, beverages, and tobacco	+	+
Textiles and clothing	+	+
Chemicals	++	+
Metals	++	++
Other manufacturing	+	+
Mining	(+)	0
Oil refining, Utility companies	+	0
Construction	(+)	+
Trade	++	(+)
Transportation	+++	−
Other tertiary services	++	−−
Total Industry	+	0

Source: Netherlands' Central Planning Bureau (1989)

Note: The estimated effect of 1992 for the industry is indicated by a minus sign, a zero, or a plus sign. The sign (+), indicates an effect between 0 and +. The estimates are based on a cumulated six-year effect.

standardization will occur in the area of food and beverage products. Because of differences in culture, personal preferences, and eating habits, these products will maintain their national, or even local characteristics. The internationalization process of eating habits in Europe has been going on for years, but is more the result of foreign travel rather than of 1992.

Another important external environmental variable is the growth, composition, and purchasing power of the European population. In "Europhoric" terms one often hears the phrase: "A single market of 320 million potential consumers." Even though this statement is correct, one has to realize that:

- The size of the total EC population is going to decrease;
- The average age of the EC population is rising;

• GDP per capita in the EC is low ($11,600) compared to the U.S. ($17,691) and Japan ($16,730).

Significant changes will also take place in the *internal environment* of the firm with a more pan-European view. Instead of working in, and with, more or less autonomous national enterprises of the various countries, a movement towards Europe-wide product-based businesses is required. Joint ventures and other forms of cooperation between firms will have implications for their organizational structures. Such agreements will not limit themselves to R&D and production. For example, five food brokers in Germany, France, Spain, Italy, and Denmark formed a so-called "community of interest." Each broker owns 51% of its own firm and 9.8% of each of the other four (Drucker, 1988).

There will be an increased need to conduct Europe-wide marketing research. Major difficulties in doing international marketing research are the frequent absence of reliable secondary data, and the lack of standardization of research methodology and analytical techniques (Douglas and Craig, 1983). As a result, meaningful international comparisons are often difficult to realize. Excellent international sources of information are available for the food and beverage market (e.g., Nielsen). However, for other (non-food) industry segments the volume of reliable market data is very disappointing.

Furthermore, efforts will be made to determine the existence of so-called "Euro-Consumers," whose places of residence and economic activity transcend national borders. One such effort was made by Vandermerwe and L'Huillier (1989), who divided the entire Western European area into six clusters. Five variables: geographic latitude and longitude, age, income, and language were used to group 173 regions into six clusters using cluster analysis. Another endeavor of Europe-wide segmentation, but on a much larger scale, was made under the title "Eurostyles Survey." This research project generated 16 different consumer segments, based on a sample of 22,000 respondents (*FEM* [*Financial Economics Magazine*], 3/24/90, pp. 63-67). Names like "Euro-gentry," "Euro-rockies," and "Euro-romantics," among others, were given to the different segment categories, referring to different lifestyles. The results of the project are somewhat reminiscent of the VALS research, done earlier in the U.S., which produced nine American lifestyle typologies (Mitchell, 1983). The suggestion that true "Euro-segments" may exist is further evidenced by the fact that, for example, Euro-rockies are concentrated in the Netherlands and Belgium, but also in Norway.

Mission Statement and Generic Competitive Strategies

In many an enterprise, as a result of 1992, the questions will be raised "what is our business?" and "what should our business be?" The answers to these questions are reflected in the cooperative agreements (e.g., joint ventures) that have taken place among firms recently. To be sure, such activities are also prompted by the question "are we big enough to survive after 1992?" In the area of high-technology, *The Economist* Intelligence Unit (London) reports 69 takeovers and mergers, and 134 joint ventures and alliances other than mergers, within Europe, for the period June 1987-September 1988 (Quelch and Buzzell, 1989). According to Translink, a U.S.-based acquisition advisory firm, 1114 EC companies (with a total value of $ 53 billion) were targets of cross-border acquisitions in 1989 (*The Wall Street Journal/Europe*, 1990a, p. 1).

The idea that size is closely related to survival is particularly evident among European airlines, where several have purchased their major domestic competitors. Examples are British Airways' 1987 purchase of British Caledonian; KLM Royal Dutch Airlines acquiring 40% of its largest competitor Transavia in 1988; and Air France's acquisition of controlling interests in UTA and Air Inter in January 1990.

Some cooperative agreements are less stringent and more aimed at increasing economic clout. Supermarket chains like Ahold, Argyll, and Casino formed the European Retail Alliance, a buying consortium working together at a European level to enhance their influence with food and beverage producers. Vendex (Netherlands), Rewe Centrale (W. Germany), and GB-Inno-BM (Belgium) together founded the Eurogroup for the purpose of joint-purchasing grocery items. Other European examples of cooperative agreements can be found in the travel industry.

Earlier, we mentioned the fears of a "Fortress Europe," expressed by the U.S. and Japan. Although these fears are probably unfounded, the White Paper did not really address the implications of 1992 for Europe's external relations. For that reason, perhaps, Europe has recently experienced a rise in foreign investment from American and Japanese firms on its markets. An article in *Marketing News* (9/26/88, p. 6) advises U.S. companies to establish "a European foothold before the 1992 deadline. . . . by doing so, they not only avoid future external trade barriers but also get an opportunity to learn the new emerging markets as they evolve" (Priovolos, 1988). Quelch and Buzzell (1989) point out that the decision by a large number of Japanese banks and manufacturers to establish themselves in Europe is not strictly based on fears of not having access to its markets. A perfectly sound economic rationale would be that it is cheaper for Japan to produce abroad because of the high value of the yen. In any event, what remains to be seen is whether these American and Japanese entities will be treated as European firms, or as foreign subsidiaries.

Implicit in the discussion above has been the notion of "competition." Consequently, we will now elaborate a bit more on competitive strategies. Following Porter's framework (1980), we can distinguish three so-called "generic competitive strategies:"

- Cost leadership strategy;
- Product differentiation;
- Focus strategy.

We expect that a single European market will lead to greater price competition based on cost leadership, and to greater technology competition based on product differentiation and/or cost leadership. Because of the elimination of entry barriers, cost differences among producers will decrease. When entry barriers prevail cost differences between existing "protected" producers and potential producers will result in higher prices than when such entry barriers are absent. In addition, costs are likely to go down because of:

- less customs documents will be required;
- lower transportation costs, partly because of less paperwork;
- lower finance costs, as a result of the harmonization of the financial markets;

- lower inspection costs, because of a greater conformity of product safety and quality regulations;
- cost savings as a result of the introduction of common technical standards.

Because of the establishment of numerous regulations and directives regarding the production and trade of many goods and services, competition will increase on the basis of differences in technology and price. Successful firms in this new era of economic integration will, primarily, be those who, on the basis of superior technology, can produce high quality or at a low price. Thus, industrial companies will be particularly affected by 1992. Export opportunities, as well as domestic sales will be threatened. The Netherlands' Small Business Economic Institute (EIM) estimates that these threats will, most likely, come from Germany (high quality), and Italy, Spain, and Portugal (low labor costs).

It seems plausible then that larger enterprises, enjoying the benefits of economies of scale and ample R&D budgets, will opt for either price competition or technology competition as a possible strategy. Smaller firms must choose a niche-strategy, i.e., focus on smaller, more specific market segments (Priovolos, 1988; Stephens, 1989). As indicated before, such niches will continue to exist. Furthermore, it is expected that because of increased globalization the number of niches will increase accordingly, improving the opportunities for small- and medium-sized companies.

In summary, we believe that competition in a single European market will intensify. However, because of mergers, take-overs, and cooperative agreements there will be greater competition among larger European businesses. As mentioned before, the expected growth in consumption in the EC, as a result of integration, will be modest (about 2%). In such a situation it is not inconceivable that supply will exceed demand, and that producers must be satisfied with smaller margins.

Marketing Strategies

The strategic marketing planning process also defines the functional strategies. We will begin our discussion with the geographic aspects (as a segmentation tool) of a marketing strategy. We distinguish between the following geographic marketing strategies:

- *Ethnocentric* approach. Focus is on the domestic market
- *Polycentric* approach. Each international market is served differently
- *Regiocentric* approach. Specific regions, regardless of political boundaries, are each served differently.
- *Geocentric* approach. International markets are served undifferentiated. Sometimes referred to as "Global marketing."[3]

After 1992, we expect that shifts in these strategies will occur. An ethnocentric approach may be difficult to maintain and will move more towards a regiocentric approach. Here one could speak of a concentrated regiocentric approach, where a firm operates on a smaller number of markets. Whenever standardization of consumption is likely, a shift from an ethno- or polycentric marketing strategy to a geocentric strategy will take place. However, polycentric approaches will prevail whenever cultural differences necessitate such strategies. In the U.S., a concentrated geocentric approach (global marketing) is sometimes propagated, as evidenced by the following citation from *Marketing News* (9/26/88, p. 6): "As to where a small U.S. company should start, the right approach is to select a small national market, get established there and, as this national market gets integrated into the larger pan-European one, swim with the stream" (Priovolos, 1988).

Product Decisions

The number of European brands on the single market will increase. Even though more products will be sold under one label,

3. The terms "Ethnocentric," "Polycentric," "Regiocentric" and "Geocentric" were first proposed by Perlmutter to describe management attitudes and philosophies towards international business (see Howard V. Perlmutter, "The Tortuous Evolution of the Multinational Corporation," *Columbia Journal of World Business*, January-February, 1969, pp. 9-18. Later, these terms were also applied to formulating international marketing strategies (see Yoram Wind, Susan P. Douglas, and Howard V. Perlmutter, "Guidelines for Developing International Marketing Strategies," *Journal of Marketing*, April, 1973, pp. 14-23.

their composition will be such that local preferences are taken into account. Certain product categories will lend themselves more easily to standardization and are thus better positioned for multi-country marketing. Examples of such products are softdrinks, instant coffee, breakfast cereals, candy bars, and frozen dinners. Successful internationalization of products will, to a large extent, depend on the elimination of variations among EC countries in technical standards, health and safety regulations, testing and certification requirements, and trademark registration procedures. Currently, there are 200 specific barriers to cross-border EC trade in ten food categories (Quelch and Buzzell, 1989). Allowing uniform (EC-wide) packaging specifications will also lead to cost savings. Such savings will be realized, primarily, by companies like Coca-Cola and Perrier, that have unique packaging in terms of their "visual symbolism" and "powerful simplicity of graphics," lessening the need for multilingual labeling (Ashby, 1988).

For certain brands the consumer is already believed to be more or less identical in all EC countries, despite 1992. BMW, the German automaker, contends that in Western Europe as a whole, there is a "typical" BMW buyer. This belief is further demonstrated by the fact that most BMW showrooms are identical in interior design (*FEM* [*Financial Economics Magazine*], 3/24/90, p. 65).

Other product decisions affected by 1992 have to do with trademarks and the protection of patents. Now there is the possibility to register trademarks that will be recognized throughout the EC. However, there is still a lot of uncertainty as to how trademark and patent laws will be introduced and implemented in the future.

Distribution Decisions

In the single European market, manufacturers will be faced with internationally-operating retailers. For example, we expect to see greater international cooperation among retail organizations (while maintaining independence) and international franchising. Earlier, we mentioned examples of cooperative agreements among grocery supermarkets for the purpose of joint purchasing (European Retail Alliance and Eurogroup). Important objectives of the members of these buying consortia is to assure higher quality of the products offered and the development of items under their own brand name, or a European brand name. Another goal is to share distribution networks, advertising and technology. However, we believe that joint purchasing of grocery items will only be advantageous if and when a large number of manufacturers are able to offer European brands. The creation of one, or two, dominant purchasing organizations is, therefore, not to be expected. Even in a large, fully integrated, market like the United States it seems impossible to build up a dominant position in the grocery trade (Nielsen Marketing Research, 1988, p. 6).

The Netherlands is a good case in point of the internationalization of the retail trade. Thirty Dutch retail organizations are active abroad, and in 1988, 203 foreign retailers had operations in the Netherlands. International franchising is likely to focus on consumer durables. Examples are Benetton, C&A, Ikea, and Marks & Spencer. Crossing borders then will be less of an issue, even if that means crossing the sea. New Look, a clothing chain operating in the south of England opened new stores in northwest France, instead of expanding in the north of England.

The efficiency of distribution in the EC is going to improve considerably. The approved single administrative border-crossing document and the elimination of the quotas on trips are but a few examples. Consequently, in the single market it will be easier to cover a larger (cross-border) territory from one distribution center. This provides an opportunity for greater internationalization of wholesalers. For smaller independent wholesalers international cooperation almost seems inevitable.

A concentration of manufacturers and distributors may possibly lead to a battle for power in present international distribution channels. This contest may exacerbate in markets which, from the supply-, as well as from the demand-side, will become more oligopsonistic in nature.

In terms of physical distribution it should be noted that 80% of all goods that flow across intra-EC borders occurs by road. Because of the increased efficiency, mentioned above, transportation costs will decline. An average reduction of 5% in road haulage prices is expected (Quelch and Buzzell, 1989). It will be worthwhile for transport companies to enter cooperative agreements, and put together pan-European networks, as to be in a better position to serve multinational clients. The Dutch transportation sector will benefit especially, because of lower operating costs (due to less restrictive national regulations).

Price Decisions

Lower costs and increased competition will lead to a decline in prices. The Cecchini Report projects an overall decline in prices between 4.5% to 7.7%. The Netherlands' Central Planning Bureau (CPB) estimates are much more modest: a 2% decline for the EC, as well as for the Netherlands itself. This percentage is based on domestic consumption. The import-export prices are expected to be 2.25% lower, according to the CPB.

Actually, the development in pricing is difficult to predict. Much will depend on EC agreements on "suggested retail pricing" rules, and on Value-Added Tax (VAT) rates. Earlier, we stated that the free flow of goods and services cannot be achieved without substantial changes in the tax rules. For example, the total percentage of taxes levied on new cars when sold, varies greatly throughout the EC. On a typical mid-size car they range from 12% in Luxembourg to 260% in Greece. Even in countries much closer economically, politically, and culturally, such as Germany (14%) and the Netherlands (51%), the tax differences are significant (*The European*, 1990, p. 24).

Other factors are the more rigorous enforcement of competitive policies and the opening up of public procurement contracts to foreigners. Evidence of the latter is Siemens' (a German technology concern) contract to build a power plant in northern England, and Britain's STC to supply computers to the German parliament (*The Wall Street Journal/Europe*, 1990b, p. 1).

Promotion Decisions

A growth in "Euro-brands" will lead to advertising aimed more at the entire European market. Today, the number of Euro-brands is still rather limited and most are "up-market" (e.g., Louis Vuitton luggage, Giorgio Armani clothes). That is not to say that we do not find similar brands all over Europe. However, most of these brands are American, or Japanese, and are prevalent in a limited number of categories such as automobiles, cigarettes, alcoholic beverages, and electronic equipment. What these brands have in common is that they are subject to pan-European communication. A lot of their advertising is done in European editions of American publications such as *Time, Newsweek,* and *The Wall Street Journal.*

Deregulation and advances in technology are changing the position of media in Europe. Independently owned and operated satellite, cable, and broadcasting TV stations are challenging Europe's established broadcasting monopolies. It has been estimated that by 1992, 21% of all European homes will be able to receive satellite television (Quelch and Buzzell, 1989). After initial difficulties, two truly commercial TV stations (SKY and Super Channel), which can be seen all over Europe, have turned profitable. *Marketing News* reported that: "countries that have resisted broadcast advertising up to now, are being forced to comply with the Europe-wide trend by allowing commercial stations, whether national or pan-European, to beam advertising to their citizens" (*Marketing News,* 1987, p. 2).

Pan-European communication may be an efficient and cost-effective concept. However, cultural differences expressed in, for example, taste and habits will remain. Another aspect of culture is language, which puts restrictions on global marketing in general, and global advertising in particular. Still, global TV advertising with an emphasis on visual impressions and music can, possibly, create a desired image for the product. In addition, local/regional media must be used to take into account local/regional differences between varieties of the same brand. We believe, different approaches are needed for different language areas to support more global messages. It points to a regiocentric marketing strategy, adhering to the view: "Think globally, act locally."

The above will lead to a greater use of multinational advertising agencies. For example, Heineken Breweries recently switched from using agencies based in local markets, to one large international agency (J. Walter Thompson) to handle all its European advertising. According to Heineken, the move to a single agency is being taken in preparation of a single European market, but does not imply it will adopt a single European campaign. A number of separate advertising campaigns will continue to be used in local markets (*The Wall Street Journal/Europe,* 1990c, p. 4) Finally, company-sponsored events, the use of point-of-purchase materials and merchandising, will also get a more distinct international flavor (Stevens, 1989).

Implementation

In this paper we have given an overview of the implications of a single European market on the marketing planning process. We have indicated the changes that may occur in the strategic and more operational decisions as a result of the 1992 directives. Although there remain several unknowns that can influence the future of the newly-unified European market, a great many variables can be considered as given. No one will have to wait until 1993 to see how everything will have worked out in reality. In fact, many changes will take place despite 1992. Internationalization, concentration, and competition are key issues here. Developments in these key factors cannot be emphasized enough in the creation of a single market.

CONCLUSION

We would like to conclude with some words of caution amidst all the euphoria. There will only be a limited blending of habits, customs, and tastes, culminating in similar preferences and buying behavior. A medium that could act as a catalyst toward such blending is television. Advertising on pan-European TV could indeed expose 320 million consumers to the same message. A major challenge is to make broadcasts that go along with such advertising appealing to a pan-European audience. Previous efforts have run into serious difficulties. Both SKY and Super Channel only recently became modestly profitable after repeated changes of management and program format. For the most part viewers still stay tuned to their local stations.

Although both SKY and Super, initially, broadcast in English only, it is not clear whether that particular aspect caused resistance with viewers. Today, SKY's "Eurosport" is presented in local languages as well. The question of language remains a major challenge in marketing. Is it possible to use one language (i.e., English) for promotional and packaging purposes? In the Netherlands yes, but what about Italy, Spain, Portugal, or even Germany? The two official languages currently in use at the level of the European Parliament and the European Commission are English and French. However, the Germans (largest EC contributors in almost every way) are lobbying hard to have their language included too. It seems that steps toward unity are often wholeheartedly and unanimously approved, as long as individual pride is not negatively affected.

Full economic and political integration will, therefore, never come into being. The expectation that after 1992 a certain type of "Euro-consumer" will, miraculously, appear is unrealistic. However, even with two major boundaries removed (physical and legal) the task awaiting the international marketer is formidable. Time and again, compromises will have to be found between a global and a more regiocentric or polycentric approach in often heterogeneous markets.

BIBLIOGRAPHY

Abell, Derek and John S. Hammond. (1979). *Strategic Market Planning, Problems and Analytical Approaches*. Englewood Cliffs, NJ: Prentice-Hall, Inc.
Anderson, P.F. (1982). "Marketing, Strategic Planning and the Theory of the Firm," *Journal of Marketing*. Vol. 46, No. 2.
Ashby, J. (1988). "European Unification in 1992 Challenges U.S. Export Packaging," *Marketing News*. Vol. 22, No. 21, p. 7.
Balassa, Bela. (1960). *The Theory of Economic Integration*. Homewood, IL: Irwin.
Calingaert, Michael. (1989). *The 1992 Challenge from Europe*. Washington, DC: National Planning Association.
Cecchini, Paolo. (1988). *The European Challenge 1992*. Aldershot (U.K.): Wilwood House.
Cecchini Report. (1988). *The Cost of Non-Europe: Obstacles to Transborder Business Activity*. Luxembourg: Office for Official Publications of the European Community.
Centraal Plan Bureau. (1989). "Werkdocument 28 *Nederland en Europa 1992*. The Hague.
Completing the Internal Market. (1985). White Paper from the Commission to the European Council.
Daniels, John D. and Lee H. Radebaugh. (1990). *International Business*. Reading, MA: Addison-Wesley Publishing Co.

Douglas, Susan P. and Samuel Craig. (1983). *International Marketing Research.* Englewood Cliffs, NJ: Prentice-Hall.
Drucker, Peter F. (1988). "Alternative Strategies for Europe's New Market," *Point of View.* Spencer Stuart.
Dudley, James W. (1989). *1992–Strategies for the Single Market.* London: Kogan Page.
Dunning, John H. and Peter Robson. (1987). "Multinational Corporations and European Integration," *Journal of Common Market Studies.* (December), pp. 103-272.
EC Commission. (1987). *Europe Without Frontiers: Completing the Internal Market.* Luxembourg: Office for Official Publications of the European Community.
The Economist. (1988). "Survey of Europe's Single Market," (July 9).
Euromoney. (1988). Special Supplement "Towards A Single Market 1992," (September).
The European, July 13, 1990, p. 24.
Financial Economics Magazine (FEM), March 24, 1990, pp. 63-67.
Gordon, Kathryn. (1987). "1992: Big Bang or Little Whimpers?" *Banker* (London), (October), pp. 18-23.
Jain, Subhash A. (1990). *International Marketing Management.* Boston: Kent Publishing Co.
Johansson, Johny K., Susan P. Douglas, and I. Nonaka. (1985). "Assessing the Impact of Country of Origin on Product Evaluations," *Journal of Marketing Research.* pp. 388-396.
KPMG Accountants. (1989). *Jaarbeeld '88.* Amsterdam.
Kotler, Philip and Gary L. Lilien. (1983). *Marketing Decision Making: A Model-Building Approach.* New York: Harper & Row.
Leeflang, Peter S.H. (1987). *Probleemgebied Marketing, Een Management Benadering.* Leiden: Stenfert Kroese.
_____. (1986). "Belang van de Strategische Marketing Neemt Toe," *Harvard Holland Review.* No. 6.
Kourvetaris, George A. (1986). "Europe Moves Towards Economic and Political Integration," *Journal of Social, Political and Economic Studies* (Summer), pp. 131-162.
Lorange, P. and R.F. Vancil. (1977). *Strategic Planning Systems.* Englewood Cliffs, NJ: Prentice-Hall.
Marketing News, March 27, 1987, p. 2.
Mitchell, Arnold. (1983). *The Nine American Lifestyles.* New York: Warner Books.
Nielsen Marketing Research. (1988). *Met het oog op de toekomst.* A.C. Nielsen (Netherlands).
Pelkmans, Jacques. (1988). "De Euroforie van 1992," *Harvard Holland Review,* No. 16.
Porter, Michael E. (1980). *Competitive Strategy.* New York: The Free Press.
_____. (1985). *Competitive Advantage.* New York: The Free Press.

Priovolos, George V. (1988). "Small Business Can Benefit from European Economic Changes If They Take Precautions," *Marketing News* (September 26), p. 6.

Pryce, Roy (ed.). (1987). *The Dynamics of European Union.* New York: Methuen.

Quelch, John A. and Robert D. Buzzell. (1989). "Marketing Moves through EC Crossroads," *Sloan Management Review* (Fall), pp. 63-74.

Quelch, John A., Robert D. Buzzell and Eric R. Salama. (1990). *The Marketing Challenge of 1992.* Reading, Mass: Addison-Wesley Publishing Co.

Stephens, N. (1989). "Europe '92 May Help Some Marketers More than Others," *Marketing News*, Vol. 23, No. 9.

Taylor, Paul. (1983). *The Limits of European Integration.* New York: Columbia University Press.

Vandermerwe, Sandra and Marc-André L'Huillier. (1989). "Euro-Consumers in 1992," *Business Horizons*, (January-February), pp. 34-40.

The Wall Street Journal/Europe, April 30, 1990a, p. 1.

The Wall Street Journal/Europe, April 14, 1990b, p. 1.

The Wall Street Journal/Europe, March 16, 1990c, p. 4.

Chapter 6

A Model for Defensive Marketing Strategy with Examples from the Europe 1992 Context

Roger J. Calantone
C. Anthony di Benedetto
Curtis E. Harvey

INTRODUCTION

A key element of an effective marketing strategy is a product's position relative to its competitors (Kotler, 1980), that is, how it is perceived by potential customers. Management of a brand's perceptual position is an ongoing concern for numerous reasons. A change in positioning may be necessary if new competitors enter the market, if customer tastes change or if new customer segments develop. Product managers could benefit from applying a conceptual positioning framework that represents their served market. The framework should also model the effects of competitive moves and counterattacks realistically. This study presents and illustrates the use of a new managerial decision tool for product positioning. This tool can assess the consequences of simple repositioning attacks and defense strategies. It can also effectively account for disruptive changes in industry structure caused by revolutionary product innovation by new entrants or established competitors. Because of important changes currently taking place in the global market, firms are facing stiffer global competition and must be more concerned than ever about maintaining competitive strength.

This chapter was originally published in *Journal of Euromarketing*, Vol. 1(1/2) 1991.

In the search for competitive advantage, new management tools for product positioning, particularly in the international arena, are taking on an unprecedented importance. For Europe, and other countries that trade with it (including the U.S.), the competitive struggle for the markets of the future has already begun. Prompted by a successful marketing campaign, the Spirit of 1992 (EC '92) has alerted business and fired its imagination. For American firms, a failure to respond promptly to the European challenge could mean a serious loss of market share abroad and the crowding out of offshore manufacturers (Magee, 1989, p. 82).

The European Community's goal of creating by 1993 an open internal market is clearly a formidable, but attainable, goal. Several sets of barriers are targeted for removal in order to stimulate the free flow of goods, services, capital and labor. Currently, these barriers still support a host of physical, technical and fiscal frontiers among the member countries; but this will soon change (Emerson, 1988, p. 33). From an economic standpoint, these barriers fall into five categories: (1) tariffs; (2) quantitative restrictions (quotas); (3) cost-increasing regulations; (4) market-entry restrictions; and (5) market-distorting subsidies and practices.

Removing these barriers and other market distortions will lead to predictable, yet still unquantifiable cost-price reductions. But as barriers fall, importers in quest of larger market shares will pass on to consumers lower costs in the form of lower prices. Domestic suppliers will follow suit by lowering profit margins, eliminating inefficiencies, and perhaps holding wage demands in check. Lower prices will lead to higher quantities of goods demanded, which in turn will stimulate investment. New investment expands capacity and, through the capture of scale economies, lowers the costs of production. This will trigger further cost-price reductions and a still more competitive market environment.

In the longer run, reconsidered and revised business strategies will result in an ongoing process of restructuring through mergers, liquidation, and other forms of revitalization. The exploitation of new, technical economies of scale will also continue unabated.

Throughout the entire process, the European consumer gains because prices decline and real incomes rise. His or her ability to purchase goods and services expands. For the economies of Europe, the expected welfare increase is the difference between the gain for consumers versus the loss in profits heretofore protected. Early estimates based on partial equilibrium calculations show that the expected total welfare gains from completing the internal European market range from 4.3 to 6.4% of E.C. gross domestic product, or an average of 5.3%. [Note: welfare (economic) gains are defined as gains by consumers and producers that approximate the increase in real income for each country.] Based on projections for 1988 gross domestic product, this translates into ECU 215 billion (Emerson, 1988, p. 155). [Based on the ECU-US$ exchange value of May 12, 1989, ECU 215 billion-US$233.6 billion.] A little less than one-half of this gain is attributable to the removal of trade barriers, the remainder to market integration based on effective competition policy.

The post-1992 market of Europe facing business will be a different market. Relative to non-Community producers, Community firms will discover reduced production costs and a competitive cost advantage. Market unification is bound to undermine the continuation of market segmentation by country with specially-designed promotional, pricing and distribution strategies. Benefits derived from such segmentation policies are destined to shrink. This is likely to occur most prominently in the pharmaceutical, life insurance, domestic appliances and German automobile industries (Davis et al., 1989, p. 7). And finally, a newly opened internal market will surely spawn new companies for whom markets were previously closed or unattractive.

MODELING COMPETITIVE ATTACK AND DEFENSE

Competitive attacks on a domestic producer can take many forms. "Flanker" brands may be launched by a manufacturer of small consumer goods (e.g., Colgate introduced a gel toothpaste to compete directly with Crest's gel product). A similar case can be cited for the European Community. In an effort to preserve environmental integrity, the Henkel A.G. introduced Persil, a phosphate-free laundry detergent. Not to be outdone, Procter & Gamble soon brought out Ariel and Unilever followed with OMO, both also phosphate free. Firms may also expand their market base by developing new geographic markets for their products (enter new European Community countries previously closed due to high entry barriers) or may use different distribution channels to reach new targets.

A costly and risky attack strategy, but one with potentially great payoff, is made possible by advancements in technology. Crawford (1987) and others referred to this as "technology push" innovation. For example, the innovating firm enters a new market with a product based on newly developed technology, which may be radically different from the brands of entrenched competitors. Examples of such "revolutionary" product innovations include the transistor replacing the vacuum tube, the electric typewriter replacing the mechanical one, the word processor replacing the electric typewriter, and many others (Assael, 1985, Ch. 7; Cooper and Schendel, 1976; Utterback, 1981, 1982; Utterback and Abernathy, 1975).

Because a revolutionary product innovation can substantially alter the competitive structure of an industry, the incumbent firms must carefully select a strategic response to the new threat (Cooper and Schendel, 1976). Relatively simple and cheap defensive strategies (such as price cuts) may not be effective or may be easily met by competitors. The alternative, new product development, will require a larger commitment of funds and time and will certainly be riskier (Crawford, 1987). The defending firms must also consider the long-run consequences of their decisions. One can already observe many transnational positioning battles in the "New Europe," as many firms entrench in both the minds of their buyers as well as their distributors to thwart the inroads attempted by larger competitors from neighboring countries. Simple product "retuning" may be a profitable short-run strategy, but a commitment to R&D may be essential to long-run survival in the industry (Bennett and Cooper, 1979).

When making strategic positioning decisions, marketing analysts locate competing brands along salient perceptual dimensions (Hauser and Simmie, 1981; Shocker and Srinivasan, 1979; Urban and Hauser, 1980). In a practical decision-making setting, an analytical positioning model should provide a view of the competitive situation. It should also be capable of answering "what-if" questions concerning potential proactive strategies and defensive repositionings. The DEFENDER model (Hauser and Shugan, 1983; Hauser and Gaskin, 1984) is useful in this regard, as is Lane's (1980) economics-based model of competition with differentiated products.

A positioning model such as DEFENDER is probably best suited for analyzing the effects of marketing-mix adjustments such as price changes, promotion reallocations or minor product improvements. Certain additional complications may arise in the case of revolutionary product innovation which might make typical positioning models inadequate. In particular, the new technology might add one or more new dimensions ("determinant attributes") to the industry structure. For example, before the advent of electric typewriters, durability and ease of service were the two determinant attributes. But once electric typewriters were introduced, speed and accuracy increased in importance. Similarly, storage capability and software availability became important attributes with the introduction of word processing.

Marketing strategists might refer to these attributes as "potentially determinant": there was latent demand for faster, more accurate typewriters that could not be met until the electric typewriter technology was developed and commercialized. The innovating firm thus successfully created a determinant attribute (see discussion in Guiltinan and Paul, 1988, Ch. 3). Currently popular positioning models represent industry structure in few (usually, but not always, two) dimensions and do not permit increases in dimensionality which may occur as a result of disruptive change in technology in the industry.

In this study, we present a conceptual framework for positioning that can be used as an analytical tool. It can handle up to three non-price attributes. We provide an illustration of our framework using real data obtained from globally competitive industries. The model presented is not meant to be a theoretical microeconomic model. Unlike Hauser (1988), Hauser and Shugan (1983), Lane (1980) and others, we do not seek to provide "rules for action" based on microeconomic analysis. Rather, we illustrate how a manager faced with a new competitive situation chooses appropriate attack or defense strategies. From a microeconomic standpoint, our model is a simple extension of those mentioned above, incorporating many of the same constraints and assumptions. Our positioning results are consistent with those obtained by previous positioning studies. This is discussed in the concluding section.

DECISION MODEL

Two-Brand Case

We present the model for the simplest case (only two competitors) in this section. A later section will permit inclusion of multiple $(n > 2)$ brands. (Technical assumptions are presented in the Appendix at the end of this chapter.)

In the three-dimensional per-dollar map of Figure 6.1, two brands, B1 and B2, are represented. The Cartesian coordinates (x_1, y_1, z_1) corresponding to Brand 1 represent the amount of each attribute obtained by the purchase of one unit of Brand 1 per dollar spent. Assumption 1 (assumptions are listed in the Appendix) permits the construction of the map of Figure 6.1, while under Assumption 5, one may assume that all customers in the market have the same perceptions of the brands as is indicated.

Figure 6.1 also provides the spherical coordinates for each brand. α Any point in Cartesian coordinate space (x_i, y_i, z_i) may be equivalently represented by spherical coordinates (r_i, α_i, β_i), where r_i represents the distance between the point and the origin, and α_i and β_i are the angles as indicated in the Figure.

Now, a given customer C_1 considers only Attribute 1 (represented by the X axis) in his or her purchase decision. He/she will choose whichever brand is highest in Attribute 1, according to Assumptions 2 and 3. If there are only two brands to consider in Figure 6.1, and using the angle nomenclature given, Brand i will be preferred if its projection on the X axis is more distant from the origin than the projection of Brand j. Stated mathematically, Brand i is preferred to Brand j if

$$r_i (\cos \alpha_i)(\sin \beta_i) > r_j (\cos \alpha_j)(\sin \beta_j); \qquad (1)$$

otherwise Brand j will be preferred. If both sides of Equation (1) are equal, the customer will be indifferent between the two brands.

FIGURE 6.1. Three-dimensional per-dollar map: Two brand case

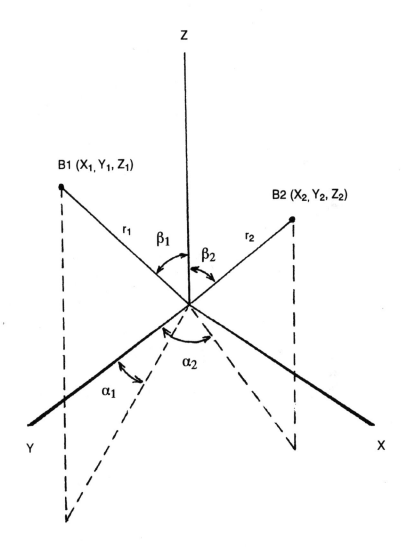

Customer C_2, who considers only Attribute 2 (represented by the Y axis) in his/her purchase decision, will choose Brand i over Brand j if

$$r_i (\sin \alpha_i)(\sin \beta_i) > r_j (\sin \alpha_j)(\text{Sin } \beta_j); \qquad (2)$$

and similarly, customer C_3 who considers only Attribute 3 will choose Brand i over Brand j if

$$r_i (\cos \beta_i) > r_j (\cos \beta_j). \qquad (3)$$

The taste preferences of these customers may be represented by rays emanating from the origin. In the case of customers C_1, C_2 and C_3, these rays are coincident with the X, Y and Z axes respectively. For example, when making his or her decision, another customer may place equal importance on Attributes 1 and 2 and no importance on Attribute 3. His or her taste preference would be represented by a ray in the XY plane with $\beta = 45$ degrees. For still other customers, a ray with $0 < \alpha < 90$ and $0 < \beta < 90$ would represent their taste preference (this would occur whenever at least some importance was placed on each of the three attributes). According to Assumption 4, any of these taste preferences are equally probable. One may therefore represent the various possible taste preferences in the market by a set of rays R emanating in all positive directions from the origin (that is, both α and β are permitted to vary between 0 and 90 degrees). Allowing α and β to vary within these bounds constrains the set of rays in R to the positive octant (the one-eighth sphere where values of x, y, and z are all positive). Assumption 4 implies that any ray which is a member of R is equally probable for any randomly chosen customer.

Equations (1), (2) and (3) may be generalized for the case where the taste preference ray is not coincident with an axis. Consider Figure 6.2, where the ray TP_i represents the taste preference of customer C_i. This ray is characterized in spherical coordinates by the angles α_0 and β_0. The reflection of Brand 1 on this ray is given by

$$r_i \cos (\alpha_1 - \alpha_0) \cos (\beta_1 - \beta_0). \qquad (4)$$

Thus Brand 1 will be preferred to Brand 2 if

$$r_1 \cos (\alpha_1 - \alpha_0) \cos (\beta_1 - \beta_0) > \tag{5}$$
$$r_2 \cos (\alpha_2 - \alpha_0) \cos (\beta_2 - \beta_0);$$

and a customer will be indifferent between the two brands if his or her taste preference ray (α_0, β_0) is such that

$$r_1 \cos (\alpha_1 - \alpha_0) \cos (\beta_1 - \beta_0) = \tag{6}$$
$$r_2 \cos (\alpha_2 - \alpha_0) \cos (\beta_2 - \beta_0).$$

Equations (5) and (6) allow the set of rays R to be divided into two subsets R_1 and R_2 (as in Figure 6.3) where R_i contains the taste preferences of all customers who will prefer Brand i. The rays in subset R_1 map out a surface M_1 on the positive octant of the sphere in the figure; the rays in subset R_2 map out surface M_2. The dividing curve between the two surfaces (indicated by 00') is the indifference curve defined by Equation (6). That is, it represents the taste preferences of all customers who are indifferent between the two brands.

The proportion of all rays in R which are members of subset R_1 is equal to the area of surface M_1 divided by the total surface area of the positive octant $(M_1 + M_2)$. For example, if the curve defined by Equation (6) exactly bisected the positive octant, the proportion of rays in R_1 would be given by

$$\text{area of } M_1 / (\text{area of } M_1 + \text{area of } M_2)$$
$$= 0.5 \ (1/8)(4 \ \pi \ r^{*2}) / (1/8)(4 \ \pi \ r^{*2}) = 0.5. \tag{7}$$

Because the surface area of a sphere is $4 \ \pi \ r^2$, the surface area of one octant is one-eighth of this area, and the radius in Figure 6.3 is r^*. Note that the choice of a value for r^* is irrelevant as it will always drop out of Equation (7): all that matters is the ratio of M_1 to $M_1 + M_2$. Because of Assumption 4 (uniform taste distribution), the proportion $M_i / (M_1 + M_2)$ is an estimate of the market share of Brand i.

Extension of Model to Three (or More) Brands

For the three-brand case, one obtains three indifference curves, each representing indifference between one pair of brands. (For n

FIGURE 6.2. A taste-preference ray in three-dimensional space

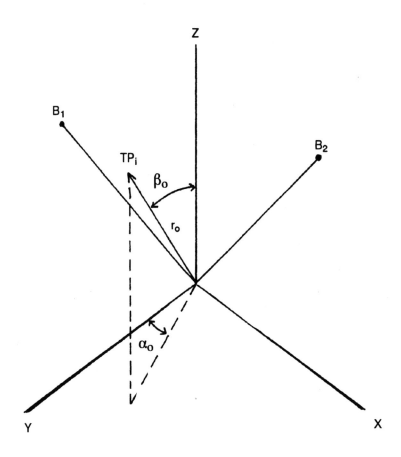

brands, one obtains (n choose two) indifference curves which equals $n!/(2!*(n-2)!)$ curves.) Figure 6.4 illustrates how these curves might divide the positive octant into six regions. A customer whose taste preference ray lies in region A1 or A2 will prefer Brand 1; similarly, Brand 2 is chosen by customers in regions B1 and B2 and Brand 3 is preferred by customers in regions C1 and C2. In Figure 6.4, the relevant portions of the indifference curves are indi-

FIGURE 6.3. Indifference curves in three-dimensional space

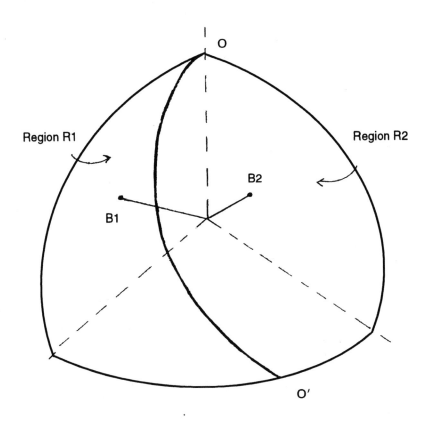

Region	Order of Brand Preference
R1	B1 > B2
R2	B2 > B1

Note: The > ("greater than" sign) stands for "is more preferred than."

FIGURE 6.4. Per-dollar map: Three brands

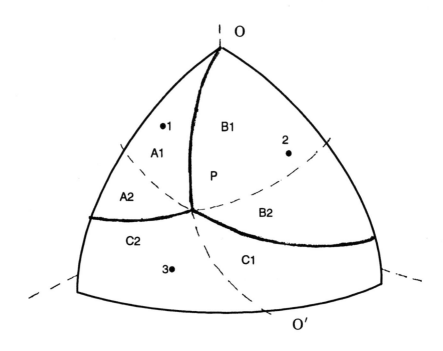

Region	Order of Brand Preference
A1	1 > 2 > 3
A2	1 > 3 > 2
B1	2 > 1 > 3
B2	2 > 3 > 1
C1	3 > 2 > 1
C2	3 > 1 > 2

Notes: The > ("greater than" sign) stands for " is more preferred than."
The relevant segments of the pairwise indifference curves are indicated
with heavy lines.

cated with heavy lines. To avoid confusion, the irrelevant portions are omitted in later figures.

Competitive Attack

We will consider two possible scenarios for a competitive attack: (1) a three-attribute, three-brand industry with global competition where one incumbent firm attacks by minor product improvement along a salient attribute or by price cutting; (2) a two-attribute, two-brand industry where the domestic incumbents are attacked by a new global entrant possessing a revolutionary, innovative product.

Minor Product Improvement and Price Cutting

Suppose that Brand 3 repositions along one of the salient attributes. Its position would move away from the origin in the direction as indicated in Figure 6.5, changing the values of r, α, and β. The figure also shows that if Brand 3 attempts to gain market share by cutting price, its position would move out along a ray emanating from the origin (that is, r increases while α and β remain unchanged). Either way, Brand 3's repositioning causes the indifference curves which cross surface M to move, as indicated in Figure 6.5, and Brand 3's market share would be projected to increase proportionately. We can assume that switching costs are negligible, but that switching is not instantaneous (see Assumption 6). That is, market shares are assumed to readjust over a period of time, finally reaching the levels predicted by the model. In this paper we assume that market shares adjust linearly, although we recognize that other patterns could also be represented.

A competitor could use the model to project the effects of proactive brand repositionings as well as of defensive countermoves by competitors. In the situation as depicted in Figure 6.5, the firm manufacturing Brand 3 would be able to project market shares resulting from a number of possible proactive and defensive moves. Knowing fixed and variable costs and market size, and assuming linear adjustments in market share, the firm could calculate the profit contribution obtained by each brand at any time up to time T, which is when market shares begin to stabilize. This information

FIGURE 6.5. Repositioning of Brand 3 and resulting indifference curve shifts

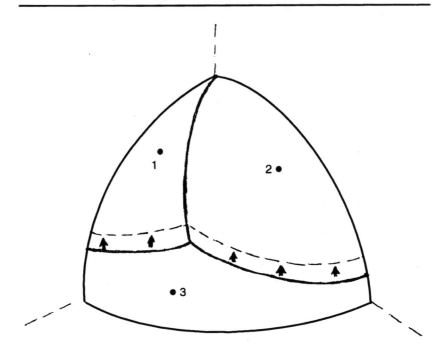

Note: Where indifference curves shift, the solid line indicates location before repositioning, and the dashed line inidicates location after repositioning.

could then be used by the firm to select the most appropriate attack strategy.

For example, the firm may believe that it will take j periods for market shares to stabilize after an attack (j will vary according to the class of product, the nature of the buying process, etc.). It would choose to undertake a competitive attack if the net impact on discounted future profits is positive. It uses a planning horizon of k periods.

For any period j, the projected discounted profit contribution could be expressed as

$$\pi_j = \frac{M_j N_j (P_j - C_j) - F_j}{(1 + r)^j} \qquad (8)$$

where π_j = contribution to the firm's profits in period j,
M_j = projected market share in period j (obtained from model described above),
N_j = industry sales (in units) in period j,
P_j = price per unit in period j,
C_j, F_j = per unit variable costs and fixed costs in period j,
r = discount rate.

Cumulative discounted profit contributions over the time horizon, $CDPC_K$, could then be expressed as

$$CDPC_k = \sum_{j=1}^{k} \pi_j \qquad (9)$$

Clearly, if the expected contribution to discounted cumulative profits without competitive attack (i.e., status quo) is $CDPC_k$ and the projected CDPC given attack and likely competitive response is $CDPC_k{}^*$, the firm would decide to attack if

$$CDPC_k{}^* - Z > CDPC_k, \qquad (10)$$

where Z is the cost of attacking (for example, the research and development expense incurred during time period 0 in order to improve the brand's performance on one attribute).

Lotus Development Corporation's entry into the European software market exemplifies this sort of competitive attack. In 1982 Lotus had four major American competitors, VisiCorp, Microsoft, Micro-Pro, and Ashton-Tate, all developing software products designed to compete against the Lotus 1-2-3 spreadsheet package. By early 1983, at least two of these (Microsoft and Ashton-Tate) had opened European offices and were preparing translated versions of their software packages. The European software market was highly segmented because of linguistic, legal and regulatory differences, and grey marketing and unauthorized copying of software were additional problems. Lotus's European expansion plans began in earnest in fall 1983 when a British distributor was hired. Extensive translation of software and support materials began soon after. In the meantime, the English version was targeted to the U.K., Scandinavia (where English is widely spoken) and Germany and France (with local language tutorial manuals and promotional materials). Recognizing that the basic needs of European buyers were essentially the same as those of American buyers, no substantial changes to the software (other than translation) were planned. Lotus hoped that successful entry into large European companies would give it an edge for competing in the small-business personal computer market, expected to predominate by the late 1980s in Europe. (Case described in Yoffie, 1990, pp. 33-47.)

Revolutionary Attack by New Entrant

This can be treated as a special case of the above model. Consider the DEFENDER-like industry model in Figure 6.6a. Two brands are depicted in XY space. These brands can be represented using spherical coordinates, holding $\beta = 0$ (angle β is irrelevant as far as the incumbents are concerned).

Now suppose that Brand 3 enters with a revolutionary innovation (Figure 6.6b). (We can assume that Brands 1 and 2 are deficient or lacking in this new attribute.) The model as depicted in Figure 6.6b could be used by the incumbent firms (1) to understand the changes in the competitive structure of the industry caused by Firm 3's attack, and (2) to assess the profit consequences of various repositioning strategies. The mathematical treatment would be identical to that of the previous case described above.

The successful launch of the Swatch watch is an example of an interesting revolutionary product innovation in a multinational setting. Traditional Swiss watchmakers were facing serious competition from Far Eastern manufacturers using electronic watch technology, yet remained extremely non-responsive to market changes: obsolete styles were continued, prices stayed high, and distribution was mainly through watch and jewelry stores. The Swatch watch

FIGURE 6.6. Disruptive change in industry structure

a. Before Attack

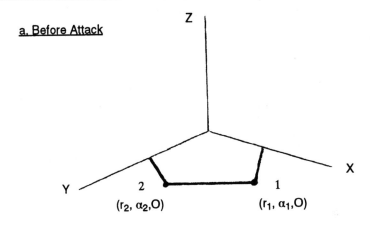

(r_2, α_2, O) (r_1, α_1, O)

b. After Attack

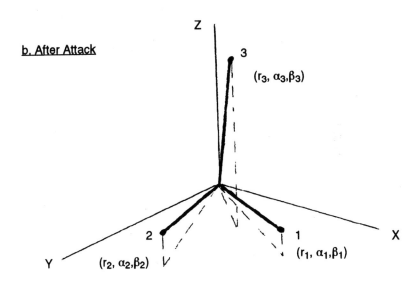

(r_3, α_3, β_3)

(r_2, α_2, β_2) (r_1, α_1, β_1)

$\beta_{12}, \beta_{2,} << \beta_3$

was developed by the Swiss watchmaking group Asuag-SSIH under the direction of a new watch division director, Ernst Thomke. Its launch was designed to help recapture the low end of the watch market. Major design and production changes were incorporated. Robots were used in manufacture and the number of parts was reduced from 91 to 51. Unconventional and fashionable styles were developed for casing, watch face and wrist band. Prices were reduced to be competitive in the 12-to-24 year old fashion market. The Swatch represented a revolutionary new watch design as well as a departure from the traditional marketing of Swiss watches, and shook up the low-end fashion watch market. It has been a major success, especially in the United States. (Case discussed in Keegan, 1989, pp. 506-518.)

SAMPLE APPLICATIONS

Application 1: Minor Product Improvement and Price Cutting

The model was used to project market shares and contributions for global competitors involved in a segment of the telecommunications industry in the United States. This is an actual application using specific industry data (company names are not revealed). The competing firms include one domestic (American) and two global competitors from foreign countries.

Three major competitors supply a particular electronic unit to the long distance United States telecommunications market. Each firm has its own unique strengths in product technology. Potential customers in the target market are quite knowledgeable about available brands and about their particular needs. The current market shares of Brands 1, 2 and 3 are approximately 22.7%, 38.6% and 38.7% respectively.

A prior market research study of the customer base has revealed that three attributes are highly important in selecting a supplier for this product category: speed of operation, flexibility in application, and reliability or durability. Price is also an important consideration to potential buyers. The study also asked the decision-making units of both potential and current buying organizations to rate each of the three major brands on each of the three non-price attributes. The average ratings for each brand appear in Table 6.1 as well as the positions of each brand in spherical coordinates.

Firm 1 (the maker of Brand 1) is considering launching a competitive attack, in order to draw market share and profits away from its competitors. Three possible alternatives are under consideration: (1) Firm 1 can cut Brand 1's price below $500; (2) Firm 1 can improve the brand's reliability/durability (currently its weak point), necessitating a substantial commitment of funds to research and development; (3) Some combination of (1) and (2). Firm 1 realizes that any of these moves could invite defensive maneuvers on the part of its competitors. Its management feels that the most likely defensive moves would be to cut price. Using the model, each of these possibilities is assessed.

Price Cutting on Brand 1

Firm 1 first explores the effect of price cutting on its brand. As Brand 1's price is lowered, its position moves away from the origin along the ray. This shifts the market share boundaries (the indifference curves), causing the projected market share for Brand 1 to increase at the expense of the other brands. Table 6.2 shows that Brand 1's projected market shares were computed as follows: for a moderate price cut to $480, projected share = 26.1%; for a deeper cut to $460, projected share = 33.1%.

Brand 1's cost structure is given in Table 6.3. With these projections of market share, costs, and Firm 1's estimates for industry growth, it would not be in Firm 1's best interest to cut price despite gains made in market share. If no price changes are made, Firm 1's CDPC over a five-year horizon would be $1,334,900. A price cut to $480 reduces CDPC to $1,249,500, and a deeper price cut reduces CDPC even more. Recall that possible competitive retaliations have not yet been accounted for, and that such competitive action would only reduce Brand 1 contribution further. Thus, even if competitors do not retaliate (and no costs of attacking are incurred, such as increased salesforce or promotional costs), Firm 1 is worse off after a price cut.

TABLE 6.1. Brand ratings on attributes and prices: Application 1

In Cartesian Coordinates:

Brand	Speed	Application Flexibility	Reliability & Durability	Price (in $00s)
1	6.7	3.8	2.0	5.0
2	4.0	6.0	3.2	4.8
3	4.0	2.8	6.9	4.8

In Spherical Coordinates:

Brand	r	α	β
1	2.592	29.5	75.5
2	1.644	56.5	66.0
3	1.761	35.5	35.5

Brand 1's Reliability Is Improved

Firm 1 now wants to determine if it is worth investing in product research to improve Brand 1's weakest point: reliability. Suppose that Firm 1's laboratories succeed in improving reliability to the point where Brand 1 is equal to the *second* most reliable brand, Brand 2. As Table 6.2 shows, the model projected a market share of 27.3% for Brand 1 in the absence of competitive defense. This share would be reduced to 24.0% if Brand 2 cuts price in retaliation, and to 22.4% (approximately the current level) if both 2 and 3 retaliate by cutting price.

Table 6.3 shows that Firm 1's CDPC increases from $1,334,900 to $1,518,800 as a result of the reliability improvement. But, if Firm 1 is certain that its attack will trigger competitive price cutting, this figure would have to be reduced accordingly. Indeed, as the Table shows, if both competitors cut prices to $460, Firm 1's CDPC would be even lower than current levels ($1,322,800). So, even if

TABLE 6.2. Summary of terminal market share projections

	Brand 1	Brand 2	Brand 3
Original	22.7	38.6	38.7
Brand 1 cuts price to $480	26.1	38.7	35.2
Brand 1 cuts price to $460	33.1	29.4	37.5
Brand 1 repositions on reliability to 3.2	27.3	38.3	34.4
Same as above, but Brand 2 cuts price to $460	24.0	40.2	35.8
Same as above, but Brand 2 and 3 cut price to $460	22.4	38.8	38.8
Brand 1 cuts price to $480 and repositions on reliability to 3.2	34.6	32.8	32.6
Same as above, but Brands 2 and 3 cut price to $460	29.1	36.4	34.5

repositioning costs incurred now (in Period 0) were negligible, the attack would still not be profitable for Firm 1.

If the decision to attack is made purely on the basis of the projected new impact on contribution, Firm 1 would choose not to attack. Nevertheless, the firm may still decide to invest in R&D to improve its product. For example, it may have reason to believe that Firm 2 or 3, or a potential new entrant to the industry, may launch a substantially improved version of the product. Improvement on Brand 1 may be the only way in which Firm 1 could survive in the industry in the long run.

Firm 1 Improves Its Brand's Reliability and Cuts Price

The last attack strategy to be considered is a combination of the previous two: Firm 1 combines a price cut with a repositioning on the reliability attribute. Table 6.2 indicates the projected market shares. If unanswered by competitive moves, Brand 1's market

TABLE 6.3. Profit contribution projections for Brand 1

Projections For Brand 1		1	2	Year: 3	4	5	Total
Original	Market Share	22.70	22.70	22.70	22.70	22.70	
	Disc. Contrib.	264.1	268.3	269.4	268.2	264.9	1334.9
Brand 1 cuts price to $480	Market Share	23.30	24.06	24.74	25.42	26.10	
	Disc. Contrib.	230.8	243.1	252.4	250.3	263.9	1249.5
Brand 1 cuts price to $460	Market Share	24.70	26.86	28.94	31.02	33.10	
	Disc. Contrib.	202.4	227.4	249.4	268.8	285.4	1233.4
Brand 1 repositions on reliability to 3.2	Market Share	23.62	24.54	25.46	26.38	27.30	
	Disc. Contrib.	276.6	293.3	306.8	317.2	324.9	1518.8
Same as above, but Brand 2 cuts price to $460	Market Share	22.96	23.22	23.48	23.24	24.00	
	Disc. Contrib.	267.6	275.3	280.0	275.4	281.9	1380.2
Same as above, but Brands 2 and 3 cut price to $460	Market Share	22.64	22.50	22.52	22.46	22.40	
	Disc. Contrib.	263.3	266.6	266.9	265.0	261.0	1322.8
Brand 1 cuts price to $480 and repositions on reliability to 3.2	Market Share	25.08	27.46	29.84	32.22	34.60	
	Disc. Contrib.	250.9	283.4	312.2	337.8	359.9	1544.2
Same as above, but Brands 2 and 3 cut price to $460	Market Share	23.98	25.26	26.54	27.82	29.10	
	Disc. Contrib.	237.9	257.3	273.6	287.0	297.8	1353.6

Note: Market shares are reported in percentages; discounted contributions in thousands.

Brand 1 Cost Information
Unit Variable Costs: $350
Annual Fixed Costs: $50,000

Assumptions
Discount Rate: 10%
Industry Sales: 10,000 units in current year, forecasted to increase by 1000 per year.
Number of years for market shares to stabilize: 5 Market share adjustment over this period: linear

share is expected to increase substantially to 34.6%. If both competitors cut price, Brand 1's market share would be contained at 29.1%. Table 6.3 shows that, even in the face of competitive price cutting, this strategy still produces a higher CDPC than the status quo ($1,353,600). This amount exceeds the do-nothing CDPC by $18,700 ($1,353,600 − $1,334,900). Thus, if repositioning costs (i.e., costs of the R&D required to improve Brand 1 reliability) are less than $18,700, this attack strategy would be recommended.

Application 2: Revolutionary Attack by New Entrant

This also is a real example taken from the telecommunications industry, and it concerns a particular kind of switching device which is sold in most European Community countries. The industry is virtually a duopoly: Brands 1 and 2 have almost 90% of the market share. A team of industry engineers possessing expert knowledge about this product type observe that the two most salient attributes for brand selection are Capacity and Flexibility (small size, mobility, ease of connecting with a wide variety of other devices, etc.). The team of engineers rated each brand on each attribute, using a seven-point scale. The average ratings for each brand, and brand prices, appear in Table 6.4.

Recently, a new brand, Brand 3, has been launched by a new foreign competitor. Although priced higher than the other two brands, its manufacturer provides a much better warranty than either Brand 1 or 2 (see entries in Table 6.4). The entry of this brand alters the industry structure in that two dimensions are no longer adequate to describe it: a third dimension, Warranty, is necessary. Further, the Warranty dimension is essentially Brand 3's strength: it possesses no advantage over existing brands on either of the other two dimensions, while Brands 1 and 2 are perceived by the engineers to have relatively poor warranties. As discussed above, Brand 3 has succeeded in transforming the Warranty dimension from a potentially determinant to a determinant attribute.

Under Assumption 4, the taste distributions are uniform. A DEFENDER type analysis was carried out and market shares of 15.6% and 84.4% for Brands 1 and 2 respectively were predicted by the model. These correspond favorably to actual market shares in the

TABLE 6.4. Brand ratings on attributes and prices: Application 2

Before Competitive Attack:

Brand	Capacity	Flexibility	Warranty	Price
1	5	2		$22
2	4	6		$21

After Competitive Attack:

Brand	Capacity	Flexibility	Warranty	Price
1	5	2	2	$22
2	4	6	2	$21
3	4	5	5	$21

duopoly before attack by Brand 3 (actual shares are 23 and 77% respectively). To project the industry market shares after Brand 3's entry, the computer program employed above was used again. It predicted that Brand 3 would draw sales away from both duopolists, but would especially hurt Brand 2's market share, due to the close proximity of Brands 2 and 3 in perceptual space. Specifically, the computer model predicted post-adjustment market shares of 12%, 54% and 34% for Brands 1, 2 and 3 respectively. Once again, these correspond relatively closely to actual data, 19%, 52% and 29% respectively. In both cases, Brand 1's share was slightly underestimated, and Brand 2's overestimated. It is possible that the taste distribution function was not uniform, and that the attributes should be weighted differently to account for this. There is some evidence, based on the above argument, that the attribute of Capacity ought to be weighted more heavily than Flexibility, since the former is the strength of Brand 1. In any case, the main point to be learned from the analysis is that both Brands 1 and 2 (but especially 2) will face strong competition and ought to consider their options regarding defensive moves. For the sake of brevity, a discussion of possible consequences of various defensive repositionings is not included here. Suffice it to note that the incumbent brands could use the procedure as outlined to develop "what-if" scenarios. This would allow them to make a more informed choice of defensive strategy.

CONCLUSION

A competitive shakeout will probably occur in the European Community beginning in 1993. One expects that this situation will have a substantial impact on all globally and regionally (in Europe) competitive firms. By this time the Community is expected to have in place an open internal market. Most barriers restricting the free flow of goods and services today will have been removed by then. Pan-European companies will become more directly competitive as they can retreat to centralized, highly efficient European manufacturing facilities. Coupled with the absence of tariff and rules restrictions, they will be able to use their cost efficiencies to compete head-on with formerly national leader brands. No longer will barriers to firms from other European countries, and the low level of foreign competition on the domestic front, be sufficient defense. Existing national market leaders in the different polities will face Europe-sized competition for valuable market shares. In this scenario the risks inherent in not assuming a proactive defensive posture are too great to be ignored. In fact, a positive outcome of the post-1992 shakeout will be larger European oligopolies to compete head-on with U.S., Japanese, and other non-E.C. manufacturers and trading companies.

The decision model presented in this paper, though based on rather simple positioning concepts, may be used to enhance the level of analysis of a proactive or reactive market repositioning in situations of more than two salient attributes, such as were encountered in the cited examples. Brand positioning may be used proactively as an important tool in competing in foreign markets. Also, a firm under attack by new global competitors must be prepared to react and defend itself in an effective manner. Therefore, this analysis may be used by firms seeking to understand better the nature of competitive forces in foreign markets and to develop effective, appropriate strategies.

The decision model makes certain predictions about the outcomes of attacks and repositionings. In particular, (1) the entry of an attacking brand will draw market share from existing brands unless they retaliate. (2) Brands which are perceptually closer to the attacking brand are likely to suffer the greatest loss due to draw (not shown in the Sample Applications but can be inferred from the mathematical derivation). (3) Price cutting by defending brands, and/or repositioning (especially in the direction of the new attacker's strength) are effective defensive strategies, and can erect an entry barrier to discourage outside firms from attacking. These results are consistent with those of Hauser and Shugan (1983), Hauser (1988), Kumar and Sudharshan (1988), and Lane (1980).

The contribution analysis carried out in the first Sample Application focuses attention on the cost structure and contribution margin of the attacker. Of course, similar calculations may be performed from the perspective of the *attacked firms*, to allow them to assess the relative merits of their retaliatory response options. The second, briefer example illustrates graphically how a radical change in an industry can substantially affect the industry structure and the relative market shares of the incumbents. This is indeed consistent with the work of Utterback (1981, 1982) who noted that certain industries were "ripe" for radical innovation and the firm that can deliver this innovation successfully to the market can disrupt the peaceful existence of the incumbent firms.

Note that we do not assume in these applications that *all* retaliatory responses are equally costly or efficient, but we did assume that only retaliatory price cuts were considered by the attacked firms. This may be relevant in many industries. Some kind of quick response may be necessary, and repositioning on non-price attributes can conceivably take too long to implement, or in the case of new product development, may not be successful. A more detailed analysis would consider the costs and benefits of more expensive and risky strategies from the perspective of *all* firms, not just the attacker.

We will conclude with a short discussion of possible theoretical extensions to the model. We have not attempted to show with mathematical rigor the conditions under which it is optimal to cut price, reformulate the product, or even attack a "ripe" industry or defend it vigorously. Given the substantial amount of theoretical advances made in positioning analysis in recent years, starting with Lane and Hauser, we suggest that future research could be aimed at developing analytic results (anchored in micro-economics) from this model that can make strong recommendations about when to implement, and when to avoid, particular offensive and defensive strategies.

BIBLIOGRAPHY

Assael, Henry. (1985). *Marketing Management: Strategy and Action.* Boston, MA: Kent.

Bass, Frederick. (1974). "The Theory of Stochastic Preference and Brand Switching." *Journal of Marketing Research* 11, 1–20.

Bennett, Roger C. and Cooper, Robert G. (1979). "Beyond the Marketing Concept." *Business Horizons*, 76-83.

Cooper, A. and Schendel, D. (1976). "Strategic Responses to Technological Threats." *Business Horizons*, 61-69.

Crawford, C. Merle. (1987). *New Products Management,* 2nd ed. Homewood, IL: Irwin.

Davis, E. et al. (1989). *1992: Myths and Realities,* Center for Business Strategy, London, U.K.: London Business School.

Day, G.S., Deutscher, T. and Ryans, A.B. (1976). "Data Quality, Level of Aggregation and Nonmetric Multidimensional Scaling Solutions." *Journal of Marketing Research* 13, 92-97.

Emerson, Michael. (1988). "The Economics of 1992." *European Economy* 35 (March), 33.

Gavish, Bezalel, Horsky, Dan and Srikanth, Kizhanathan. (1983). "An Approach to the Optimal Positioning of a New Product." *Management Science* 29(11), 1277-1297.

Green, Paul and Srinivasan, V. (1978). "Conjoint Analysis in Consumer Research: Issues and Outlook." *Journal of Consumer Research* 5(2), 103-123.

Guiltinan, Joseph P. and Paul, Gordon W. (1988). *Marketing Management: Strategies and Programs,* 3rd ed. New York: McGraw-Hill.

Hauser, J.R. (1988). "Competitive Price and Positioning Strategies." *Marketing Science* 7(1), 76-91.

Hauser, J.R. and Gaskin, S.P. (1984). "Application of the DEFENDER Consumer Model." *Marketing Science* 3(4), 327-351.

Hauser, J.R. and Shugan, S.M. (1983). "Defensive Marketing Strategies." *Marketing Science* 2(4), 319-360.

Hauser, J.R. and Simmie, P. (1981). "Profit Maximizing Perceptual Positions: An Integrated Theory for the Selection of Product Features and Price." *Management Science* 27(1), 33-56.

Hauser, John R. and Wernerfelt, Birger (1988). "Existence and Uniqueness of Price Equilibria in DEFENDER." *Marketing Science* 7(1), 92-93.

Hendler, Reuven. (1975). "Lancaster's New Approach to Consumer Demand and Its Limitations." *American Economic Review* 65, 194-199.

Horsky, D. and Rao, M.R. (1979). "Properties of Attribute Weights Estimated from Preference Comparisons." Working paper, University of Rochester, September.

Keegan, Warren J. (1989). *Global Marketing Management.* Englewood Cliffs, N.J.: Prentice-Hall.

Klahr, D. (1970). "A Study of Consumers' Cognitive Structure for Cigarette Brands." *Journal of Business* 43, 190-204.

Kotler, Philip. (1980). *Marketing Management: Analysis, Planning and Control,* 4th ed. Englewood Cliffs, NJ: Prentice-Hall.

Kumar, K. Ravi and Sudharshan, D. (1988). "Defensive Marketing Strategies: An Equilibrium Analysis Based on Decoupled Response Function Models." *Management Science* 34(7), 805-815.

Ladd, George W. and Zober, Martin. (1977). "Model of Consumer Reaction to Product Characteristics." *Journal of Consumer Research* 4, 89-101.

Lancaster, Kelvin. (1971). *Consumer Demand: A New Approach.* New York: Columbia.

Lane, W.J. (1980). "Product Differentiation in a Market with Endogenous Sequential Entry." *Bell Journal of Economics* 11(1), 237-260.

Lucas, Robert E.B. (1975). "Hedonic Price Functions." *Economic Inquiry* 13, 157-158.

Magee, John F. (1989). "1992: Moves Americans Must Make." *Harvard Business Review* (May-June), 82.

Pekelman, D. and Sen, S. (1974). "Mathematical Programming for the Determination of Attribute Weights." *Management Science* 20, 1217-1229.

Pekelman, D. and Sen, S. (1979). "Improving Prediction in Conjoint Measurement." *Journal of Marketing Research* 16, 211-220.

Pessemier, E.A. (1979). "Managerial Aspects of Market Structure Analysis and Market Maps." Marketing Science Institute Research Paper, Technical Report 79-101.

Pessemier, E.A. (1982). *Product Management: Strategy and Organization.* New York: Wiley.

Ratchford, B.T. (1975). "The New Economic Theory of Consumer Behavior: An Interpretive Essay." *Journal of Consumer Research* 2, 65-75.

Ratchford, B.T. (1979). "Operationalizing Economic Models of Demand for Product Characteristics." *Journal of Consumer Research* 6, 76-84.

Reibstein, D.J. (1978). "The Prediction of Individual Probabilities of Brand Choice." *Journal of Consumer Research* 5, 163-168.

Shocker, A.D. and Srinivasan, V. (1979). "Multiattribute Approaches for Product Concept Evaluation and Generation: A Critical Review." *Journal of Marketing Research* 16, 159-180.

Silk, A.J. and Urban, G.L. (1978). "Pre-Test Market Evaluation of Packaged

Goods: A Model and Measurement Methodology." *Journal of Marketing Research* 15, 171-191.

Srinivasan, V. (1975). "A General Procedure for Estimating Consumer Preference Distributions." *Journal of Marketing Research* 15, 159-180.

Stefflre, V. (1969). "Market Structure Studies: New Products for Old Markets and New Markets (Foreign) for Old Products." In Bass, King and Pessemier (eds.), *Applications of the Sciences to Marketing*. New York: Wiley, 251-268.

Urban, G.L. and Hauser, J.R. (1980). *Design and Marketing of New Products*. Englewood Cliffs, NJ: Prentice-Hall.

Utterback, J.M. (1981). "The Dynamics of Product and Process Innovation in Industry." In *Technological Innovation for a Dynamic Economy*, Proceedings of a Symposium for Senior Executives, C.T. Hill and J.M. Utterback (eds.), Massachusetts Institute of Technology.

Utterback, J.M. (1982). "The Innovative Process: Evolution Vs. Revolution." In *The Innovative Process: Evolution Vs. Revolution*, Proceedings of a Symposium for Senior Executives, Cambridge, MA: MIT.

Utterback, J.M. and Abernathy, W.J. (1975). "A Dynamic Model of Product and Process Innovation." *Omega*, 3, 639-656.

Yoffie, David B. (1990). *International Trade and Competition*. New York: McGraw-Hill.

APPENDIX: ISSUES IN MODEL DEVELOPMENT

Our model addresses the managerial issue of how customers respond to changes in product offerings made by competing firms (domestic incumbents or new global entrants). This analysis is accomplished by positioning the various competitive brands on a three-dimensional per-dollar map. The model suggests how consumer preferences would change through time as a result of a competitive attack, and examines the defensive response of the leader or other brands to the attack.

Some of the assumptions made here are consistent with those in Hauser and Shugan (1983) and other microeconomic models. Certain DEFENDER model assumptions are relaxed, while a few additional constraints are introduced.

The following assumptions are made in this study.

1. It is possible to represent competing brands in a given marketplace by points in multiattribute space. The marketing literature supports the concept of product positioning (Kotler, 1980; Pessemier, 1979, 1982) and shows that individual consumers tend to have

similar perceptions of the positions of existing brands (Stefflre, 1969; Klahr, 1970; Day, Deutscher and Ryans, 1976; Gavish, Horsky and Srikanth, 1983). Price scaling, that is, dividing attribute levels by price in order to produce "per-dollar" maps is also frequently done in the marketing literature (Lancaster, 1971; Ratchford, 1975, 1979; Urban and Hauser, 1980; Hauser and Simmie, 1981).

2. Each customer chooses his or her utility-maximizing brand. Some studies have indicated that this is a realistic assumption at the market level (Green and Srinivasan, 1978; Pekelman and Sen, 1979; Shocker and Srinivasan, 1979). At the individual level, customers will choose their most preferred brand most often but not always (Bass, 1974; Reibstein, 1978; Silk and Urban, 1978; Gavish, Horsky and Srikanth, 1983).

3. Utility is linear in the product attributes. This assumption allows the rank ordering of preferences by each customer to be accomplished relatively easily using a linear response function.

4. Customers will be heterogeneous in their taste preferences or importances attached to the various attributes (Pekelman and Sen, 1974; Srinivasan, 1975; Horsky and Rao, 1979). In the DEFENDER model, Hauser and Shugan (1983) assumed a taste distribution function which showed the proportion of customers who would prefer a given brand. In this study we assume uniform taste distribution; thus, market segment considerations are suppressed at this stage.

5. All customers are aware of all brands; that is, each customer's *evoked set* contains all brands. Hauser and Shugan (1983) relax this assumption in the DEFENDER model, as all consumers of frequently-purchased branded goods are unlikely to evoke all brands (Silk and Urban, 1978). For the case of large industrial products bought by professional buyers, this assumption is probably not unreasonable.

6. As a result of a price cut or other repositioning action, the utility-maximizing brand of some customers will change. This study assumes that all customers will eventually choose the utility-maximizing brand in the long run, but that in the case of a changeover, the change will not occur immediately for all customers. This is a reasonable assumption, as a customer may have a long-term

contract with its existing supplier; he or she may want to conduct "trial runs" before switching brands or may simply be reluctant to change because he or she is quite satisfied with the current brand choice. Nevertheless it is assumed that, in the long term, all customers will have switched to the utility-maximizing brand.

Chapter 7

Marketing Mix Strategies in the Europe of Post-1992

Gianluigi Guido

The fragmentation of the European market, coming from the existence of national regulations and non-tariff barriers, has for years discouraged companies from operating in more than one country. By the end of 1992, the European Community's plan for the completion of the Internal Market should remove most of the physical, fiscal, and technical barriers to trade among the 12 EC nations and this should create a single European market of more than 320 million consumers, in which goods, services, labor, and capital can freely move without borders.

The resulting changes in national regulations and standards will force firms to redefine their role in the Single Market, taking an active, ongoing approach to 1992 not only for the exploitation of the opportunities of this integration process, but also for the mere survival in this modified environment. Firms cannot opt out of Europe: even if their management decides not to trade with the new EC, they will still face increased competition in their own market.

CHARACTERISTICS OF THE "EURO-MARKET"

Competition in the Unified Europe. Two elements are necessary to understand the nature of this integration process, as discussed by Quelch, Buzzell, and Salama (1990):

This chapter was originally published in *Journal of Euromarketing,* Vol. 1(1/2) 1991.

1. Every eventual gain is a supply-side-led one: the improvements in economic performances (e.g., growth, increased demand, etc.) are contingent on the companies' ability to decrease prices as a result of both low costs and increased competition. The EC program, in fact, does not focus on demand. Consumers in Europe are not asked to change their preferences and, presumably, they will not soon become considerably homogenous for the existence of different cultures, languages, and economic situations.

2. Not all the benefits will be immediate or direct (such as those coming from the elimination of frontier controls), but most of them will require the company's action or reorganization (such as those which will be derived from enlarged competition, economies of scale, reallocation of resources, and increased innovation and dynamism). The threat of a more competitive market, presently, has driven companies toward a wave of consolidations, both via mergers and acquisitions (for gaining control of distribution channels, spreading administrative overhead costs on larger bases, etc.), and through strategic alliances (for exchanging technologies, participating joint ventures, and so on). This process of concentration, however, could be very harmful, especially for those firms in which large scale economies exist but have been impeded by national regulations (such as banks, telecommunications, publishing, transportation, construction, etc.), which now could be acquired or forced out of business.

Exporting versus Marketing. In the international arena, the greatest changes will take place in exporting rather than in marketing (van Mesdag, 1988). The 1992 reforms grant to every EC company the possibility to sell in one Community country what it can legally sell in another. This means that small companies previously not organized for complex export trade will be able to move across borders with the same ease as U.S. multinationals, suddenly contending with established market leaders. Exporting will become simpler and easier, but marketing will still involve difficulties. Its main purpose will continue to be that of handling 320 million different people, each with their own individual necessities and desires, most with increasing wealth, autonomy, and choosiness.

The problem is that governments cannot make markets. If they could, there would be no need for marketing and 320 million consumers should be suddenly transformed in 320 million euro-clones, drinking euro-beer, eating euro-hamburgers and watching euro-satellite television. Even if the EC's plan will allow businesses to sell their home-market products abroad or to sell standardized merchandise throughout the Community, this will not imply that customers will want to buy it.

The 1992 reforms in Europe will make the single national markets more accessible, not more identical. With expanding competition, the responsibilities of marketers will increase. They won't decrease in spite of fewer and simpler rules.

A PAN-EUROPEAN APPROACH

The Myth of "Euro-consumers." We should believe that treating the EC market as a global one, with marketing standardization and homogenization of products, is an over-simplification, not always applicable. Nevertheless, it would be a big mistake for marketers not to plan a strategy which could take advantage of possible scale economies allowed by the European program. The companies who could be easily beaten by the competition would be those who will wait and not search for the opportunities of a pan-European approach.

A quarter-century of research about the evolution of the marketing practices by U.S. international companies has shown that, in Europe, a standardization of marketing is possible. It should be related, however, to (1) types of product, (2) market clusters, and (3) market segmentation.

Three connected studies spanning 25 years (Terpstra, 1963; Boddewyn and Hansen, 1977; Soehl, 1985) suggest that standardization of marketing varies in relation to the kind of products. In the case of industrial goods and consumer durables (such as cameras, toasters, watches, and portable radios) standardization is fairly advanced. For consumer non-durables, such as foods, standardization, instead, is difficult to achieve, primarily for differences in hard-to-change national tastes and habits.

According to a research developed in Geneva by S. Vandermerwe and M. L'Huillier (1989), the European market is also reasonably homogeneous in its needs and purchasing behaviors if divided in six major "clusters." These clusters have similar demographic and economic characteristics cutting across cultural and national boundaries (see Figures 7.1 and 7.2). Managers working in those markets should be able to reach larger cross-cultural Euro-consumers' groups without marketing separately. The clusters indicate im-

FIGURE 7.1. The Six Clusters and Their Population (1990, in 000's of people)

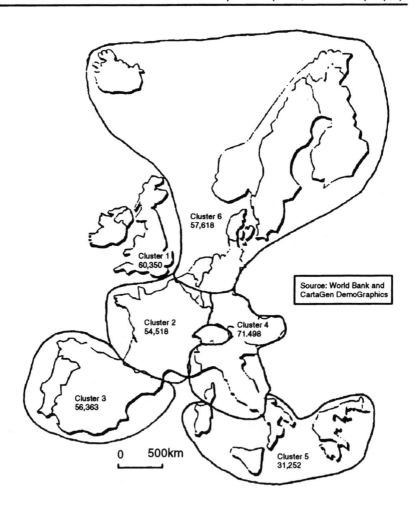

Cluster 6
57,618

Cluster 1
60,350

Source: World Bank and
CartaGen DemoGraphics

Cluster 2
54,518

Cluster 4
71,498

Cluster 3
56,363

0   500km

Cluster 5
31,252

FIGURE 7.2. 1992: The Implications of Pan-European Marketing

	Effects of the EC Plan	Does Say	Does Not Say
CONSUMERS	The 1992 reforms focus on supply rather than demand	Firms should act to exploit market economies	Consumers will change considerably their preferences
MARKET	Exporting will become easier, not marketing	National markets will become more accessible	National markets will become more identical
MARKETING STRATEGIES	Standardization of marketing is possible depending on —type of products —geographic clusters —market segmentation	Marketers should be aware of: —changes —threats —strategic options in each area of marketing mix	Marketers are able to wait before exploiting the opportunities of the EC Plan

143

portant changes in market configuration, but within each there are segments that share life-style and specific psychographic needs.

As reported by Martin (1988) and Kossoff (1988), three distinct segments, or social groups, have been identified by a recent study conducted by Eurisko, an Italian research company, as being ready for the pan-European approach. First, the young people, who have unified tastes, across Europe, in music, sports, and cultural activities. Second, the trend-setters and climbers, who are the wealthier and highly educated Europeans, who tend to value independence, refuse consumer stereotypes, and appreciate exclusive products.[1] Third, Europe's business people, who are a rich target audience of six million. They are about forty years old, regularly travel abroad and have a taste for luxury goods; they are almost exclusively male.

A Possible Scenario. On these bases, a standardization of marketing is possible. In planning a common market program, however, marketers should be aware of certain factors emerging from the EC directives and from the marketing environment which could threaten their own pan-European strategies. We attempt, as follows, to address the kind of changes and problems likely to be encountered by marketers, and some of the possible responses in relation to the specific areas of the marketing mix (4-Ps): (1) Product (brand and packaging); (2) Pricing (price structure and taxes); (3) Promotion (advertising and positioning); and (4) Place (distribution and direct marketing).

PRODUCT STRATEGIES

National Product Standards. In 1992, the harmonization of different product standards, testing, and certification procedures should be highly beneficial to producers by avoiding costly product modifications and lengthy delays due to varying country-specific requirements. To comply with them, a product, for example, must be built in different versions, thus creating all kinds of inefficiencies and a lack of economies of scale. The results are: more complex manufacturing processes (assemblers have to be trained to make the product in different ways with increasing possibilities for errors), loss of purchasing power, and bigger storage facilities.

---

1. Heineken, Coca-Cola, and Marlboro are typical brands that position themselves toward this group.

Some European standards organizations (namely CEN, CENE-LEC, and ETSI, for non-electrical, electrotechnical, and telecommunications products, respectively) are working to satisfy the guidelines listed in the EC directives. Thousands of products, however, will be allowed to be marketed because of the principle of "mutual recognition" contained in the EC directives that grants to every EC company the possibility to sell in one Community country what it can legally sell in another (see Table 7.1).

Part of these directives, still in their pre-ratification phase, are creating some concerns to companies both for their untimeliness, given the fact that marketers have to plan in advance their product strategies, and for their eventual protectionist meaning.[2] Especially for non-EC manufacturers, insurmountable obstacles could be raised by issues such as "rules of origin" and "local content." The former require that the major production process be made within the EC; the latter calls for a minimum European content, for avoiding stiff tariffs or for bidding in government procurement. The EC might also engage in restrictive tactics by refusing to recognize product tests administered abroad, forcing foreign producers to ship off goods to the EC at a high expense for testing and sale without the assurance of certification.

Euro-products and Euro-brands. Handling new products could also be difficult, at least during the run up to 1993. The challenge of assessing profitable areas to enter and the potential response of customers could be complicated by marketing research, traditionally less developed in Europe, which would not provide homogenous information about products. For example, lemon-flavored Perrier could be classified as mineral water in France, but as a soft-drink in Italy.

As more uniform technical requirements and standards are introduced, firms are likely to try to develop pan-European products and brands. Standardization should imply fewer stocked units in storage, less sale forecast errors, more reliable production and logistic

---

2. Until final ratification by individual countries, nobody knows how much time it will take to pass some directives and how they will affect marketers and advertisers. Even if some regulations can severely affect competitiveness in the market, companies must move ahead for the single market, so as not to remain unprepared. For instance, still subject to approval are restrictions for ads using tobacco-product brand names for non-tobacco products; "fresh" and nutrient labeling for food; ban of duty-free sales at airports; and so on.

TABLE 7.1. Product Strategies in Europe of 1992

Changes Affecting Strategies	Threats to Marketers' Planning	Management's Strategic Options
– Harmonization in product standards, testing, and certification procedures – Common protection and branding – Consumer protection regulations – Harmonization in packaging, labeling, and processing requirements	– Untimeliness of directives – Rules of origin – Local content rules – Differences in mktg research	– Consolidate production – Obtain mktg economies – Shift from brand to benefit segmentation – Shift from brand to market management – Extend strong national brand names in the EC – Standardize packaging and labeling where possible

planning. The result will most probably be a smaller total number of new products introduced in the 12 nations, but each with more potentialities because targeted at a wider population. New-identified pan-European consumer segments, and the acquisitions of strong national brand names able to be extended throughout Europe, should let us think that common positioning strategy and package design will become more widespread in the Community. In spite of the difficulty of an acceptable common name in different languages, more basic goods, such as detergents and household cleaners, should be marketed as Euro-brands across the Community.

Two directional changes will influence product strategies (Schultz, 1989). The first one is a shift from brand to benefit segmentation. This means that, in the future, products will be sold putting more emphasis on their benefits rather than on their attributes. The second subsequent shift will be from brand management to market management. People do not have needs for brands: they have needs for products that solve problems. Organizing marketing by consumer use rather than brands should also allow avoiding internal competition among brands.[3]

Patenting and branding of the products will also become more significant, because a successful product will potentially have more market than before. The Community is currently seeking a "single patent system," which could lower registering and reviewing patent costs in Europe (presently very high), and unifying the law on protection of trademarks and copyrights particularly significant in combatting piracy in computer software.

Packaging. Reduced barriers will also push toward standardized packaging and labeling, providing considerable savings. In this process, new technologies will affect the packaging and distribution process, improving production. The "aseptic packaging system," for example, should increase shelf life and allow products to be shipped over greater distances. This development, in combination with the principle of "mutual recognition" should permit consolidated production. For instance, a large yogurt supplier with plants in France, where its product is not pasteurized today, and in other EC countries, where it is pasteurized, could centralize its production in one place to serve all markets.

Marketers will still face the problem of capturing the Imagination of 12 different nations. This issue is particularly important for U.S. marketers approaching the European market. The aesthetic standards are higher in Europe, so that if U.S. products use the blatant approach which sells in their domestic market, in Europe, they will be perceived as low-quality. For example, flagging on packaging is considered cheap (Goldman, 1989).

In addition, while in the U.S. the brand name is one of the most important elements on packaging because of faith in well-known brands, in Europe brand name is deemphasized. Europeans are interested in products with natural purity, and packaging should

---

3. "Handling so many brands can be confusing and costly." It's what occurred to Unilever in Fall 1989. Having bought several cosmetic firms, controlled brands, "Calvin Klein, Passion, and Elizabeth Arden each launched a men's fragrance, which competed against each other" (Konrad 1989, p. 102). Another example is given by Richardson-Vicks, which sells "Oil of Olay" in the U.K. but "Oil of Olaz" in Spain and Italy. Such approach is against an efficient pan-European branding.

address these needs. Finally, packaging has to look like it is aimed at the individual. This can be found in the European private label products, which are often packaged in a more attractive, imaginative, and appealing way than the generic, low-priced look of U.S. private label products.

PRICING STRATEGIES

Price Competition. The European market of the future will be typified by surplus production and, wherever there is surplus, price is always the dominant form of competition (see Table 7.2). This trend should be intensified after 1992. Price will be pushed downward for the following reasons (Quelch and Buzzell, 1989):

1. Decreased costs;
2. The opening up of public procurement contracts to broader competition;
3. Foreign investment that increases production capacity;
4. More rigorous enforcement of competition policy; and
5. The general intensified competition generated by the 1992 reforms.

The European Commission has estimated that the prices of goods and services throughout the EC could decrease as much as 8.3%. In industries as ubiquitous as chemicals, consumer goods, and financial services, there are enormous price differentials for the same product among countries that cannot be justified in any case with the costs of raw materials, labor, or transportation, and that will be unsustainable in a more competitive environment. The withdrawal of existing restrictions to foreign producers, particularly important in the case of auto-makers, and the tendency of the European Commission to strongly enforce anti-monopoly measures, should further heighten competition.[4]

---

4. According to the European Commission, to make excise taxes uniform in each country, Spain would have to increase the price of cigarettes by 120%, distilled spirits by 90%, and beer by 18%; while the U.K. would have to slash beer price by 37%, distilled spirits price by 37%, and cigarettes by 6%.

TABLE 7.2. Pricing Strategies in Europe of 1992

Changes Affecting Strategies	Threats to Marketers' Planning	Management's Strategic Options
– More competitive environment – Withdrawal of restrictions to foreign products – Antimonopoly measures – Widening up of the public procurement market	– Parallel importing – Different taxation of goods – Less freedom in setting transfer prices	– Exploit different excise and value-added taxes – Understand price elasticity of consumer demand – Launch new higher-margin products – Introduce visible low-cost brand names – Promote efficiency

In the short run, price cutting (in the form of temporary trade or consumer promotions rather than reductions in list prices) could be used by firms before realizing cost savings on suppliers in order to build market share. In the long run, although the average price should be lower than before the integration, the role of pricing in the marketing mix could depend on the effective competition coming from non-EC countries, especially those based in Asia.

Different Price Structures. In a Europe without barriers, the major concern of manufacturers is that products sold in different countries at lower prices could more easily find their way into other countries where the pricing structure for the same products is higher. Price differences among countries can reflect diverse positioning based on the stage of product life-cycle in each market, exchange rate fluctuations, different distributors margins, national social costs, delivery clauses, and so on, but, principally, they are caused by different excise and value-added taxes. "Parallel importing," which is not illegal in Europe, but which is stopped until now by complex customs and shipping procedures, could prosper in a unified Europe thanks to strong retail chains.

To survive and remain profitable with lower margins, manufacturers, especially small companies, will have to improve efficiency, considering that other factors will also influence the pricing decisions: less freedom in setting transfer prices; pressures on manufacturers' margins from the consolidated distributors' side; savings in distribution and warehousing costs; and economies from lower cost locations.

Pricing Strategies. According to Quelch and Buzzell (1989), what manufacturers should do to face these trends is to:

1. Understand the price elasticity of consumer demand for each product in every single EC nation, and identify the product substitution effect at different price points;
2. Launch higher-margin new products before 1992 in the low-priced markets, to convince consumers to buy them;
3. Introduce visible low-cost brand names, to discourage parallel importing;
4. Try to increase control of distribution channels in high-priced markets, to cross-subsidize aggressive pricing in other markets.

PROMOTION STRATEGIES

Pan-European Campaigns. In the issue of global versus local marketing, the essential question seems to be if it is possible to run a truly pan-European promotional campaign. While in Europe, major players, like the world's largest advertising conglomerate Saatchi & Saatchi, strongly believe that the European village people are growing much alike in lifestyle and attitudes (a trend which it calls "cultural or consumer convergence"), in the U.S., the world's biggest mass-market, companies are moving to regional and local sales and marketing. It could be seen as a signal for European marketers that U.S. companies, such as Colgate-Palmolive, Procter & Gamble, Pepsi-Cola, Campbell Soup, and others have been reorganized to focus more closely on small geographic targets (see Table 7.3).

A pan-European (or "global") campaign could have appropriate results when the same product specification is sold in each country to the same target consumers, for the same end application, against competitors that offer the same mix of advantages and disadvan-

TABLE 7.3. Promotion Strategies in Europe of 1992

Changes Affecting Strategies	Threats to Marketers' Planning	Management's Strategic Options
– Common guidelines on television broadcasting – Deregulation of national broadcasting monopolies – Uniform standards for TV commercials	– Restrictions on alcohol and tobacco advertising – Limits on foreign TV production – Differences in permitted promotional techniques	– Coordinate components of promotional mix – Exploit where possible advant. of pan-European media (ad space, standardized ads, etc.) – Position the product according to local mkts – Provide promotional programs with "residual market value" – Encourage brand loyalty

tages, and with a comparable market maturity. Even if this happens, despite the efforts to communicate the same message with the same promotional tool, only one thing remains certain: consumers will respond to any marketing strategy as individuals. The customer does not make differentiations in terms of segmented communications: advertising, sales promotion, and public relations. He or she simply takes information from magazines, dealers, and word-of-mouth. Therefore, it is vital for a company to speak with one voice: integrated communications which require the coordination of the components of promotional mix, including advertising, sales promotion, direct marketing, publicity and point-of-purchase material.

Communications in the Common Market. The influx of the new press and broadcast media will contribute greatly to the development of pan-European advertising. Presently, there are no real European newspapers or magazines, and the reasons for this are various. The most obvious of these is language: the majority of readers prefer their native language. English is becoming the "lingua franca" of the EC, but only very slowly. Another reason could be that multinational companies, owners of many media, don't want their paper to have an international viewpoint because their interests are better served by "playing a national game" inside the country.

The necessity to regulate the media sector has brought the Council of Europe to advance a draft convention on common guidelines on television broadcasting, specifying the minutes of advertising permitted per hour, the placement of ads during and between programs, etc. In addition, the European Commission has proposed common restrictions on alcohol and tobacco advertising and limits on foreign TV productions to encourage European programming by setting a minimum air time European programming of 30%. (The 60 networks in Europe require 125,000 hours of programming, of which only 25,000 hours should be originated in Europe. That gives a considerable quota which could be exploited by U.S. competitors.)

Ever since it was developed, European television has largely remained under strict government control and has been financed by the same viewers through annual fees. Advertising is severely restricted not only in the time (which resulted in artificially maintained high prices), but also by the different national broadcast regulations governing advertising. For example, a thirty-second Kellogg cereal commercial, if introduced in three different European countries, should actually require the following adaptation to comply with different laws: in the Netherlands, deletion of references to iron and vitamins; in France, deletion of the child actors; in Germany, deletion of the claim that "Kellogg make their corn flakes the best they've ever been" (Kotler, 1986). If the 1992 program achieves uniform standards for TV commercials, the savings in production costs would be substantial by using the same spot across Europe, only differing in voiceovers.

These promotional strategies will become significant when viewed in conjunction with the deregulation of Europe's national broadcasting monopolies, because competition from commercial pan-European satellite networks will force European governments to allow new precious ad time. European television, for example, has been shaken by the arrival of satellite channels, like Sky Channel and Super Channel, conceived from the beginning as an advertising medium, whose penetration level is expected to reach 21%, capturing 8% of EC television advertising by 1992.

Advertising in Europe. Deregulation of markets is almost always accompanied by increased spending, and Europe's advertising expenses are expected to increase by at least 30%. Higher spending on advertising should be justified in the transitional phase for supporting entries in new markets, and in the long run by the larger gross margins and increased availability of media. Presently, European ad business is half the size of that in the U.S., but is growing at 12% a year, twice the U.S. rate. The growth is expected to be greater in France, Italy, and Spain.

The trend for European media cannot be totally exploited by the agencies in developing standardized advertising, because different languages, cultures, needs and attitudes do not create the conditions for the ultimate ad: one selling message directed to 320 million people. However, limited attempts at pan-European advertising have already been done, where the product and the market have shown connotations of homogeneity prevailing over elements of differentiations.

From the front of global marketing, advertisers promoting products on a pan-European basis should avoid "slice of life" advertising and adopt less referential, more symbolic ads. In such occurrences, opportunities exist for advertising that emphasized a common graphic language, like two campaigns of Saatchi & Saatchi.[5]

From the front of local marketing, it should be noted that advertisements often exhibit national features that are unintelligible beyond their frontiers. British ads, with their tradition of creativity, are often too subtle and indirect for continental Europeans. France, with its more relaxed attitudes to nudity, creates ads that would be banned as pornography in puritan England. German advertising utilizes

---

5. The Johnson & Johnson's campaign for Silhouette sanitary napkins and Gillette Co.'s campaign for Natrel deodorant were the first attempt at approaching Europe as a single market, rather than a collection of separate countries. Johnson & Johnson's campaign features origami birds that turn from white to blue, instead of words, to convey a message about the product's absorbency. In the Natrel ads, a nude man and a woman in the forest appear to be part of a tree, giving the feeling that the product is in harmony with nature.

unemotionally factual headlines. Spaniards use melodrama; Italians, songs and shouts; and so on.

Positioning. There is a temptation for many consumer-goods marketers to imitate the "one sight, one sound, one sell" dictum governing the sales of the few global products like Coca-Cola, Pepsi, and Marlboro cigarettes. But even Coca-Cola, the arch-exponent of globalism, tailors the advertising of its other drinks, like Fanta, to appeal to different markets.

The fact is that dissimilarities exist in the way products are viewed within countries of the European Community. The Renault 11, for example, may be a good economy car in the U.K., but in Spain, it is still perceived as a luxury item. These ways of thinking, desires, needs, and consumption habits are not going to change considerably, and this cannot be ignored in positioning a product. Toothpaste and oral care are another example of products which cannot be marketed in the same way across Europe. In Spain and Greece, toothpaste is regarded as cosmetic, so their commercials look glamorous, like soft drink ads. In the U.K. and in Holland, instead, toothpaste is seen as a therapeutic product and its consumption is three times as high as in Spain and Greece.

Firms with a mass-market product should concentrate on micromarketing too, because different positioning will be required by many other products, from beer to household appliances, computers, and so on. The motto of the new Europe should be: "Plan globally, act locally."

Public Relations and Sales Promotion. No company should assume, for as big as it is and could be, that it is easily well recognized across Europe. Companies like ICI, Hanson, and BAT Industry, are difficult to identify even if they are among the 100 largest public corporations in the world. Size alone does not give presence. It takes solid, consistent communications.

In order to improve communications, promotional programs in the 1990s have to provide "residual market value" and "relationship value" (Schultz, 1989). The first is defined as the image about the product or service which remains after the promotion is over. Consumers shouldn't simply take advantage of the promotion (e.g., a discount of 15%), and then forget and move on. The second, "relationship value," refers, on the other hand, to the bond created between the customers, the company and the brand. Since people buy from companies they like, loyal customers should be encouraged.

The scope of public relations will always be to make the companies look good. But to succeed in a competitive environment like the European market, firms need to know the needs and motivations of the clients and understand their own responsibilities. Images cannot be created: they are by definition a reflection of something that already exists. Public relations, nevertheless, can help to change the existing image of a company and improve it. Also, use of non-traditional agency services, such as event marketing, package design, or direct marketing, is forecasted to be expanding in the years to come. For the moment, a maze of national regulations hinders the growth of pan-European promotion and EC directives have not been proposed other than to regulate promotion for only specific industries, like toys or drugs.

DISTRIBUTION STRATEGIES

Transportation in Europe. The unified Europe will have a larger population than the U.S. or Japan, yet most of the manufacturers and consumers live and work within a radius of 800 km. They are located in an area which is only 12% of the land area of the U.S. In spite of this favorable concentration, transportation in the EC has been overburdened with regulations and associated administrative paperwork, resulting in high inefficiencies. For example, it was calculated that a truck traveling from Glasgow to Athens, a distance of 2,368 miles, and crossing five national boundaries, including a sea crossing, will travel at an average speed of eight miles per hour. The Commission has estimated that, on average, truck drivers spend 30% of their time at border crossings just waiting or filling out as many as 200 forms. Border delays have increased overall prices by 2% and cut the EC firms' profit by 25% (see Table 7.4).

The Community transportation policy should reduce formalities and harmonize regulations, so that goods could more quickly cross national boundaries. Since January 1988, one 13-page EC customs document, the Single Administrative Document (SAD), has already replaced two pounds of forms previously required by the national

TABLE 7.4. Distribution Strategies in Europe of 1992

Changes Affecting Strategies	Threats to Marketers' Planning	Management's Strategic Options
– Simplification of national transit documents and procedures – Elimination of customs formalities	– Increase in distributors' margins – Lack of direct mktg infrastructures – Restrictions in the use of computer databases	– Consolidate manufacturing facilities – Centralize warehouses and distribution centers – Implement JIT production and EDI technology – Develop non-traditional distribution channels (direct mktg, telemarketing, etc.)

regulations. Other improvements and harmonization are expected to be in the following areas:

1. Cabotage, the prohibition against a driver from picking up or delivering loads outside his country of origin.[6]
2. Restrictions on backhauls, the freight motor carriers haul on their return trip (fully 40% of the commercial vehicles crossing internal borders are empty, according to the EC report);
3. Fiscal, technical, and social barriers (highway user fees and fuel taxes; truck size and weight limits; working conditions and duty hours).

Transportation deregulation is expected to cause a significant shakeout both for the European transportation industry, which will

---

6. Today, truck freight hauled within a single country can only be carried by a motor carrier who is citizen of that country, but the EC Court of Justice has already ruled these restrictions as not allowed under the Single Market Act's liberalization of services.

become smaller and more competitive, and for the ability of European firms to compete globally, which will be encouraged by lower freight and fewer trade barriers. Now, the challenge is to rationalize manufacturing and distribution to cope with customers that are growing in size, increased competition, and uniform standards. It is no longer necessary to set up plants in the host countries to be able to conform to national product and transportation standards. Companies can justify consolidated manufacturing facilities, which allow economies of scale and replacement of small warehouses with centralized, highly mechanized distribution centers–while maintaining, or even improving, customer service.

Pan-European franchising will probably increase, following the removal of trade barriers, while inventory holding costs should decrease, since fewer safety stocks will be necessary to protect against road haulage delays. In the area of inventory reduction, European manufacturers will increasingly implement Just-In-Time (JIT) production, which requires frequent deliveries and no delays (therefore, free borders).

Finally, the growing use of electronic links will enable transportation companies to provide new services to their clients. These might include database of routes and prices, access to information on market trends, reports on new packaging, loading and distribution techniques, and possibly even distribution of performance statistics. Companies with the technology in place to support EDI (Electronic Data Interchange) may have a great advantage with European customers. EDI allows sending invoices, orders, customs documents, and design drawings between trading partners via computers rather than on paper.[7]

Retailers and Supermarkets. The major companies, especially American ones, are presently moving toward mergers and acquisitions to build strong product lines across Europe, as are retailers, distributors, and brokers in order to consolidate their buying power.

---

7. EDI transfers the information without the delays and the errors typical of the printing process. Adding bar code scanning to the EDI system, the transaction becomes truly paperless. The bar coding is an international language: the worker on the dock uses a scanner to read the code and transmits all the detailed data to a computer; at any prompt, these data can he programmed to appear in any local language.

All this activity derives substantially from the same phenomenon that consolidated America's food industry in the 1970s: the growing power of supermarkets. Big European chains like to stock only top brands backed by strong consumer advertising. Concentrating production will become common for Europe's food giants as 1992 eliminates transportation barriers. Nestle, for example, is producing its new Yes candy bars in Berlin for distribution throughout Europe. Quaker Oats Co., which has a 30% annual growth in Europe for its ready-to-eat cereals, says it will suspend two of its 15 European plants and merge purchasing units.

As a direct consequence, brands which are not among the top three positions in terms of market share will find difficulties in securing market shelf space at the retail level. This should allow distributors' power to increase, as manufacturers' margin decreases. Part of the benefits of large buying-programs should also be passed on to consumers by means of lower prices.

A proposal of the European Commission is likely to block acquisitions and mergers. Distribution arrangements which affect trade or restrict competition are already prohibited by the Treaty of Rome. Article 85(3) of the Treaty, however, provides an exemption for those exclusive sales agreements that contribute to the production or distribution of goods or to the promotion of technical and economic progress. This allowed the EC Commission to grant automatic exemption to certain types of exclusive licensing arrangements meeting certain criteria. Nevertheless, the Community does not want an irreversible market situation where the whole supply comes from a few big companies, which appears to be happening as Europe's giant chains rush to attain control of the market.

Direct Marketing. Much of the sales strategy of consumer goods' makers are now addressed at tailoring products to even more specialist and thus narrow markets. The latest trends in distribution strategies, direct mail and allying powerful consumer databases, give them instruments to develop and exploit, rather than blur, national and regional peculiarities.

Europe will remain, for the immediate future, a challenging environment for direct marketers. Still the hope exists for developing a more mature receptive environment for direct selling, telemarketing, and other nontraditional distribution channels (one medium expected to introduce broad opportunities is satellite TV). On the other hand, European direct marketers face several difficulties:

1. Europeans are not as used to buying direct as Americans and, in some quarters, perceive direct marketing as intrusive;
2. They speak different languages and a universal message will find difficulties in "travelling";
3. Inclusion of direct-response telephone numbers in TV spots is forbidden by the privacy laws of member states, such as West Germany;
4. Information about potential clients is fragmented and almost unobtainable;
5. Supported infrastructure for direct marketing is weak because credit cards, toll-free numbers, and computer databases (which could provide larger and better documented lists) are in their infancy in Europe.

Nevertheless, the European Community remains a main target because it's large, rich, and it's the logical alternative for expanding beyond the saturated U.S. market.

CONCLUSION

As regulatory barriers within the EC break down, marketers (both inside and outside Europe) should define strategies to grasp new opportunities from what will become one of the largest, most stable, and wealthiest markets in the world. Although some multinationals have occasionally regarded Europe as one market, most corporations have had to deal with a number of small segments regulated by individual national laws. In spite of the integration, the markets for some products and services will remain puzzling and local for some time, but, in line with global tendencies, the euroconsumers will generally continue to become more homogenous.

For 1992, corporations must determine to what extent they can treat the enlarged market as one entity and how they can structure their organization. By adapting their marketing strategies to the new realities, firms can take advantage of the unified Europe.

Dallmer, chief executive officer of an important European corporation, once told a story which symbolizes the situation of Europe:[8]

Two people were walking through the Black Forest where it was rumored a very dangerous lion lurked. They took a break and were sitting in the sun when one of them changed from his big hiking boots to jogging shoes. The other one smiled and laughed and asked, "You don't think you can run away from the lion with those jogging shoes?" "No," he replied. "I just need to be faster than you."

The integration of Europe is a complicated process and the implications for marketing are not immediately apparent. What we do know, though, is that the companies that will lose will be those who wait. There is no need to be first. What it takes is to be faster than the others.

BIBLIOGRAPHY

Boddewyn, J.J. and Hansen, D.M. (1977). "American Marketing in the European Common Market." *European Journal of Marketing*, (11), 548-563.

Goldman, T. (1989, March). "Packaging for a Unified Europe." *Marketing Communications*, pp. 26-27.

Konrad, W. (1989, November 27). "The New, Improved Unilever Aims to Clean Up in the US." *Business Week*, pp. 102-106.

Kossoff, J. (1988). "Europe: Up for Sale." *New Statesman & Society*, 1(8), 43-44.

Kotler, P. (1986). "Global Standardization—Courting Danger." *Journal of Consumer Marketing*, 3(2), 13-15.

Martin, J. (1988, July 11). "Beyond 1992: Lifestyle Is Key." *Advertising Age*, pp. 57.

Quelch, J.A., and Buzzell, R.D. (1989). "Marketing Moves Through EC Crossroads." *Sloan Management Review*, 31(1), 63-74.

Quelch, J.A., Buzzell, R.D. and Salama, E.R. (1990). *The Marketing Challenge of 1992*. Addison-Wesley Publishing Co.

Schultz, D.E. (1989, March). "New Directions for 1992." *Marketing Communications*, pp. 28-30.

Soehl, R. (1985). "U.S. Marketing in the European Common Market, 1963-1983: A Longitudinal Study." *MBA Thesis*, Baruch College, City University of N.Y.

---

8. See: "Fortress Europe" (1989), *Target Marketing*, 12(6), June, 12-14.

Terpstra, V. (1963). *American Marketing in the Common Market*, New York: Praeger Publishers Inc.

Vandermerwe, S. and L'Huillier, M. (1989, Jan/Feb). "Euro-Consumers in 1992." *Business Horizons*, pp. 34-40.

van Mesdag, M. (1988). "1992: The Cant Dispelled." *Industrial Marketing Digest*, 13(4), 49-55.

Chapter 8

Marketing in Europe Beyond 1992: The Challenge of a Mix Between Global and Local Marketing Strategies

Riccardo Varaldo
Andrea Piccaluga

EFFECTS OF THE COMPLETION OF THE EUROPEAN SINGLE MARKET

The 1992 program of trade reforms has been designed–among other reasons–to improve the efficiency of EC (European Community) industries, stimulate economic growth, and thus make the EC economy more competitive in global markets (Quelch, Buzzell, and Salama, 1990). New market opportunities which will be generated by the completion of the Single Market after 1992 (Emerson, 1988; Cecchini, 1988) will represent remarkable incentives for firms all over the world. In fact, the integration process will bring about income growth effects which will certainly increase European demand both in industrial and consumer goods sectors.[1]

---

1. The new European market is first of all expected to offer a series of savings to member countries, as a consequence of the elimination–or at least the strong reduction–of costs arising from a situation of poor integration among nations. These costs, often referred to as "non-Europe" cost, are mainly linked with:

i. *administrative obstacles:* such as the duplication of documents in many transactions, border controls, and a general heterogeneity of procedures;

ii. *technical barriers:* including different technical standards for similar products, different jurisdictional disciplines, preference for national firms in awarding public contracts, etc.;

iii. *differences in fiscal regimes* (VAT, excise taxes) (Stanton and Varaldo, 1989, p. 479).

More precisely, it is to be expected that firms will operate in a new competitive framework, characterised by the presence of a more international competition and consumers who will increasingly assume a common European identity, though keeping national characters as well. Some authors (Quelch, Buzzell, and Salama, 1990, p. 9) focus their attention on the fact that the integration process will cause essentially a supply-side-led gain. This means that improvements in performance will be mainly due to firms reacting to the new cost structures and improved competitive conditions, while, on the other hand, the increase in demand should be merely a consequence of falling prices, which are the result of lower costs, greater competition and economies of scale.

At firms' level, the new competitive scenario is going to create conditions for a greater selection of the initiatives, determining a sharper differentiation between firms able to exploit the new opportunities and those which are destined to suffer from the greater competition which will characterize European markets after 1992.

Marketing policies and instruments will play an important part in the success of European firms in the future. This is because firms will have to be able to operate and compete in more dynamic markets, since the abolition of trade, tariff and technical barriers will diminish the defences of national markets.

Nevertheless, it is not possible to indicate precise principles for the reorganization of marketing activities connected to all environmental situations and to every type of firm. Rather, in the new Europe we will witness–beside a general increase in the importance of the role of marketing, as an instrument for development and cooperation–a differentiation of firms' behaviors with regard to the strategies which will be adopted. In this chapter, attention is essentially focused on the factors which differentiate marketing policies in consequence of the completion of the European Single Market.

First of all, two main development alternatives are considered: (1) the increase in the number of European markets in which to operate, and (2) the increase in the level of covering and penetration in single markets. Second, a discussion is presented about global marketing at European level and local marketing, as a policy of adapting to differentiated market conditions within single countries.

THE CHANGING MARKETING MIX

The new European framework will undoubtedly influence the management of marketing mix variables (Quelch, Buzzell, and Salama 1990). For example, the harmonization of technical standards will perhaps make it easier to elaborate long term product policies for firms which will have resources to invest in R&D. Larger firms seem therefore to be the most likely beneficiaries of this effect. Similarly, the possibility of obtaining certifications which will be valid all over Europe will probably induce firms to launch simultaneously a certain product in a number of European countries, targeting to a similar segment in every one of them.[2]

Prices are generally expected to decrease–despite some sectorial differences–since the downward effect caused by stronger competition should be greater than upward effects caused by the new primary demand created by trade reforms. It is also likely that in the first post-1992 period price reductions will be intensively used to build higher shares in European markets even if integration effects will influence firms' cost structures only after some time.

With regard to distribution, transports should generally become easier and less expensive; at the same time there will be stronger competition to occupy retailers' shelves and it will be possible to organize more efficient common purchases all over Europe from single countries.

Finally, it is expected that promotion expenditures will increase, both in the short and in the long run; in fact, pan-European media will be increasingly available and these, as well as other instruments, will be broadly used, especially when entering new markets.

THE DIFFERENT GROWTH STRATEGIES IN THE EUROPEAN MARKETS

After 1992, together with changes in specific marketing mix variables, firms will also have to face problems about the general

---

2. This strategy is based on the so-called horizontal homogeneity, since it reflects consumer similarity across countries; on the other hand, vertical homogeneity represents consumer similarity within a particular country (Onkvisit and Shaw, 1990).

management and control of marketing activities, in order to exert their own specific influence over the market. Under this aspect, the situation will be much different with regard to the various types of firms, with a clear difference between large, and small and medium size firms. Large firms will tend to strengthen their sale organizations, made up of commercial subsidiaries, sale offices, concessionaires and so on, coordinating their activities with a greater orientation towards marketing activities. These are the firms which in perspective will be most favored in experimenting the adoption of marketing strategies conceived in a European dimension, counting on the greater homogeneity which characterize the markets of the various European countries.

In order to take full advantage of the general growth effects of the completion of the European Single Market, firms will have to face a number of new strategic challenges. In particular, they will have to choose among different marketing strategies, referring their decisions not only to old parameters, but to new and less predictable ones as well. One of these decisions is between expansion and penetration strategies. The first one–expansion on European markets–will be adopted by firms wishing to increase their total sales in Europe by expanding their activities by serving the largest possible number of single countries. The second strategy–penetration in selected markets of single European countries–consists in a greater coverage (i.e., more areas and/or more points of sale) of the countries where a certain firm is already present. Figure 8.1 shows the directions in which the two different strategies develop.

Given the proposed matrix, one can see that expansion strategies develop horizontally, adding new countries to single firms' national markets. Nevertheless, firms can operate in the different countries in dissimilar ways; in fact, firms may have spent more years producing and/or selling in specific countries or they may have just entered other national markets. Therefore, their experiences and efforts are generally more relevant in "older" markets, where they have been present for a longer period of time.

On the other hand, penetration strategies have a vertical direction, and their objective is to intensify the presence in single national markets. Of course, all this must not be taken as an absolutely rigid decision, since firms will continuously take into account the

FIGURE 8.1. Expansion and Penetration Strategies

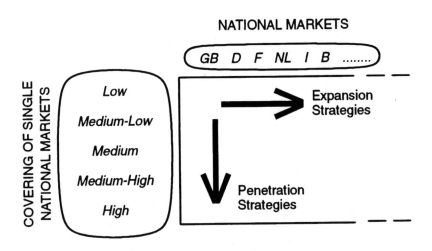

possibility and the opportunity of adding a new country to their portfolio, and at the same time intensifying efforts in the vertical direction.

It is most likely that different types of firms will implement these two strategies. Generally speaking, expansion strategies should be followed by two main groups of firms. First, they will be adopted by firms which are less experienced in operating abroad and which prefer to exploit easy commercial opportunities in single countries, without being present with strong brand identity and structural involvement, and are therefore more likely to prefer to increase the number of markets they sell to. Many small firms fall into this category and some of them may also be national leaders in specific sectors, even if their sizes are not relevant in the broader European context. As these firms decide to go abroad, they chose to enter the easiest markets, which sometimes are those closer to the country of origin from a geographical and cultural point of view.[3] These firms may encounter difficulties in dealing with a variety of different mar-

---

3. Some of the most common examples of cultural and geographical proximity are: (1) Austria, Germany, and Switzerland; (2) Italy and Southern France; (3) Italy and Spain; (4) Great Britain, Benelux, and Scandinavian countries, etc.

kets. A possible consequence is that firms following expansion strategies will enter one or two European markets and will be satisfied with serving a portion of these countries (often, only one or a few areas), without aiming at a stronger market penetration. Also, since they often adopt costs-saving entry strategies, they will probably suffer the competition of larger firms. The tendency to enter a certain number of European countries, serving only a few areas and a small number of points of sale, is justified by the fact that these firms (1) do not have some of the material resources and know-how necessary to reach a large market coverage and, (2) tend to sell abroad what they already produce for the domestic market with only minor product adaptations. Therefore, these firms prefer to exploit the easiest sales opportunities which do not imply particular efforts and investments. In some cases, however, they employ refined sales techniques, such as direct selling to selected potential customers through a clever use and promotion of their quality image.

A second group of firms which follow expansion strategy are those which sell their products in a standardized way, so that the degree of market coverage is limited by the structural characteristics of distribution. This is the case, for example, of multinational companies which sell consumer goods and whose only possibility to expand their activity in the European market is to sell to modern distribution structures, that is, marketing channels which require the commitment of human and material resources. Nevertheless, as we will see, these same firms might also choose to be present only in a limited number of areas within single countries, following an expansion strategy.

On the other hand, penetration strategies in single markets will be followed by firms which are already present in one or more European countries and show interest in intensifying their presence in some of them. This strategy implies efforts on the reorganization of sales procedure and structure, and often leads to a modification of entry strategies in foreign markets. In fact, it may be that simultaneous to the decision of entering a new area of a country (e.g., northwestern France for an Italian firm already present in southern France), a firm will have to find new agents, modify advertising, pricing and product policies, or create new local production facilities. This type of strategy will also allow firms to reach certain economies of scale which will open the way to more efficient distribution and production policies in the new European environment. The firms which will be more interested in adopting penetration strategies will probably be those operating in industries where the new competition will bring a greater concentration of production and distribution facilities and where size will become a key factor. To obtain market success, firms will have to reach critical turnover threshold for each European market they decide to enter. Only through the achievement of large sale volumes, will firms be able to invest enough resources for sale and marketing activities.

We can therefore affirm that growth effects generated by the completion of the Single Market will most likely oblige European as well as non-European firms to reconsider their competitive position in the new framework. Of course, since some industrial sectors probably will be more affected than others the evolutive pattern will not be the same for every one of them (Onida, 1990a). Nevertheless, one of the first decisions to make will be that between expansion and penetration strategies–or a mix between them–which we briefly described.

MARKETING STRATEGIES IN EUROPE: GLOBAL vs. LOCAL ALTERNATIVES

A second important set of decisions will stem from realizing that the European market will become increasingly global after 1992. European consumers are already rather homogeneous in some aspects, and the completion of the Single Market will further abolish some of the barriers which at present do not allow firms to consider Europe as a single potential market.

The second critical set of choices, which firms already present in the EC–as well as those wishing to enter it–will have to consider, therefore, regards the degree of globalization of marketing. Concretely, this set of strategic decisions generates two main possibilities:

a. a *full exploitation of marketing globalization opportunities*, enjoying the growing homogenization of technical standards and national legislations, and a broad diffusion of common cultural characteristics;

b. a *choice towards customization*, being present in several countries and regions with different marketing policies according to specific market characteristics.

The problem will arise especially for those firms which are not only present in several countries, but are or will be intensively present in every one of them. In fact, Figure 8.1 discloses issues which are not only related to dealing with dissimilar national realities, but also with local and regional situations which constitute a "patchwork" of heterogeneous sub-national frameworks. In past years, firms operating in several markets without a high level of covering, implemented a sort of "skimming" strategy: that is, they tried to make the easiest sales, those from consumers who were most similar to those in the domestic market; more difficult sales, i.e., those requiring greater marketing efforts, would be eventually left for a later time. In our competitive scenario, which–as already pointed out–will imply an increase in the critical turnover threshold to be reached for each single European country that will be served, firms will not be able to limit themselves to exploit the easiest market areas, but, in order to reach high sales volumes, they will have to adopt strategies of penetration in single countries. To implement these strategies, firms will perhaps have to deal with differentiated local market conditions, which will have to be taken into account when choosing specific marketing policies.

In the changing technological and economic environment which characterize European countries, firms will face a sort of a strategic dichotomy. In fact, on one side there are tendencies towards market integration, both from the demand and the supply side, which encourage global business strategies; on the other side, there are also evidences of market fragmentation and diversification, which seem to foster the adoption of differentiated business strategies to deal with single national markets.

As a matter of fact, stimuli towards market globalization (Levitt, 1983) operate through a set of relationships in which the evolution of technologies and the homogenization of demand smooth the way for market unification and for the globalization of competition and business strategies (Abravanel, 1987). Therefore, in global markets, firms look for points of similarity and aggregation among countries and benefit from planning common strategies to exploit the advantages arising from integrated planning and structures (Porter, 1986). Nevertheless, firms, especially those that adopt penetration strategies, will find out that, as they go deeper in a national market, they will probably find more difficulties in adopting the same strategies in different markets, since regional differences will become relevant.

The European Single Market, which is on its way towards com-pletion, has already demonstrated, in some cases, that globalization strategies might be inadequate, especially in the field of marketing activities. In fact, contrary to what might be the case for production, procurement and research and development (R&D), which can be more easily integrated and concentrated on an international basis, it is more difficult for marketing activities to follow principles of unification.

For example, the European market of household appliances, notwithstanding that a large amount of exchange flows among Germany, Great Britain, France and Italy, still represents a non-unified market, since a series of heterogeneities can be noticed (Fuller and Stopford, 1988; Varaldo, 1991):

- European demand for household appliances is fragmented, since consumers' preferences are differentiated according to cultural and climatic factors;
- the penetration of international brands in single markets is relatively limited; in fact, even if some brands are present in the four countries which have been mentioned, they frequently have little market shares if compared to domestic companies;
- for a same product there are often price differences among various countries, which shows that a European market does not exist and that competition on single markets is more important than global competition;
- the structures of the distributive systems in various countries are not homogeneous, and there are differentiated conditions in trade marketing policies; on the other hand, in some countries, fragmented trade structures still exist, which leaves market opportunities for products with local or national brands.

As a consequence, the absence of a unified European market has induced some of the most important producers to change from global to national strategies. Market fragmentation, in fact, has nullified many of the advantages resulting from the economies of scale generated by large plants, so that new and smaller plants have started to be used. As a matter of fact, some ten years ago the best size for a plant was about one million units per year, while nowadays the typical plant produces about 150,000 units per year. Also, plants used to produce a variety of models for several countries, now only produce a few models for one or two countries.

Differences in market situations can be noticed not only among various European countries, as showed by the previous example, but also within single countries. It is a well known reality that European countries are not very internally homogeneous. A good example is Italy, with its north-south differences in income and fertility (Dawson, 1987; Varaldo and Marbach, 1991). In fact, per capita gross domestic product (GDP) in southern Italy is about half of that of northern Italy, and southern final consumptions are about 75% of those in the north; recent statistics showed that in the north 21.6% of total income was spent on food consumption, 26.5 in the center and 28.3 in the south.[4] Also, great differences can be found in the levels of employment, demographic tendencies and other economic indicators.[5]

In Europe, the differentiation of consumer behaviors goes often beyond national borders, i.e., relevant differences can be noticed within single countries. Therefore, firms will have to face a variety of different situations within single served countries. It is then likely

---

4. Source: Varaldo and Marbach, 1991.

5. Some of the most visible indicators of north-south differences show the following values (north and center = 100):

Indicators	Values for Southern Italy
Per capita GDP (1987)	54,1
Final per capita consumptions (1987)	75,3
Per capita family disposable income (1987)	63,5
Family per capita consumptions (1987)	70,0
Transfers as % of family income (1987)	117,3
Deposits (1989)	54,2
Investments (1989)	39,1

Source: CENSIS elaborations (1990) on data from ISTAT and Bank of Italy.

that many firms will have to follow, alternatively or at the same time, global and local marketing strategies.

One of the main determinants of differentiation of the market situations concerns the nature of the product. In fact, four major categories of consumer needs can be identified in relation to territorial and cultural homogeneity in Europe and the nature of consumers' need. Products in section 1 and 3 of Figure 8.2 are connected to functional needs, such as technical and objective exigencies (computers, credit cards) or to specific exigencies, such as demographic and structural factors (cars, household appliances); for them a global marketing strategy can be implemented only if territorial heterogeneity is not important, as it is the case for products in section 3. On the other hand, in sections 2 and 4 there are products which satisfy psychological needs, such as universal lifestyles (perfumes, cigarettes) or local cultures and traditions (food, classical clothing), but again, a global marketing strategy can be adopted only for those needs which are not influenced by territorial heterogeneity.[6]

THE MIRAGE OF THE EUROCONSUMER

As a matter of fact, Euroconsumers do exist in some sectors (Ryans and Rau, 1990), even if they are difficult to identify since firms, when measuring the similarity among European nations, must take into account economic and demographic variables as well as psychological factors (Chadraba and Czepiec, 1988). In reality, a true European consumer does exist only for some specific products and services, such as baby food or products and services for young people (clothing, entertainment, sports equipment, etc.), high-tech products (computers, hi-fi etc.) and fashion items.

Technological progress, though diminishing the importance of spatial and temporal barriers, and increasing living standards, does not imply the overcoming of some relevant cultural distances. In many cases, consumer behavior is "culture bound," and European governments have often showed a growing concern about maintaining this kind of national and subnational characters.

---

6. For a survey on the studies in the field of cross-cultural behavior in marketing see Mårtenson (1988).

FIGURE 8.2. Different Types of Needs and Territorial Heterogeneity

	FUNCTIONAL NEEDS	PSYCHOLOGICAL NEEDS
TERRITORIAL HOMOGENEITY	Needs linked to objective, technical exigences. e.g. computers, credit cards.	Needs linked to universal life styles. e.g. pefumes, cigarettes, luxury products.
TERRITORIAL HETEROGENEITY	Needs linked to specific exigences, such as demographic and structural factors (climate, income, etc.) e.g. cars, electrical household appliances, furniture.	Needs linked to pre-existing and consolidated local cultures and traditions. e.g. food, classical clothing.

(Between quadrants are boxes numbered: 1 2 / 3 4)

As a matter of fact, generally speaking, a true European consumer does not exist. This is because in Europe there are a number of differentiating factors, such as:

a. different languages and cultures;
b. different alimentary traditions (so that even products such as beer, coffee, chocolate, orange juices, etc., will have to be adapted before their introduction in different countries with regard to quality, packaging and product characteristics).

Also, at consumers' level and not at national level, there are growing tendencies towards individualism, so that people increasingly refuse mass consumption and standardization,[7] making it even more difficult to elaborate strategies based on common con-

7. As a matter of fact, this search for individualism often turns out to be a massification process; this may be the case, for example, of Swatch, which is sold as something with "particular" and "unique" characteristics but is owned by a huge number of people.

sumption patterns. Some of these factors also play an important role not only at sub-national, i.e., at regional and local levels, but also, immigration flows in Europe have generated several seemingly homogenous groups (which may have a common religion or origin), but that show considerable heterogeneity at the same time.[8] Consequently, market clustering can be used as a combination between standardization and market segmentation, seeking similarities to form clusters, but acknowledging that a single, homogeneous market does not exist (Onkvisit and Shaw, 1990).

In Europe, two tendencies are particularly strong which characterize post-industrial markets; these are (1) fragmentation, through the process of personalization of consumptions and (2) variability, because of the continuous modifications in consumers' needs and preferences. The high degree of differentiation among European consumers will definitely require local marketing efforts on the part of large multinational corporations as well as smaller firms wishing to enter several European markets.

GLOBAL MARKETING STRATEGIES

Global marketing is the most common strategy that will be pushed forward as the European integration process proceeds. After all, the EC represents a group of 325 million consumers which under many points of view show similar characteristics and in some fields are getting even more similar, so that it should be reasonable that firms will try to benefit from a further homogenization of demand.[9]

Integration processes in Europe started many years ago, and after 1992 consumer behavior is expected to be even more homogeneous for several reasons:

---

8. This situation is rather similar to that of the United States, where the Hispanic segment, for example, comprises consumers from many different backgrounds (Quelch, 1989, p. 2). In Europe, good examples might be Muslims in Great Britain or Germany and the immigrants coming from Eastern Europe.

9. For example, in the last ten years, Germans, Belgians, Dutch, Danish, and Irish have decreased their beer consumption by 5% and have increased wine consumption by 3%. In the same period, French, Italians, Portuguese, Spanish, and Greeks have decreased wine consumption by 16% and increased beer by 30%, so that European consumption patterns for these products are more homogeneous.

i. After 1992, TV programs and other services will be more broadly available throughout Europe so that consumers will receive identical promotional messages and, as a consequence, cross-cultural differences should slowly decrease;

ii. Similarly, after the internationalization of distribution European corporations will try to export their most successful "national products," with the hope that they will be appreciated in other countries as well;

iii. Minor border controls and new legislation on labor mobility will make the process of transferring fashions and tendencies across European countries much quicker than it used to be;

iv. Population mobility: 65% of Dutch, 45% of Germans, and 30% of English people spend their holidays in southern Europe, and this accelerates the diffusion of common life styles.

Moreover, it must be emphasized that the extension of globalization processes in Europe is not only a quantitative issue, i.e., the mere reproduction of traditional operating models, but, more precisely, it is a qualitative issue, which comprises innovative trends in the organization and operating procedures of markets (Varaldo and Bonfiglio, 1989, p. 535; Varaldo, 1987b). In fact, what seems to be particularly important is not the globalization process that regards sectors which have naturally acquired a global dimension (Porter, 1986) or are going to do so, but the globalization of national or even local sectors, which become at least partially global because of new environmental forces such as communication technologies, information networks, markets deregulation, common technical standards and so on. It is this second type of globalization which should be particularly favored by post-1992 conditions.

Nevertheless, we must not conclude that the European market is definitely on the way toward the globalization of every type of product. There are forces which push toward that direction, but there are also important factors which contribute to slacken the process. Recent studies (Picard, Boddewyn, and Soehl, 1988) do not support the hypothesis that the era of total global marketing standardization has arrived. Although an increased degree of standardization can be perceived—in accordance with Levitt's theories—even industrial-good manufacturers recognize that their products still require great adaptation efforts to meet customers' needs.

LOCAL MARKETING STRATEGIES

Local marketing means the tailoring of one or more aspects of a broad marketing program–or the use of supplementary programs–to meet local consumers' or trade needs (Quelch, 1989, p. 77). This can be done, for example, on a geographical basis (a specific program for a region, a city or a zip code), or even on a trade account basis (a different program for a particular retail chain, a division of the chain, or an individual store). Of course, local marketing is nothing new, since it merely involves customizing one or more elements of the marketing program in order to achieve higher profits than would be achieved with a standardized program.

Producers of consumer goods and service companies normally devote more resources than other firms to local marketing activities. Among these, product adaptations are quite common, as shown, for example, by the different types of coffees sold in European countries, different flavors and colors for soft drinks, different packages for similar products and so on. Promotion might also need some adaptations, as is the case of airlines offering bonus mileage to fliers on routes where their competitive position is weak, etc. Distribution policies may vary according to firms' initiatives, but also as a consequence of the characteristics of the distributive structure of particular regions. Price policies, on the other hand, are to be dealt with more carefully in order to avoid dangers of price discrimination.

Curiously, in some cases, local marketing in Europe will be a sort of a cross-national campaign, since there are special ethnic groups which show quite homogeneous characteristics across two or more nations, such as German speaking people in northern Italy and Switzerland, or Basque people in Spain and France.

Local marketing is not only something that will have to be done in Europe, a sort of defensive and necessary move, but it will represent a source of competitive advantage for firms. However, it should not merely consist of an ad hoc collection of localized sales promotion events. Rather, it should represent firms' willingness to analyze and exalt different behaviors of European consumers through a continuous segmentation effort.

CUSTOMIZATION vs. STANDARDIZATION

Substantially, after 1992, firms will increasingly find themselves involved in a sort of a strategic dichotomy. On one side, success in the European market will be strictly linked to their ability to customize their marketing mix, and in particular their products, in order to meet the needs of diversified consumers. On the other side, other firms–often because institutional changes in the EC will decrease the importance of segmentation–will try to sell products which will be able to reach the largest possible market share, through a standardization process (Onida, 1990b, p. 35).

Which sectors and which firms will follow one of the two strategies will be mainly a matter of meeting specific needs and making personal decisions on common problems. Obviously, it will also be possible to adopt intermediate strategies, adapting certain aspects of global marketing variables to meet local needs (Blackwell, Ajami, and Stephan, 1991). This is something that European firms have learned to do some years ago, while perhaps American firms will meet some more difficulties, since only large multinational corporations have in the past acted locally after doing global planning.

Many business cases show that before actions are standardized at an international level, management's thought must be internationally harmonized. Globalization strategies often require changing the rules through which international organizations manage their businesses, but the changes come mainly from outside local markets.

In the future, firms operating in Europe will need a multinational management able to interact with people from everywhere; also, firms' identification with the country of origin is generally expected to decrease.[10] At the same time, the completion of the Single Market is likely to cause an increase in the number of collaboration

---

10. A good example of this tendency is given by a non-EC country, Sweden, whose multinational corporations, with some minor exceptions, have succeeded in reaching a real international dimension, and are not necessarily seen as Swedish companies in the international marketplace.

agreements between firms, and more and more mergers and acquisitions will probably take place (Emerson, 1988). In these cases, the ability of the management to work in an international framework will be important; also, managers from different countries will often have to work together after mergers and acquisitions, and this has recently appeared to be quite a challenging problem in several cases.

With regard to management's ability to operate in the international framework, Nestlé's management, for example, has a strong international experience, an official language does not exist in the corporation, only four out of Nestlé's ten top managers are Swiss and new talents are employed in every European country. Without going so far in the process of internationalizing the managerial workforce, firms of every size will have to keep in mind that before globalizing their marketing mix they must be internally ready to deal with a differentiated multinational European market.

CONCLUSION

In short, our opinion is that after 1992 firms will have more incentives to enter European markets different from the domestic one. In some cases these firms will operate in European countries for the first time; in other cases, more frequently, firms which already sell in Europe will operate–after 1992–in a larger number of countries or will increase the coverage of single markets. Moreover, some firms which already operate in a number of European countries will modify some of their strategies, in order to take full advantage of post-1992 globalization opportunities and prevent the danger of treating differentiated markets in a standardized way.

The extension of the number of countries to be served will put firms in front of the problem of managing a variety of market situations. Despite integration effects, different countries will continue to present dissimilar characteristics and market conditions with regard to demand, distribution, competitors, etc. Moreover, as firms tend to increase their presence in European countries, they will have to deal with heterogeneous situations inside single countries. These situations represent a limit to the adoption of global strategies.

It is therefore reasonable to say that in order to deal with the

European market firms will have to think global and act local. This means that they should be able to standardize parts of their activities and deal with them in a centralized way, while others will be customized and often decentralized. Examples of the activities which are likely to be customized, even with regard to subnational characteristics, are typically marketing mix adaptations, such as local brands and products, management of relationships with distribution facilities, promotional activities and the recruitment of managers.

BIBLIOGRAPHY

Abravanel, Roger. (1987). "Shaping Effective Responses to the Globalization Challenge," in Varaldo, Riccardo (editor), *International Marketing Cooperation*, ETS, Pisa.

Blackwell, Roger, Ajami, Riad and Stephan, Kristina. (1991). "Winning the Global Advertising Race: Planning Globally, Acting Locally," in *Journal of International Consumer Marketing*, Vol. 3(2), 97-120.

Cecchini, Paolo. (1988). *The European Challenge 1992. The Benefits of a Single Market*. Wildwood House: Aldreshot.

Censis. (1990). *Rapporto sulla situazione sociale del Paese*, Roma.

Chadraba, Petr and Czepiec, Helen. (1988). "Euroconsumers? A Three-Country Analysis of the Feasibility of Product Value Standardization," in *Journal of Global Marketing*, Vol. 1(4), Summer.

Commission of the European Community. (1988). *La sfida del 1992*, Sperling & Kupfer, orig. title *The European Challenge 1992. The Benefits of a Single Market*.

Dawson, Leslie M. (1987). "Transferring Industrial Technology to Less Developed Countries," *Industrial Marketing Management*, 16(4), November, 265-271.

Eliasson, Gunnar and Lundberg, Lars. (1990). "The creation of the EC Internal Market and its Effects on the Competitiveness of Producers in Other Industrial Economies," in Siebert, Horst, ed., *The Completion of the Internal Market*, Institut fur Weltwirtschaft an der Universitat Kiel, Tubingen.

Emerson, Michael. (1988). "The Economics of 1992. An Assessment of the Potential Economic Effects of Completing the Internal Market of the European Community," in *European Economy*, March.

Fuller, Charles E. and Stopford, John. (1988). "Globale o nazionale: scelte strategiche e performance delle imprese nell'industria europea degli elettrodomestici bianchi," in *L'Industria–Rivista di economia e politica industriale*, April-June.

Kaynak, Erdener. (1988). Editor, *Transnational Retailing*, De Gruyter, Berlin.

Levitt, Theodore. (1983). "The Globalization of Markets," in *Harvard Business Review*, N. 61, May-June, 92-102.

Mårtenson, Rita. (1988). "Cross-Cultural Similarities and Differences in Multinational Retailing," in Kaynak, E., editor, *Transnational Retailing*, De Gruyter, Berlin.

Onida, Fabrizio. (1990a). "Europe 1992: Macroeconomic Sustainability and Implications for Patterns of Industrial Specialization," *CESPRI Working Paper N.38*, September, Università L.Bocconi, Milan.

_____, a cura di. (1990b). *Competizione e crescita delle imprese sul mercato europeo*, SIPI, Roma.

Onkvisit, Sak and Shaw, John J. (1990). "Global Advertising: Revolution or Myopia?" in *Journal of International Consumer Marketing*, Vol. 2(3), 97-112.

Picard, Jacques, Boddewyn, Jean J. and Soehl, Robin. (1988). "U.S. Marketing Policies in the European Community: A Longitudinal Study, 1973-1983," in *Journal of Global Marketing*, Vol. 1(4), 5-23.

Porter, Michael E. (1986). *Competition in Global Industries*, Harvard Business School Press, Boston, Ma.

Quelch, John A. (1989). *How to Market to Consumers. 10 Ways to Win.* John Wiley & Sons, New York.

Quelch, John A., Buzzell, Robert D., Salama, Eric R. (1990). *The Marketing Challenge of 1992*. Addison-Wesley.

Ryans, John K. and Rau, Pradeep A. (1990). Marketing Strategies for the New Europe: A North American Perspective on 1992, The American Marketing Association, Chicago.

Stanton, William and Varaldo, Riccardo. (1989). *Marketing, Il* Mulino, Bologna.

Varaldo, Riccardo. (1987a). Editor, *International Marketing Cooperation*, ETS, Pisa.

_____. (1987b). "Competizione globale e marketing internazionale," in *L'Impresa*, N.2.

Varaldo, Riccardo and Bonfiglio, Luca. (1989). "La dimensione globale dei mercati e delle strategie competitive," in *Rivista Internazionale di Scienze Sociali*, N.3-4, luglio-dicembre, 533-556.

Varaldo, Riccardo. (1991). "La dicotomia marketing indifferenziato/marketing differenziato nel contesto internazionale," in *Studi in onore di Carlo Masini*, forthcoming.

Varaldo, Riccardo and Marbach, Giorgio. (1991). *The Changing Consumer in Italy*, forthcoming.

SECTION III.
EUROMARKETING STRATEGIES:
EASTERN EUROPE

Chapter 9

East and Central European Marketing: 1992 and Beyond

Gabor Hovanyi

INTRODUCTION

Meditating on "European Marketing: 1992 and Beyond" from the point of view of Hungary and the other East European countries, one has to calculate with more risk factors than usual on the risk-interwoven East European scene. Some of the distinct characteristics of the Central and East European markets can be summarized as follows:

- There are basic uncertainties in the different possibilities of the economic development of the East and Central European countries, and all of the possibilities have completely different marketing consequences and implications.
- The effects of the new economic conditions of the *European Community* after 1992 on the marketing efforts of the East and Central European countries are also important risk factors.
- Economic and technological transformations of the *world economy* can profoundly influence the future of the East and Central European countries. These stem from the political events in the Middle East related to the problem of oil prices to a permanent negative balance of payments and a significant slowdown of economic growth in the U.S.
- A basic uncertainty surrounding the East and Central European countries is the political and economic future of the Commonwealth of Independent States influencing import and ex-

port possibilities, as well as the conditions of an economic "take off" in the region.

To restrict the above-mentioned risk factors, one has to analyze the present economic situations of the East European countries, including their existing marketing practices. Here, the purpose is not to forecast turbulent changes taking place in European or world-wide economic environments. The analysis and prognosis were stated with the Hungarian situation first, then broadening our view later on to the East and Central European scene as a whole. What concerns the role of marketing in Eastern and Central Europe? To answer this question, one must discuss not only the marketing concepts and practices of East and Central European firms, but also to forecast the marketing practices of Western companies in the East and Central European markets. These companies cover traditional trade activities as well as problems of industrial cooperations, joint ventures, Western investments, with 100% ownership, etc., from the point of view of marketing requirements.

THE HUNGARIAN SCENE: RECENT, PAST, AND PRESENT SITUATION

Here the author presents some figures concerning the current state of the Hungarian economy. In these figures, one can notice some of the main problems of the economy. That is, the decrease of the volume of investments in recent years, the real price of the growth of exports, namely the frightful figures of the terms of trade, and the decrease of final consumption (i.e., of the living standards). The consequence of all this was the increase of the layers of the society living in absolute or relative poverty to the limit of 15 and 30%; the increase of the inflation rate to the critical limit of 30% a year; the increase of the debt of Hungary to Western creditors representing today a frightful amount of US $22 billion. Also, one has got to know that on the average, 85% of the profits of the Hungarian state-owned companies were "centralized" by the state; with less and less funds for investments, the technology of the large Hungarian companies became more and more outdated. The highest level of the personal income tax system was 56%, which hindered the development of entrepreneurship and put brakes on the increase of productivity. In spite of all this, Hungary opened up her economy more and more to the West. This situation is proved also by the increasing numbers of joint ventures between Hungarian and Western companies.[1] (See Table 9.1)

Now let us summarize some general problems inherited by the first freely elected government and dated more or less from the last 40 years of pro-communist regime:

- The Hungarian economy has a lot of *structural problems* being manifested by the weight of the different sectors of the economy and industry, and by the size of the huge, overcentralized state-owned companies.
- The *regulatory system* of the economy was in many respects a voluntarist one; the unforseen, rapid changes of the system did not make possible any forecasting.
- For the first time in their history, the companies have faced *scarcities*; the lack of supplies raised costs and prices, and loosened disciplines in production as well as in trade.
- The administration's buildup of a large *bureaucracy* which was also reflected at the micro level.
- The governmental budget had a huge *deficit*, mainly as a consequence of the bureaucracy, the activity of lobbies, and unfounded company subsidies.
- The *infrastructure* of the economy became more and more outdated.

As the basis and consequence of all this, the value system and the direction and functioning of the economy became a deteriorated one in the economic sense–prices, costs, profits, etc.–as well as in work ethics in general, quality consciousness and productivity. These problems of the management of the economy were, in most cases, linked with problems of Hungary's foreign economic relations.

Due to a long-term relationship, Hungary had to rely on other former socialist countries. For instance: (1) Hungary became too dependent on the supply of energy and raw materials; (2) the quality of products, their range and timing of shipments of the imported

---

1. *Yearbook of the Hungarian Statistical Office,* Budapest, 1990.

TABLE 9.1. Characteristic Trends of the Hungarian Economic Scene in 1980-1989

	Years			
	1980	1985	1987	1989
GDP	100.0	109.1	115.2	115.3
Output of Industry	100.0	109.8	114.9	115.3
Output of Agriculture	100.0	108.2	108.1	112.0
Investment	100.0	(80.3)	105.0	(77.6)
Export	100.0	140.2	138.7	(155.3)
Imports	100.0	108.8	115.2	114.8
Terms of Trade	100.0	(92.0)	(89.7)	(91.1)
Final Consumption	100.0	108.1	(114.5)	(106.0)

( ) = Main problem areas

Source: *Yearbook of the Hungarian Statistical Office*, Budapest, 1990.

goods had many problems; (3) the low quality requirements and poor paying capabilities of the East-European importers lessened the R&D efforts of the Hungarian firms; (4) the main importer country, the former USSR, accumulated a huge negative balance of payments in respect to Hungary; and (5) the costs and profits of the main trade agreements and joint ventures between Hungary and the Eastern partners—especially the USSR—cannot be appreciated because of the blocked information flows and the deteriorated value systems where prices, in most cases, do not reflect either the costs of used resources or the judgements of the market. But it must also be stressed that in many cases, these Eastern European markets with low product quality standards represented the only possible export markets to reach for the Hungarian manufacturing industry.

What does affect the foreign trade relations of Hungary with the West? Hungary has had problems with low and changing quality, outdated products, and late shipments of products due to physical distribution problems. In spite of growing export trade, the terms of trade have become somewhat unappealing. Last but not least, the whole Hungarian economy is partly blocked, partly threatened by the huge debt of the economy of US $22 billion.

With this background in mind, let us now turn to the main problems of the Hungarian companies. In the Hungarian industry, with very few exceptions, state-owned companies produce 90% of the total industrial output. It was proved during the last decades that these companies did not have real owners, so they did not have real responsibility for goal setting and resource management. Many of the companies functioned like monopolies. As such, they were highly centralized, but not large enough for world standards, without competition, so they could transfer their cost increases as price rises to the customers. The counterproductive wage regulation system created the phenomenon of "unemployment behind the gates" by decreasing productivity and dissolving work ethics. In the average corporation, taxes were extremely high, so the companies had no investment funds to modernize their technology. But through the lobbying system, they could get subsidies from the state. This also decreased their productivity and the work ethics of the employees even more. As a consequence of the lobbying system, personal links and not managerial skills became important. Along with low productivity, the wages were also low; but with low wage quality, productivity decreased even more. At the end, employees had no identification with the goals of the companies, and they had no confidence either in their company management or in the management of the economy.[2]

Looking at the marketing consequences of this economic scene, we can come to the following main conclusions:

- On the *domestic market*, some elements of the marketing concepts, techniques, and practices (such as market research, product planning, promotion campaigns, and new sales organizations) have been introduced by Hungarian companies; and these have been proved useful and necessary. Utilization of advanced marketing programs were exceptional. In most cases,

---

2. More details in the Report of the Research Institute of Industrial Economics of the Hungarian Academy of Sciences prepared for the PHARE-ACE project in 1990.

the effects of economic scarcity, the administrative regulatory system (managing by non-economic interference), the monopolistic position of companies, and the lobbying system which compensates the market losses by governmental subsidies, made the existing marketing programs superfluous.

- In the *East-European* former socialist *markets*, general economic and foreign trade agreements were contracted at governmental level, and companies entered into contracts only with later specifications. In this situation, marketing agreements were contracted by influencing the potential customers to urge their governments to sign agreements on Hungarian imports and to engage in industrial cooperations and joint ventures.
- Real marketing was needed in *Western markets*. But even there, two high barriers were always present. The shortage of hard currency to buy sophisticated market research to finance efficient promotion campaigns, and the rigidity of the production system at home that was the consequence of the restricted possibilities to make investments and technological changes, of the low level of productivity, of the outdated managerial skills, and of the lack of real interest rates which paralyzed efforts to follow the quick changes of the markets. Having this rigid production system, at the very most, caused a *luxurious marketing* to be executed on the competitive Western markets.

After even this brief analysis of the marketing scene in Hungary, we can draw the following conclusions: on the eve of the 1990s, most of the Hungarian economists, managers, and other professionals at company level admitted *in theory* the decisive role of marketing in modern business; but in *daily practice*, only some elements of marketing have been introduced, leading not once to high profits, but never forming an organic philosophy of the whole company.

THE PLANS OF THE HUNGARIAN GOVERNMENT FOR THE 1991-92 PERIOD

This was the general situation in Hungary when the new, freely elected government took over in May of 1990. What have been the targets of the new government? All were very honorable aims:

privatization, the buildup of a market economy with competition, the payback of the international debts of the country, the decrease of the inflation rate and of the bureaucracy, the balancing of the government's budget, the stimulation of Western investments to modernize the technology, the cutting of subsidies to companies, the creation of a stock exchange leading to a public appreciation of the performance of the companies, decreasing corporate and income taxes, and the buildup of a new social security system solving the problems of the unemployed and of the pauperized population. But these honorable aims altogether suggested a very dubious possibility: that the Hungarian economy could achieve a higher growth rate with a lower inflation rate and with no increase in the unemployment rate.[3]

At the end of June of 1990, therefore, the general scene suggested the idea that the new government: (a) could not find the appropriate main economic targets and could not balance the supporting and opposing subtargets for a successful and consistent economic policy; (b) could not create the clearly determined and efficient means to achieve the main targets of the economic policy; and (3) could not reach or did not want to reach for political reasons, namely the eventual social unrest and the necessary speed for a "take-off" (i.e., for a renaissance of the economy, including the changes in economic policy, direction system, and economic climate in general). This was the program of National Renewal of the Hungarian Democratic Forum. It was the largest political party in the coalition government in Budapest in 1990.

All this means–at least during the autumn of 1990–that the development of the Hungarian economy for the 1991-92 period, and very likely beyond this period, can follow four potential courses, thereby creating four different avenues for the development of marketing concepts and practices. These are: the radical, the slow, the mixed, and the retrograde courses.

1. The *radical course* needs a quick buildup of a market economy in view of the significant competition of imports and a quick priva-

---

3. Based on the Report from the Tunel published in 1990 by the Hungarian Financial Research Institute, Budapest.

tization with Western takeovers. This course is based on huge Western investments–helped by advantageous package deals–for the modernization of the outdated Hungarian technology. In parallel, bureaucracy and subsidies of the government must be abolished, the structure of the economy and the product range of the companies have to be changed in a dramatic way, and the inflation rate must be reduced rapidly. All of these efforts may create a quite large unemployment level, maybe also social unrest, which should be balanced by new social aid and retraining systems. The radical course also needs the strong support of the government and of financial institutions, such as banks, to establish many small and medium-size enterprises and to build up a new infrastructure of the economy. This is partly included in the package deals developed by Western governments and businessmen. The radical course also needs new managerial skills which means personal changes and new confidence on the part of the employees that will be manifested also in new quality consciousness and in higher productivity, if the results go hand in hand with wage increases. Naturally, all of these will create big social problems in the present day in a more or less egalitarian society.

2. The *slow course* is a much more cautious one with a nationalist flavor. It will be more closed for Western competition and Western investors, therefore privatization and structural changes will be slower; this will also lead to slower abolition of the government's subsidies. All of this means that unemployment will reach only a moderate level and there will be less risk for social unrests, at least in the short run. As a disadvantage, the inflation rate will remain high, mainly because of the low level of the international competitiveness of Hungarian products, manufactured in outdated plants with outdated technology. But social differences will be small and mutual confidence will rule–at least among the different strata of the society. Therefore, the big risks of the slow course will come to light only in the long run, but then with an overwhelming force.

3. The *mixed course* tries to marry the advantages of the two previous courses without the mentioned disadvantages. This means that it wants to prepare good conditions for Western investment and takeovers, influenced in many details by the government; to abolish the

bureaucracy while maintaining an efficient central power; to decrease the inflation rate and the subsidies paid to companies in a medium term, also setting back the explosion of unemployment. This course drags out the most needed changes into a period of 2-3 years and decreases all the above risk factors except one: the risk of the widening gap between the level of development of the Western economies and Hungary, between Western and Hungarian technology.

4. The *retrograde course* means the return of the economy to shortages. In this case, no market economy, no competition exists, but the economy is managed centrally by the government. Without Western investments, it is impossible to modernize the outdated Hungarian technology; therefore, the gap between Hungary and the West grows in a hopeless way. The country falls down quickly and for a long time from the economic and cultural level of the European community: practically it will miss the last moment of closing the gap.

To make a decision on the most efficient course, the decision maker and a marketing expert making a forecast have to know that the factors and risks are not static ones. The factors, their weight, and the risks change as regards time. This is represented in Figure 9.1. The graphs show that the sizes of the risks change as each course proceeds. Therefore, the time span in risk taking is as important as the risk factor itself or the advantages and disadvantages of the actors of the courses. In the decisions on the courses of economic development, i.e., on economic policy and business strategy, the changes of risks are always as important as the changes of the advantageous and hostile factors of the scene.

MARKETING CONCEPTS AND PRACTICES OF THE DIFFERENT COURSES OF ECONOMIC DEVELOPMENT

If the *radical course* could be realized, a real market economy can be created in a short period of time with intensive international competition of products and services. As a result, the supply will be abundant, exceeding the demand; after a painful period of setback,

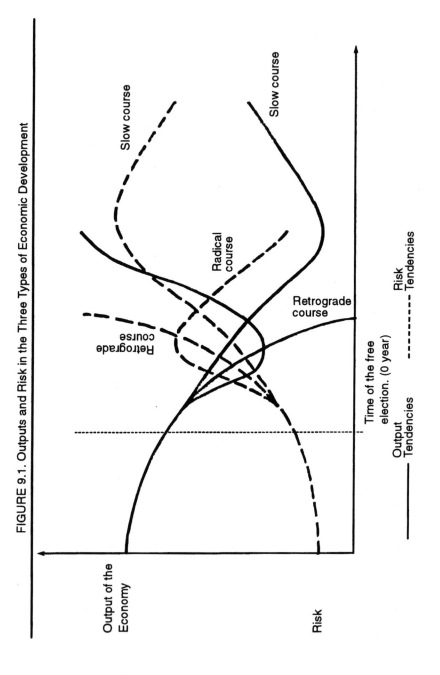

FIGURE 9.1. Outputs and Risk in the Three Types of Economic Development

Slow course

Slow course

Radical course

Retrograde course

Retrograde course

Time of the free election. (0 year)

Risk Tendencies

Output Tendencies

Output of the Economy

Risk

the buying power will grow significantly, although some smaller strata of the society will have to continue their fight against pauperization.

This means the following for the Hungarian companies from the marketing point of view. There will be a strong tendency to integrate the presently disintegrated elements of marketing concepts and practices into marketing strategies, market programs, and marketing mix projects. Integrations will be established at corporate level between the marketing and the other functions, such as R&D, production, and finance of the enterprise. No difference will exist between the Western and the home market-oriented marketing of the same enterprise. This new marketing can be characterized as *full marketing* in the Western sense.

What concerns the marketing of Western companies interested in the Hungarian market is that they have to calculate with a dynamic market and economic environment, where changes take place at an ever higher speed, where the costs of the resources and the volume of sales will go up hand by hand. There will be advantageous possibilities to reinvest the accumulated profits. For Western companies, a plant in Hungary, joint ventures, or international cooperations in production and marketing–with low cost level, high skills, and modernized technology–will ensure an efficient springboard for overseas markets. All this means an *offensive, multi-target marketing*.

The *slow course* as a long-term process results in the survival of the actual quasi-market until 1994-95, with few domestic and even less international competition. The effects of scarcity will influence the economy more and more, and there will be less and less differences in the demands of the market segments. In comparison with the radical course, this one will postpone the social troubles; but at a later stage, their intensity and probability of occurrence could be higher.

For the practicing Hungarian companies, all this means a survival of certain elements of marketing without an integration into a planned, marketing program. Neither will marketing have a real influence on the activities of other functions of the enterprises. When Hungarian firms are producing for Western markets, the procurement of raw materials, component parts, and the acquisition of government subsidies will be more important than their market research or product planning. Marketing will not play any role as a philosophy of top management; but as a partly paralysed function, it will suffer all the disadvantages of a schizophrenia of a two-fold–Western and domestic market–orientation. Therefore, this will be a *stuttering marketing*.

If this course of development takes place, the marketing professionals of Western companies will have encountered a recession in Hungary or at least a very slow growth in certain sectors of the economy. The costs of resources in joint ventures and in Western-owned companies will be very low, but the Hungarian buying power will also be very weak. There will be good opportunities for investments as costs are high, but the favorable ROI should be taken into consideration. This means that a plant in Hungary can be an excellent springboard to the third markets overseas, especially if the production has, in an increased degree, Western sources for the procurement of some raw materials and component parts. Naturally, this increases the originally low level of costs. All this means an *overseas oriented marketing* for the Western businessmen.

The third potential course of development is the *mixed one*. If this should be realized, real market and up-to-date technology islands will be established in the quasi-market arena blended with more or less outdated technologies. This means also heavy international competition of products and services, but only in some areas of the overall market. The same is true for the ratio of demand and supply; it depends on market segments and manufacturing sectors, and, in this case, demand will exceed supply. In parallel with this, quite intensive growth and quite severe decrease of the purchasing power can be forecasted for the same period of economic development.

For Hungarian marketing, this means an outstanding challenge; namely, to find and exploit the future islands of the real markets and up-to-date technologies. Naturally, here again integrated marketing is needed for the exploitation of the islands; the marketing elements must fit into a homogeneous marketing concept, plan or program. And in all the islands, marketing has to work as a basic function of the enterprise, influencing basically all the other functions. This appears also on the domestic market between the market-islands and the large sea of quasi-markets. All this suggests the appearance of an *ambiguous marketing*.

In this course of development, the existence of a dynamic marketing and technological island also depends on the investments of Western capital, including a given company and its competitors in investing. Therefore, this course is dominated by a risk factor for the Western businessmen–and one of the main tasks of marketing is to forecast not only the right islands for investments, their costs, profits and ROI figures, but also the risks of island competition. Based on good forecasts, there will be profitable islands for investments, with sales on the domestic and overseas markets. Because of the existence of the islands, marketing activity also has to handle with care the problems of procurement. Last but not least, the same "island syndrome" helps diversification efforts whereby one witnesses the setting up of new islands and the fast expansion of a Western business in Hungary. All this can be characterized as an especially *risk-conscious marketing*.

The *retrograde course* means a total regression and creation of a periodical recession in the economy. In this case, no market will exist, scarcities will be usual phenomena, costs and prices will be completely deteriorated from the market values, the inflation rate will be extremely high, payments of international debts will be postponed, necessary imports, even for continuous production, will be largely stopped, the government's budget will be steadily unbalanced, the living standards will go sharply down, the technology will become more and more outdated, and the gap between Hungary and the West will widen over the limit of a foreseeable closing up.

In this situation, not even a simple market niche exists for real marketing. As such, the retrograde course is completely *clear of marketing* for the Hungarian enterprises and also for the Western companies.

If we make an analysis of the most decisive factors influencing the four potential courses of action, we can refer to the following:

1. The economic policy of the *Hungarian government* is influenced by the duty to pay back the international debts of the country and by the requirements of the IMF. The first influ-

ence points to the mixed, the second to the radical course of economic development.

2. The *Western assistance* needed to take part in the privatization process, in the setting up of a market economy and in the import of up-to-date technology, managerial skills, and marketing expertise. The assistance or the lack of it can open up the possibilities of the realization of the slowness to the radical course. Western assistance in privatization as it was materialized in mid-1991 was less than 10% of the total state-owned assets of firms to be privatized in Hungary. This has been a far too low rate for an economic recovery.[4]

3. The growth rate of the *world economy*. Taking into account the present-day forecasts as a single factor, this could stimulate the radical or the mixed course.

4. The flourish, the stagnation, or the collapse of the other East-European economies (mainly the *Russian economy*) will influence the possibilities of all four courses, and not as much in the procurement of raw materials and energy supply as in the marketing of semifinished and finished products. Namely a huge part of Hungarian R&Ds, technologies, and products have been oriented to the requirements of the Soviet market; and the collapse of that market would result in the fact that a big part of the Hungarian output could not be sold. It follows that the collapse of the Soviet market would push Hungary–or at least many branches of the Hungarian industry–toward the retrograde courses. Only one-third of the lost exports of the Hungarian firms could be converted into Western markets during the first half of 1991.[5]

These examples show that the forecast of the most likely course is a multi-factor puzzle. And some factors of the puzzle can be forecast with higher certainty from the West, some other factors can be better perceived by the locally trained sensitivity of the East. The conclusion is that a realistic business forecast should be a joint venture between East and West. During the summer of 1990, it

4. Report of the State Property Agency, Budapest, 1991.
5. Report of the Market and Economic Research Institute of the Ministry of Foreign Economic Relations, Budapest, July, 1991.

turned out that the Hungarian government chose the slow course; but it was forced later on by growing economic and social difficulties to switch over in 1991 to the mixed economy course.

OUTLOOK TO THE OTHER EX-COMMUNIST COUNTRIES' "MARKETING POTENTIAL"

Making a comparison between Hungary and the other ex-Communist countries, one notices the same main problems in all countries. Naturally, some of the problems have a different shape or weight. But everywhere you strike against low productivity, high inflation rate, unbalanced government budget, the lack of a real market and real competition, more or less insignificant private sectors, outdated technology, uncompetitive products, basic structural problems, underdeveloped infrastructures, low salaries without real incentives, low work moral, starting unemployment, etc. Therefore, some general features and effects can be stressed, valid for all the countries in this region–depending on the potential course of development the different countries will follow in the future. Those general features and effects must influence the marketing concepts and practices of Western companies making investments in the region. Some of these effects are summarized in Table 9.2.

But behind the above general features, we have to take note of the differences as well. Especially for Western businessmen considering investments in the area, a scrutinizing analysis is indispensable. This analysis needs a scrupulous checking of facts, influencing factors and potential effects which is different from country to country, from industrial branch to branch, from business to business. Table 9.3 serves as background of a detailed analysis which has to take the risk of making mistakes, not so much because of the lack of the necessary information, but because of the fast changes of political and economic events in the area. Therefore, it should also be the task of the meticulous analysis to prove the points described in Table 9.3. The importance of certain factors has already changed during the turbulent events which have taken place in Central and East European countries. For instance, the inflation rate has decreased in Poland, and political risk has substantially increased in Yugoslavia.

TABLE 9.2. Effects to be Considered by Western Companies Investing in East European Countries

Basic effect Potential courses	Main marketing targets	Main sources of procurement	Characteristics of risk taking in marketing	ROI expectancy	Investment of gained profit
Radical course	Domestic market and Western markets	Domestic market	Western-type risks everywhere	Better than usual Western expectancies	Many good possibilities on the domestic market
Slow course	Mainly Western markets	Western markets and partly the domestic market	Very risky on the domestic market	Good expectancies only on Western markets	Advantageous only if Western sales can be realized
Mixed course	Western markets and partly the domestic market	Domestic market and partly Western markets	Very risky on certain segments of the domestic markets	Good expectancies also on some segments of the home market	Good possibilities on some segment of the home market
Retrograde course	Western markets	Western markets	Very risky for every kind of investments	Doubtful expectancy depending on the speed of the recession of the economy	Decreasing possibilities

TABLE 9.3. The Role of Economic Factors in the Development of Marketing Concepts and Activities in East European Countries

				Countries			
Factors Examined	BG	CS	H	PL	RO	RU	YU
Size of the economy/market	−	−	−			+	
Level of development of the economy/not only GDP/head/	−	+	+				
Homogeneous character of the economy including competition		+	+		−	−	−
Potential development of a market system of the economy	−	+	+		−	−	
Progressiveness of the direction system of the economy		+	+	+	−		+
Balance of the budget of the government/ including domestic and foreign debts/			−	−			
Inflation rate			−	+			
Energy and raw material resources	−	+				+	
General level of technology	−	+			−	−	
General/international/competitiveness of products	−	+			−	−	
Level of the development of the infrastructure of the economy	−				−	−	
Skills and work moral of labor	−	+	+		−		+
Managerial skills/on the international scale/		+	+	+			+
Political and business risks in general	−				−	−	

201

What does all of this mean from the point of view of marketing concepts and practices of the *home-based companies* on the domestic market? It is certain that basic technological, economic, and governmental changes must take place in Bulgaria, Romania, and Russia before it will be possible to use techniques and concepts of marketing on the general economic scene. Closest to switching over from production-orientation to full marketing-orientation are Czechoslovakia and Hungary. But their time span to reach this limit or fall back again depends significantly on the type of course of the development of their economy. Poland is between the two above categories.

This also means that Western companies selling at these markets will need to plan and run real marketing programs in the Western sense to be highly competitive in the Czechoslovakian and Hungarian markets–if these countries will follow the radical course of economic development by 1993 and beyond. In all the other countries, elements of Western marketing, mainly market research, product planning and promotion will be enough to be competitive should these countries select to follow the radical course of development. If the latter countries could not follow the radical course, no marketing at all or a kind of *pervert marketing*, tailored on an economy of scarcity, will be needed on the part of Western companies.

Looking at the problems of East and Central European countries from the point of view of Western companies considering investments in the SE ex-Communist countries, the situation is a little different:

- The two most favorable countries are Czechoslovakia and Hungary, the first mainly for her relatively high technological skills and standards, the second for the relatively developed market economy system and the entrepreneurial-minded attitude of large parts of the population. But for Hungary, the huge international debt of the country is a risk factor.
- Yugoslavia is in a sense between Czechoslovakia and Hungary, but the unevenness of the development of her economy could become quite a high risk factor in the future. The recent political and military events in 1991 and in 1992 have justified this forecast which was made in mid-1990.

- Poland follows these countries with two main problems: the unbalanced budget of the government and the high inflation rate. Both are big risk factors even at the present time, and the general economic situation is also characterized by long lasting scarcities of products.
- Russia's advantage is the size of her market and the country's rich energy and raw material resources. But for the investor, the present political and economic risks are troublesome due to the territorial problems, the chaotic political power centers, the scarcities in all sectors of the economy, and the completely unreal cost and price system. In the long run, even the size of the market is a doubtful advantage, because the closing up of Russia to Europe can take place only on a territorial basis in case of a radical course of economic development. There are also a great many differences in the cultural, economic, and technologic levels within the Commonwealth of Independent States.
- Behind the above countries comes Bulgaria and Romania. At the present time, their political and economic situation is equally risky; nobody can trust the systems on the surface–and the potential political or economic turbulences can easily produce multiplying effects in the other areas and vice versa.

To make some general closing remarks we can point to the following factors: (1) Marketing in its full Western sense is basically important for the former socialist countries when they want to do business with the West in 1993 and beyond. But the question remains if they will be able to follow the requirements of marketing by activating their other resources in R&D, production, finance, etc. (2) Marketing will be important for some of those countries in their domestic markets in 1993 and beyond if they can follow the radical course of economic development. (3) Full marketing concepts and programs or elements of marketing will be needed by Western companies selling in the East European markets, depending on the given country and its course of economic development. (4) Very sensitive marketing strategies, based on local expertise, must be worked out before a Western company decides to invest in an East European country, wants to buy shares, or goes into a joint venture with a seemingly promising East-European partner.

Chapter 10

U.S./Hungarian Joint Ventures: An Opportunity for Entering New Markets

Robert D. Hisrich
Jan Jones

INTRODUCTION

Bordered by the market-oriented country of Austria and, until 1989-90, the planned economy countries of Czechoslovakia, Romania, Yugoslavia, and the Soviet Union, Hungary is situated in the center of Europe. With two-thirds of the 93,030 square km area of the country being plains under a temperate continental climate, Hungary is the "breadbasket" of Eastern Europe as well as the Soviet Union. The joke in Hungary is that if you can find any fresh fruits and vegetables in Moscow, they had to come from Hungary.[1]

While some reforms have been occurring since 1980, a more significant reform movement started in 1989. These reforms have: guaranteed freedom of the press and trade unions; guaranteed impartial justice; and dropped all mention of the "Communist leading role." Reform in the Hungarian political structure and other areas is helping to create the environment for economic restructuring–the movement from a planned to a market-oriented economy. Two new

---

1. An overview of the general country conditions can be found in: Beracs and Papadopoulos (1990) and Hisrich and Vecsenyi (1990).

This chapter was originally published in *Journal of Global Marketing*, Vol. 5(3) 1992.

major pieces of legislation were enacted and implemented in January, 1989–Act VI (The Company Act) and Act XXIV (Investments by Foreigners in Hungary Act). The Company Act regulates the legal corporate structure of foreign firms operating in Hungary while providing guarantees similar to those of the European Community. Among other things, the Investments Act provides an easy mechanism for foreign investors to repatriate forint profits (soft currency) into original investment currency (hard currency). Other important provisions of the Act include: tax benefits for foreign investments, 100% foreign ownership allowed in certain situations, and duty-free importing of production equipment.

The Hungarian economic and political reforms are in line with the taste of the populace for Western styles of living. This taste has emerged from previous years of various wars and living under different rulers such as the Hapsburgs. It has been refined further through contact with relatives living in Western Europe and North America, some of whom fled following the crush of the uprising in 1956.

Some recent factors have particularly impacted the country's movement from a planned to a market-oriented economy. A deterioration in the level of trade combined with the rising rate of inflation, unemployment, the lack of hard currency, and the near bankruptcy conditions of many large companies and the entire country, are just some of the problems that confront Hungary today.

Three particular problem areas have developed from the years as a controlled economy. The first is the emphasis on heavy industry, which is also energy inefficient. The physical plants of these industries have deteriorated significantly with the average age of the machinery being 16 years and new products accounting for less than four percent of the total output of the plants (Belassa, 1988, p. 14). The second is the dependence on Comecon trade, particularly with the Soviet Union, which has encouraged the production of "soft goods" that cannot be traded with the West. The third major problem is subsidizing all companies, including those continually sustaining a loss, thereby reducing the resources available for investing in more profitable growth industries. These problems as well as the increasing debt, low growth and high inflation, unemployment, the decrease in personal income and consumer demand, and the new personal income tax, have contributed to Hungary's current economic difficulties.

This chapter is based on a survey of the population of U.S. firms with operating joint ventures in Hungary. It focuses on an examination of their performance in the light of the unique environment in Hungary and Eastern Europe, and their potential role as a bridgehead to other European countries. It should be noted that while the paper views Hungary in the context of an Eastern European country, consideration of contemporary phenomena is difficult in view of the dramatic changes in that region and can become outdated quickly. In fact, Eastern Europe's trading block, the Council for Mutual Economic Assistance (Comecon), was dissolved in January, 1991, as this chapter was being finalized.[2] Therefore, the discussion emphasizes the long-term aspects of Hungary's position rather than short-term developments.

METHODOLOGY

In order to examine economic development in general and specifically the results of the established U.S./Hungarian joint ventures, a three-stage research study was undertaken. First, all secondary sources of information in both Hungary and the United States were thoroughly investigated from an economic development and joint venture perspective. Names of U.S. joint ventures in Hungary were obtained from the Commerce Department and the U.S. Embassy in Hungary, and the population of 16 that were operating (as opposed to being registered but not yet in operation) was selected to be surveyed (see Table 10.1). Second, a questionnaire designed to obtain information on the type of joint venture, relative importance of decision factors in establishing the joint venture, management capabilities in Hungary, the operation of the joint venture compared to other joint venture activities of the company, and general compa-

---

2. At the time of writing the potential of future trade associations involving East European countries is unclear. Forecasts range from replacing Comecon with another Eastern trading block, to some Eastern countries applying for membership in the European Community, to remaining without a trade association for some time.

TABLE 10.1. Hungarian-U.S. Joint Ventures in 1989

BCR and LILLY CO., LTD.
CITIBANK Budapest Corp.
COMPUTERWORLD INFORMATICS Ltd.
FOTEC
McCAN ERICKSON-INTERPRESS
BABOLNA-McDONALD'S Restaurant Ltd.
PANGUS Rubber Products Co.
QUALIPLASTICS Co., Ltd.
RADELCOR Co., Ltd.
HEMINGWAY Computer International Ltd.
LEVI STRAUSS Budapest Co., Ltd.
SCHWINN (USA)-SCEPEL Ltd.
PUSKI-ISIS Ltd.
HUNGARD Ltd.
OGILVY & MATHER-MAHIR Budapest
INTERNATIONAL MANAGEMENT CENTER

ny demographic information, was sent to the U.S. marketing manager of each operating joint venture company. The final stage involved developing a similar questionnaire, in Hungarian, for the Hungarian managing director of the joint venture. Each individual completed the detailed questionnaire and participated in an in-depth personal interview lasting from one to two hours.

FINDINGS

The results of the study will be discussed in terms of the aspects of joint ventures in Hungary, the views of the managers in Hungary and the U.S., and joint venture difficulties encountered.

Aspects of Joint Ventures in Hungary

There are several advantages for U.S. firms establishing joint ventures in Hungary. In the survey, the most frequently mentioned reasons for establishing a joint venture in Hungary were: lower labor costs, access to Hungarian markets, and access to Western European markets. The labor costs in Hungary are significantly lower than in Western Europe: "The difference in average wages depend on the country but can reach a ratio of 1:10" ("Joint Ventures in Hungary" 1988, p. 8). Due to these lower labor costs, Levi Strauss is able to operate its Hungarian factory at 30 to 40% cheaper than its operations in other European countries. The labor market in Hungary also has a sufficient number of skilled workers who are able to work in higher technology industries. Given the relatively small size of the Hungarian population (approximately 10 million), few companies can afford to produce only for this market. When the Hungarian market is combined with potential Western European markets, there is enough sales potential to warrant locating in Hungary. Nonetheless, in some cases the Hungarian market alone is of sufficient size. McDonald's in Budapest has little competition for its type of fast food and has become the number one McDonald's in Europe in terms of number of transactions.

The access to Western Europe is an important reason for establishing a joint venture in Hungary. Hungary was the first Comecon country to make a trade agreement with the European Community. This agreement eliminates over 2,000 quantitative trade restrictions in three stages, allowing Hungary by 1995 to export "very sensitive items" to the EC. These lessened restrictions favorably affect any investment in Hungary. Exporting to Western markets provides a favorable hard currency balance necessary for companies needing to import raw materials or component parts.

How easy is it for a U.S. company to establish a joint venture in Hungary? In spite of the country's late start compared to Yugoslavia and Romania, with its first joint venture established in 1972, Hungary has more joint ventures registered (310), but not necessarily operating, than any other Eastern Block country (Yugoslavia has 230, Poland 53, Bulgaria 20, Czechoslovakia 19, and Romania 5) or the Soviet Union which has 270 (see Table 10.2). This reflects in part the ease of obtaining permission to establish a joint venture in Hungary versus the other controlled economies. If the foreign partner's share of the joint venture is 50% or less only a simple registration of the proposed joint venture is needed. When the foreign share exceeds 50% then a permit issued by the Ministry of Commerce needs to be obtained. Even when this is the case, it is still easier to obtain permission for a joint venture in Hungary than what transpires when dealing with the ministry or agency designated in other controlled economies. In granting permission to start a joint venture for companies with more than 50% foreign ownership, the Hungarian Ministry "only considers what the activity of the joint venture would do to the foreign exchange balance of the country. Consequently, it is undesirable, particularly in the case of foreign majority ownership, to limit the products of a joint venture to those intended for the Hungarian market" ("Joint Ventures in Hungary" 1988, p. 6).

Another area favoring establishing a joint venture in Hungary is in the repatriation of profits. While in a Hungarian joint venture the entire profit can be changed to hard currency and taken out of the country, the policy in most other Eastern Block countries is that only the hard currency portion can be repatriated. For example, repatriation in a joint venture in the USSR can only occur for the hard currency portion of the return (see Table 10.2). In other important areas of consideration for establishing a joint venture, such as percentage tax on dividends and special deals for establishing the venture, Hungary is similar to the other former members of Comecon. In terms of the joint venture's tax rate as a percentage of profits, Hungary's is slightly higher, at 40% on profits up to 30 million forints and 50% on all profits exceeding this amount. Tax rates in other Eastern Block countries range from a low of 10% in Yugoslavia to a high of 40% in Czechoslovakia and Poland. Those of the U.S. companies surveyed that also have other joint ventures in market economies, reported that it was the same or more difficult to establish and operate the Hungarian venture. However, in comparison with their joint ventures in non-market economies, the Hungarian joint venture was found to be easier to establish and operate (see Table 10.3). As is indicated, doing business in Hungary is perceived as being easier than in the People's Republic of China or the Soviet Union. These favorable evaluations occurred even though most of the joint ventures were established prior to two new acts (The Company Act and The Association Act) which eased considerably the regulatory aspects of establishing a joint venture in Hungary.

From the Hungarian perspective, joint ventures are advantageous as they bring technology, managerial expertise and the all-important hard currency to the economy. According to Tamas Beck, Hungary's Minister of Trade, "With more resolute efforts in the future to promote foreign initiative in Hungary through the founding of joint ventures and representations in Hungary, I am sure we will be able to achieve long-term, profitable alliances with foreign units who will in turn be able to help Hungary realize its own economic objectives" ("Invest in Hungary" 1989, p. 8).

The interviews of the managers of 13 of the 16 U.S./Hungarian joint ventures indicated that the most important reason for forming the joint venture was access to European markets. Other reasons given, in order of importance, were: the experience and connection with a well-known company, high technology, supplying the U.S. market, and tax incentives. The reasons given by Hungarian managers to this same question reflect to a significant extent the interests of the government–wanting to increase exports to Western markets and improvements in technology and managerial know-how.

Managerial Views

The need to improve the managerial skills of Hungarian managers is a top priority in a country becoming more market- and profit-oriented. Presently, Hungarian managers are not profit-motivated as in the past the state has skimmed off any profits of successful firms and bailed out any failures. In addition, any profits of Hungarian firms are taxed at a 60% rate. This high tax rate is viewed by the Hungarian managers that were surveyed as being detrimental to their companies. In comparison, joint ventures have a lesser tax or none at all for the first five years. Another problem in Hungary is that the highly developed marketing systems and practices that are found in the West do not exist in Hungary. In fact, there is no word in Hungarian that translates with the same meaning as "marketing." In discussions with Hungarian managers, the need for greater marketing skills was frequently mentioned.

Both the U.S. and Hungarian respondents were asked to compare Hungarian to U.S. managers in general in the areas of experience,

TABLE 10.2. Rules Governing Establishing Joint Ventures in Eastern Europe

	Bulgaria	Czechoslovakia	Yugoslavia
Year of First Joint Ventures	1980	1985	1968
Number of Joint Ventures	41	20	230
Permit Issuing Authority	Council of Ministers	Individual ministries, following consultation with other authorities	Varies according to republic, in special cases – the federal government
Joint Ventures Tax Rate as a Percentage of Profits	30	40	10
Special Deals for Establishing Joint Ventures	Special tax free status can be requested for first 5 years		
Tax on Dividends as a Percentage	10-15		
Repatriation of Profits	Only hard currency portion	Only hard currency portion	Only hard currency portion

Poland	Romania	Soviet Union	Hungary
1976	1971	1988	1972
170	5	685	628
Agency dealing with foreign investments	Council of Ministers	Council of Ministers	Ministry of Commerce and Finance if the foreign share exceeds 50% otherwise registration insufficient
40	30	30	Up to 3 million forints – 40 over 3 million forints – 50
First 3 years are tax free, an additional 3 can be requested. Value of new investments can be deducted from tax base.	The first year is tax free. Second year 15% tax and 20% reduction if the profit is not taken out of the country.	First 2 (3 in the Far Eastern areas) years are tax free. Lower taxes in far East later as well.	Depends on amount capital, percentage of foreign capital, type of activity. The special reduction can even be 100% in the first 5 years.
30	10	20 Special Reduction possible	20 Private individuals pay personal income tax, economic organizations do not pay
85% of surplus export	Only hard currency portion	Profit covered by convertible export	The entire profit can be changed to hard currency and taken out of the country with no limitations

TABLE 10.3. Hungarian Joint Ventures

U.S. Companies Comparison of their Hungarian Joint Venture with their other joint ventures:

In Market Economies

	More Difficult	Same	Easier
Financing from local sources	2	2	1
Financing from home sources	1	4	
Gov't. red tape	2	2	1
Local management	1	4	
Exporting prod.	1	3	
Distribution	3	2	
Advertising	1	3	1
Setting prices	2	3	
Setting wages	3	2	

In Non-Market

	More Difficult	Same	Easier
Financing from local sources		4	1
Financing from home sources		4	
Gov't. red tape		2	1
Local management			4
Exporting		1	3
Distribution		2	2
Advertising		2	2
Setting prices			4
Setting wages		1	3

Note. The numbers in this table are absolute frequencies. The number of respondents varies due to non-responses (concerning companies without comparable ventures outside Hungary).

efficiency, authoritarian style, use of group consensus, profit orientation, timeliness, and detail. Fifty percent of the U.S. managers thought that Hungarians were less experienced, less efficient and less profit-oriented than U.S. managers. Eighty-three percent thought that Hungarians used group consensus less than Americans. Although the impressive qualifications and excellent language skills of the Hungarian managers became evident in the personal interviews, they frequently cited the need to obtain good managers in making the joint venture a success; 91% rated their fellow Hungarian managers as less efficient than American managers; 73% found Hungarians to be less profit-oriented and timely; and 55% found Hungarians to be less experienced. One major difference between the Hungarian and the American ratings was in the use of authoritarian style. While 64% of Hungarians perceived Hungarian managers as less authoritarian, 50% of Americans perceived the Hungarians as more authoritarian. Overall, the Hungarians rated Hungarian managers as less qualified than American managers they had encountered. These findings indicate that the skill level of Hungarian managers, particularly in managing a market-oriented business, is perceived to be lower than necessary, accounting for the continual emphasis on the need for finding the "right" person to manage the venture.

The Hungarian managers had more interest in risk-taking than expected. Perhaps this reflects their decision to work for a U.S./Hungarian joint venture, a relatively new form of business in Hungary. Most of the managers exhibited strong personalities and readiness to accept new challenges (see Table 10.4). When asked how certain they were in trying something new, 79% indicated that they were very or usually certain of success. In adopting a new business procedure, 57% felt there was some danger, 36% felt there was not much danger and 7% saw no danger.

With regard to their employment, it was anticipated that a long period of time would be mentioned as employment contracts for indefinite time periods are the norm in Hungary and turnover is generally low. Yet 43% of respondents anticipated staying with the company less than five years as they expected to move on to new challenges. Still, the majority (57%) expected to stay with the company for more than 5 years or until retirement. Surprisingly, the

TABLE 10.4. Risk and Uncertainty Avoidance: Hungarian Managers' Responses

I. Certainty of success at trying something you have not tried before:

Very Certain	Usually Certain	Sometimes Certain	Never
29%	50%	21%	

II. Danger perceived in trying a new business procedure.

Great Danger	Some Danger	Not Much Danger	No Danger
	57%	36%	7%

III. Rules: A Company's rules should not be broken —even when the employee thinks it is in the organization's best interest.

Strongly Agree	Agree	Undecided	Disagree	Strongly Disagree
8%	15%		69%	8%

IV. Employment Stability
How long do you think you will be working for this company?

2 years	2-5 years	more than 5 yrs	until retire
7%	36%	29%	29%

V. Level of Stress
How often do you feel nervous or tense at work?

very frequently	frequently	sometimes	seldom	very seldom
	8%	46%	46%	

managers experienced a fairly low level of stress at work with the most often reported amount being only "sometimes" or "seldom." In terms of adhering to certain rules and expecting employees to adhere to these rules, most of the managers disagreed with the statement that an employee should not break the rules even if it is in the best interest of the company.

Problems Encountered

In establishing a joint venture in Hungary, U.S. business should be aware of some potential problems. The most frequently mentioned difficulty was with the telecommunications in the country. This aspect of the Hungarian infrastructure presents a serious barrier to efficient business procedures. With the exception of the firms that installed their own overseas lines, most managers indicated that they usually had telecommunications problems. In fact, the manager at Schwinn-Csepel said that his staff had "nervous breakdowns" trying to send fax messages to the U.S. prior to installing special equipment. Seventy-seven percent of the Hungarians surveyed usually or often had problems with telecommunications.

Cultural problems did not seem to be an important issue with most of the Hungarian managers, although 67% of the American managers reported occasional cultural problems. In the interviews, most Hungarians indicated that Americans accustomed to working with Europeans have an easier time working in Hungary as the culture shock would not be as great. A few of the Hungarians expressed the importance of being tolerant of the customs of another country, such as "not demanding drinks with ice."

In general, language also did not present a problem. In the few interviews of managers with weak English skills, excellent company interpreters were provided. These managers recognized, as do most Hungarians, that English-speaking people probably do not know Hungarian. Most managers showed a desire to become more fluent in English. The Levi Strauss Hungarian manager was requiring all his employees to learn English.

Several managers questioned the real value of the lower labor costs, due to the inefficiency of the workers which in turn is due partly to their working second jobs in the "black economy." Bela Belas, managing director of Qualiplastic, did not think that labor was significantly cheaper due to the bureaucracy and ineffectiveness of the workers.[3] This problem can be resolved to some extent by paying workers higher than average wages in lieu of them not holding a second job. Many managers suggested that an adjustment period should be implemented for workers who were not used to working up to the standards required by the American partner. The Hungarian McDonald's is experiencing about a 30% turnover even though higher wages are paid, due in part to the fact that the young

---

3. Interview in Budapest, May 29, 1989.

people find the work very hard. Even though many Hungarians are employed through indefinite time contracts, a joint venture should hire workers under limited contracts making it easier to dismiss incompetent workers when their contract expires. Although some managers indicated that "you can't transplant American ideas right away," the workers in many cases were more than capable of attaining the desired standards than was anticipated.[4] For example, at Schwinn-Csepel, the number of quality control people was reduced from 60 to five without any negative impact. Eventually, this same reduction was able to be implemented at Pangus Rubber. The manager at this latter company indicated that she had problems with her first staff of white collar workers due to their inflexibility and being accustomed to different working ways and standards. However, she feels there will be little, if any, problems with additional staff. Pangus Rubber also had problems in turnover among factory workers due in part to the ease in finding other jobs.

Companies operating in Hungary also need to be aware that the government or labor unions might meddle in some situations. At Schwinn-Csepel, the manager complained about time-consuming and inefficient regulations. A great deal of paperwork was needed for one interview at Csepel Iron Works due to the tight security regulations. The company also had to hire a full-time equipment inspector who was only needed occasionally. Managers also felt that in the smaller towns outside of Budapest high ranking Communist Party officials had even more influence on the managers. To offset these problems, joint ventures can institute policies prohibiting party or union activities during working hours. One Communist Party member commented that it was important to separate politics from any business operation.

Another problem area in doing business in Hungary centers around ordering supplies. In most cases, lead times are much longer than in the West. Companies having a short lead time usually obtain their supplies either from the parent company or a branch in Europe. The quality of materials is particularly a problem when hard currency is lacking and components are purchased from Eastern Block countries. This was a particular problem for Schwinn-Csepel

---

4. Interview at Schwinn-Csepel, Budapest, June 1, 1989.

in making bicycles using components from the other socialist countries. The quality of these bicycles was not high enough for sale in Western markets.

Hungary as a Bridge to Eastern Europe

Since Hungary depends upon foreign trade for approximately 50% of its net material product, exports play a critical role in the overall economic picture. As a result of its membership in Comecon, Hungary still does about 55% of its trade with Comecon countries, the Soviet Union being Hungary's most important trading partner. While Hungary's major exports are agricultural products, machinery and semi-finished manufacturing, its major imports are fuel, semi-finished products and machinery. The dual aspect of Hungary's foreign trade with Comecon countries (soft currency economies) and with Western markets (hard currency economies) has meant the need for two different national trading policies. This dual trading situation reflects some of the difficulties encountered in trying to combine planned and market economic structures.

Notwithstanding its dissolution, several characteristics of trade within Comecon are worth noting since they continue to exist or have exerted significant influence on the development of trade among its members. The first involves the trading of "soft" goods–goods that cannot be sold in the free market at the prices assigned to them. Many of these products cannot be sold in Western markets due to their deficient quality. For example, the previously mentioned bicycles produced with Eastern Block components were not saleable in Western markets. Another problem occurs in that the fuel from the Soviet Union is imported at prices established in advance which lag the price changes in the world energy markets. Also, any currency in the Comecon countries does not convert into hard currency. This causes differences in exchange rates for transferable rubles, dollars, and forints that would not exist if the currencies were subject to arbitrage on the free market.

Hungary's trade with Comecon countries is the "planned" part of its foreign trade with five-year trade agreements established. Not only does the Soviet Union account for 30% of Hungary's exports, it supplies almost three-quarters of Hungary's energy imports. For Hungarians, the Soviet oil imports appear "cheap," because they are paid for in the "soft" low-quality goods exported to the Soviet Union. On the other hand, this "cheap" energy has contributed to the country not developing a national energy policy. "The opportunity to export more to the Soviet market is a very mixed blessing. As it stands in the late 1980's it has kept part of Hungarian industry at a relatively low level of development and even requires additional investment in activities that should be curtailed rather than increased if industry is to be restructured" (Kerpel and Young, 1988, p. 64).

Some foreign companies, particularly those in the U.S., evaluating establishing joint ventures, plan to use Hungary as a bridge to the USSR. The low fluctuating valuation of the ruble makes this export somewhat difficult. Because of Hungary's interest in developing a positive hard currency balance through exports, Hungarian officials have not been enthusiastic about establishing joint ventures designed primarily to develop markets with soft currency countries. Marer (1987) suggests that Hungary would be better to have a more long term view, using access to the markets of its former Comecon counterparts to lure foreign direct investments:

> . . . can JVs be instrumental in helping Hungary to break out of a vicious circle of deteriorating trading position in both the CMEA and Western markets? The answer would seem to be in the affirmative: by promoting deals that are likely to yield significant long term advantages for the national economy, even if they may involve some risks in the short run. Specifically if an important consideration in attracting MNCs to invest large sums in Hungary is to offer the JVs access to the Soviet market, then Hungary should seriously consider using this trump card.

At present, Hungary prefers to export goods to Western countries which indeed helps the hard currency trade deficit. Yet, in order to trade more with the West, Hungary needs to improve the quality of its goods, the most often cited barrier to this trade in the interviews with the Hungarian managers. To increase the quality, more imports from the West are needed to upgrade the technology, which in turn requires more hard currency expenditure–a dilemma that needs to be resolved.

As a member of the Warsaw Pact, Hungary is restricted from importing technologically sensitive items from the United States. This restriction limits high technology imports to Hungary from the U.S. as well as developing wariness on the part of Hungarians in using U.S. technology that may be later restricted. Hungary has been granted Most Favored National (MFN) trade status since 1978, subject to annual review. The Hungarian government would like to see this review extended beyond a yearly renewal basis, feeling that a longer-term MFN would facilitate longer term trade agreements.

One boost to U.S. investment in Hungary is the recent Congressional approval of Organization for International Economic Cooperation (OPIC) status which allows companies investing in Hungary to insure their investments. While Hungary was denied OPIC status in June, 1988, it was approved in 1989. This confidence level, along with the dollar being relatively low compared to the Deutsche Mark and other EC currencies, gives the U.S. an edge in its exports to Hungary.

Hungary is faced with increased competition from developing countries making it difficult to maintain market share for light industrial products such as textiles, clothing and leather goods. Hungary's share of total world exports dropped from 0.75% in 1973 to 0.46% in 1980 and 0.42% in 1985. In total Organization for Economic Cooperation and Development (OECD) imports, Hungary's market share decreased to 0.19% by 1985. According to Kerpel and Young (1988, p. 71), "While Hungary could probably compete successfully with the newly industrialising countries on wages and skilled labour, the economy has been inflexible and slow in responding to challenges."

CONCLUSIONS AND RECOMMENDATIONS

In moving toward a more market-oriented economy, Hungary will need to address its many problems, particularly the hard currency deficit. One solution is to export more products to the West. In order to effectively export to the West, in many instances Hungary will need to import the technology, quality components, and expertise to raise the quality of its products. This need will necessi-

tate channelling resources to the lighter industries, allowing any
heavy or unprofitable industries to fail. Also less reliance needs to
be placed on the Soviet Union for energy sources, thereby decreasing the production of the "soft goods."

Joint ventures with Western companies offer a method for creating a more flexible, market-oriented economy in Hungary. The
influence of the Western companies through these joint ventures
cannot be underestimated. The managing director of Hunguard
Glass summed up this importance:

> Until we got joint ventures we didn't see where the problem
> was . . . the difference in attitude is due to the ownership factor
> . . . Even though the Hungarians wanted to increase profits,
> they felt that the dividend did not go directly to them . . . As a
> manager of a state-owned enterprise the reports were for the
> government, but here no one is looking for reports but every-
> one is looking for results.[5]

The future of Hungary's economy depends significantly upon the
commitment of Hungary's leaders to the reform measures. There
are various scenarios on Hungary's future based upon varying degrees of government reforms. One "middle of the road" scenario is
based on the reforms being only partially implemented due to financial constraints and lack of commitment of the leadership. An alternative "see-saw" scenario alternates implementation of reforms
with government interference. In a third scenario, "sink or swim,"
the reforms are carried to a logical conclusion. "As many of Hungary's radical reform economists argue, the only way out that offers
hope in the long term is through a thorough liberalization of the
economy" (Kerpel and Young, 1988, p. 107).

With the problems of inflation, debt rescheduling, political interference, and dual export markets, Hungarian reformers have a difficult road ahead. If the government cannot maintain reforms along
with the often contradictory austerity programs, the real benefits to
the economy from restructuring may not be realized. One good way
for Hungary to solve its external financial problems is through the

---

5. Interview with Lajos Sapi, Managing Director of Hunguard Glass, May 30,
1989.

export of saleable goods in Western markets. While Hungary's major export prospects to the U.S. include buses, machinery parts, light bulbs, chemicals and pharmaceuticals, women's shoes, and food products, the best prospects for exports to Hungary from the U.S. are in telecommunications, electronics technology and computers, food processing equipment, agricultural equipment, pharmaceuticals and energy conservation systems.

Hungary's liberalization of joint ventures is a step toward achieving the needed higher-quality goods. In addition to the products themselves, joint ventures with the West offer Hungary an opportunity to improve managerial expertise and gain experience in free markets. By providing needed skills in marketing and in responding to changes in the marketplace, the ventures can raise the level of Hungarian management and company efficiency. The concept of the joint venture between partners from both the market and non-market economies provides a means for the integration of market mechanisms into the rapidly changing planned economy of the country.

As the respondents in this study made clear, for U.S. companies the joint venture in Hungary provides access not only to the Hungarian market but to markets in other Eastern Block countries as well as the European Community. Not only are the markets more geographically accessible, but the understanding gained by dealing with one country will facilitate trade with the other former members of the Comecon trading block. Given Hungary's present and anticipated status in the European Community in the next few years, joint ventures in Hungary will also have easier access to the large markets of the European Community.

BIBLIOGRAPHY

Belassa, B. (1988). "The New Growth Path in Hungary," in J.C. Brada and I. Dobozi, eds., *The Hungarian Economy in the 1980s*, 42-69.

Beracs, J. and Papadopoulos, N. (1990). "Marketing in Eastern Europe: The Case of Hungary," in V. Kirpalani, ed., *International Business Handbook* (New York: The Haworth Press, Inc.).

Hisrich, R.D. and Vecsenyi, J. (1990). "Entrepreneurship and the Hungarian Economic Transformation," *Journal of Managerial Psychology*, Vol. 5, 11-16.

Invest in Hungary. (1989). Vol. I (Budapest: Interpress).

Joint Ventures in Hungary–A Newsletter of CW Informatika Kft. (1988). Vol. 1, No. 1 (December, Budapest).

Kerpel, E. and Young, D.G. (1988). *Hungary to 1993: Risks and Rewards of Reform* (London: The Economist Intelligence Unit).

Marer, P. (1987). "Can East-West Joint Ventures in Hungary Serve as a 'Bridge' to the CMEA Market?" Paper Prepared for *Academy of International Business 1987 Annual Meeting* (Chicago, November) 12-15.

Chapter 11

Decision Processes in Strategic Alliances: Designing and Implementing International Joint Ventures in Eastern Europe

Arch G. Woodside
József Kandikó

The rapid increase in the formation of international joint ventures is one result of the dramatic political and economic changes in nearly all Eastern European nations in 1989. In 1989, the number of Hungarian-U.S. joint ventures has doubled to 70. In Poland, where the basic law governing business was liberalized late in 1988, the number of joint ventures involving U.S. companies has jumped from 4 to 40 in 1989 (Hansen, 1989). In Russia, the number of registered international joint ventures increased 700%, from 200 to 1,400, in 1989 versus 1988 (cf. Dyson, 1989; Holusha, 1989).

Elaborate planning and regulatory structures for creating and operating international joint ventures (IJVs) were abolished in Hungary late in 1988. A new IJV law (Act XXIV, 1988), highly favorable for foreign enterprises, was passed by the Hungarian Parliament in December 1988 and became operational in January 1989. A similar new IJV law became operational in Poland in 1989 (Holusha, 1989).

A less reported fact is that most international joint ventures are not operational. For example, fewer than 50 of the estimated 1,400 international joint venture agreements signed between the U.S.S.R.

This chapter was originally published in *Journal of Euromarketing*, Vol. 1(1/2) 1991.

and foreign enterprises are actually operating (Dean, 1990). A total of only ten of the 70 existing U.S.-Hungary international joint ventures were operating in 1990 (Dyson, 1989).

Also, one joint-venture specialist, Richard Dean, who heads the Moscow office of Coudert Brothers law firm predicts that perhaps only 100 IJVs have much prospect of ever making a profit in the U.S.S.R. (Keller, 1990).

News reports of specific IJVs operating in Eastern Europe are available in popular business publications, such as *Forbes* (Dyson, 1989) and *Advertising Age* (Hume, 1990). However, based on a review of the 1988/89 literature, detailed reports on the decision processes occurring in designs and implementations of specific IJVs (in Eastern Europe and elsewhere) are unavailable in the business press or scholarly business-related journals.

Our aim in this chapter is to describe and present the research results of a micro-analytical study on the decision processes used in designing and implementing two specific IJVs in Eastern Europe. The design of the study and this report is grounded in several theoretical perspectives of strategic decision making. However, our primary interest is to describe why and how IJVs may be designed and implemented, not to test the validity of alternative theories of decision making.

The reasoning for using a micro-analytical research method is provided in the next section. Details of the specific method used appears in the third section of the chapter. Sections four and five include the findings of the study and implications for strategic management.

THEORETICAL AND METHODOLOGICAL PERSPECTIVES

The study is focused on the "realized strategies" (Mintzberg, 1988) of IJVs, that is, the strategies that actually occur in the streams of decisions, interactions and behavior of persons in committing organizations to an action. For the study, a decision is defined as "a specific commitment to action" (Mintzberg, Raisinghani, and Theoret, 1976). International joint ventures are business enterprises created by two or more parent organizations headquartered and operated in two or more nations.

Initiating the need or opportunity for a decision, acquiring relevant information for making a commitment, processing the information, evaluating alternatives, and making a commitment have been identified as phases in decision processes (e.g., Witte, 1972; Howard, Hulbert, and Farley, 1975; Mintzberg, Raisinghani, and Theoret, 1976; Mintzberg, 1988).

Two key empirical findings on decision process phases are useful particularly for theory development and for planning research on IJV designs. First, specific phases in decision processes can be identified and described but these phases rarely follow a planned sequence (from problem formulation, search for alternative solutions, evaluation, choice, and implementation). Second, organizational decision processes are complex and dynamic, with iterative steps permitting all phases to be observed in every time unit occurring during the process.

The complex, dynamic nature of international business decisions has been emphasized in several classic studies. For example, Aharoni (1977, pp. 176-177) notes that "a foreign investment decision is a very complicated social process . . . It contains various elements of individual and organizational behavior, influenced by the past and the perception of the future as well as the present. It is composed of a large number of decisions, made by different people at different points in time. The understanding of the final outcome of such a process depends on an understanding of all its stages [phases] and parts."

Research and theory building for describing and explaining IJV decision processes most likely require some use of "direct" research (Mintzberg, 1979). Several semi-structured face-to-face interviews with several persons at several points in time, as well as the analysis of documents and the mixing of qualitative and quantitative methods (Jick, 1979; Denzin, 1978), are necessary for mapping the flow of decisions, behaviors, and interactions of people involved with all phases of IJV decision processes.

The need and use of direct research studies has been reported in several international business studies on decision processes. For example, Kelly (1981) used both questionnaires and semi-structured face-to-face interviews in a study of foreign direct investment (FDI) decision processes. She concluded that "a questionnaire approach, while valid for documenting current practices and discovering general relationships, was not sensible enough to discern the intricacies of the decision process. Thus, the personal field interviews provided invaluable perspective on the relationships in the decision process" (pp. 175-176).

Using a similar direct research method, Bjorkman (1989) provides thick descriptions of the decision processes occurring for 12 Finnish Foreign Direct Investments (FDIs). He offers several theory-building conclusions based on these 12 case analyses. For example, "FDI decision-making almost entirely consisted of development of one and only one FDI alternative at a time. This concerned both the country to be investigated, the location within the country, the choice of whether to acquire a firm or to make a greenfield investment, the choice of JV partner, and the choice of which firm to acquire. Although earlier studies have shown that the development of alternative solutions is relatively uncommon, the consistent absence of such activities was striking in our data" (p. 163).

A second conclusion from Bjorkman's 1989 study is worth noting. In many of the cases on FDI, decision processes he examined were solution-driven, not problem-driven–the emergence of an FDI opportunity triggered decision making without prior problem formation or search for FDI alternatives. Why may solution-driven decision-processes occur? Bjorkman (1989) suggests four explanations: (1) managers might view solution-driven decision making as the best approach from a cost-benefit point of view. It can therefore be seen as unwise for organizations to spend time and resources on a problem to which the chances of finding a solution are perhaps relatively small (March, 1981). (2) Serious constraints occur on managerial attention (cf. Cohen, March, and Olsen 1972). As a result, managers can only engage themselves in a limited number of issues. Managers are therefore more liable to raise a decision-making problem when there is a solution ready to attach to the issue. (3) A third possible explanation is that decision-making problems and criteria for finding their solutions are not well specified. A number of solutions can therefore be linked to almost any problem, provided they arise at approximately the same time. (4) Managers may be expected to make decisions that convey to the environment that they are competent executives. Therefore, when ideas that concur with this aspect of the managerial role come to the attention of managers, they are likely to be implemented. Additionally, if new norms for organizational action are emerging in the society, managers are likely to adopt these norms in order to gain environmental legitimacy for themselves.

The theoretical and empirical work of Kogut (1988) complements Bjorkman's (1989) contributions to some extent. Kogut (1988) provides persuasive support to the argument that most statements on the motivations for joint ventures are reducible to three factors: transaction costs, strategic behavior, and organizational knowledge and learning.

Transaction cost theory posits that firms transact by the mode which minimizes the sum of production and transaction costs (Kogut, 1988, p. 322). This theoretical perspective relates directly to Bjorkman's first explanation for solution-driven triggering of FDI decision-making processes.

Strategic behavior posits that firms transact by the mode which maximizes profits through improving a firm's competitive position vis-à-vis other rivals or consumers. Kogut (1988, p. 322) emphasizes that this perspective has not been investigated and the prediction of which firms will joint venture is unlikely to be the same for both transaction cost and strategic behavior perspectives.

> Whereas the former predicts that the matching should reflect minimizing costs, the latter predicts that joint venture partners will be chosen to improve the competitive positioning of the parties, whether through collusion through depriving competitors of potentially valuable allies. (Kogut, 1988, p. 322)

Organizational knowledge and learning as a motivating force for joint ventures occurs under two conditions: one or both firms desire to acquire the other's organizational know-how and one firm wishes to maintain an organizational capability while benefitting from another firm's current knowledge or cost advantage.

The three perspectives of transaction cost, strategic behavior, and organizational learning provide distinct, though at times overlapping, explanations for joint venture behavior. Transaction cost analyzes joint ventures as an efficient solution to the hazards of economic transactions. Strategic behavior places joint ventures in the context of competitive rivalry and collusive agreements to enhance market power. Finally, transfer or organizational skills views joint ventures as a vehicle by which organizational knowledge is exchanged and imitated efficiently (Kogut, 1988, pp. 323-4).

To what extent are these three perspectives, as well as competing perspectives,[1] found to occur distinctly or as overlapping motivators for joint ventures? Similar to Bjorkman's (1989), Aharoni's (1977) and Kelly's (1981) views on the study of foreign investment decisions, Kogut (1988) perceives that transaction cost and organizational knowledge explanations involve microanalytic detail which is difficult to acquire for one firm, not to mention for a cross-section of joint ventures. "For this reason it is likely that case studies of industries or a few ventures will be the most appealing methodology to provide initial insight into transaction cost and transfer of organizational knowledge motivations" (Kogut, 1988, pp. 329-30).

In the present article, the applicability is explored of the theoretical and empirical based observations of Bjorkman (1989) on FDIs as solution-driven versus problem-driven decision making and the three theoretical perspectives of Kogut (1988) as distinct, but possibly overlapping motivators, for joint ventures. The reported microanalytic examinations of two international joint venture decision processes offer findings similar to the results of Bjorkman's (1989) study. While strong evidence is found for more than one theoretical perspective as motivators for each IJV, based on the results of the study one of the three motivating perspectives proposed by Kogut (1988) is likely to be observed to be the dominant reason for each IJV creation.

METHOD

Decision systems analysis (DSA) (cf. Hulbert, Farley, and Howard, 1972; Howard, Hulbert, and Farley, 1975; Hulbert, 1981) was used to collect the data for the study. DSA involves a series of personal interviews with several managers participating in one or

---

1. For example, joint ventures as a form of bandwagon behavior (cf. Kogut, 1988).

more phases of the decision process, as well as an analysis of available documents related directly to the decision process. The aim of DSA is to describe the structure and flow of how and why a decision process actually occurs.

In the process of using DSA, series of flow diagrams of the decision phases, specific decisions, behavior and interactions of managers are prepared. In follow-up interviews, these flow diagrams are shown to the managers initially interviewed to learn additional details of the decision processes and to make corrections. The initial diagrams are revised based on additions and corrections noted as necessary for completeness and accuracy by the managers. After completing the suggested revisions, the diagrams are shown again to the managers in a third round of interviews, as well as being shown to other managers who had observed the decision process but who had not been directly involved as participants. Final versions of the flow diagrams are then prepared based on the third set of interviews.

DSA was used to collect data on the design and implementation decision processes for two manufacturing IJV enterprises. During each phase of the DSA interview process; open-ended semi-structured interview forms were used. Personal face-to-face interviews were used for each round of interviews. During each of the initial interviews with participants in the decision processes, the written IJV agreements, correspondence between the participating managers, and related internal memoranda were examined.

A second round of interviews was completed one to two weeks following the first set of interviews with the same respondents, and after preparing the initial flow diagrams of the decision processes. All of the diagrams prepared using each individual's responses were shown and discussed with each respondent. Each respondent was requested to make additions, corrections, and to comment on the reasons for each decision node and event shown in the diagrams.

The responses from the second round of interviews were used to revise and combine the individual flow diagrams into a summary diagram of the IJV decision process. The summary diagram was shown and discussed with the respondents in a third round of interviews, held one to two weeks after the second set of interviews.

During the third round of interviews, one additional manager in the IJV (who did not participate in the first two rounds of interviews and who was involved in the IJV creation) reviewed the summary flow diagram and made an assessment of changes needed for accuracy and completeness.

Interview Form

A ten-page, open-ended survey form was used in all the initial interviews. The survey form included questions about all possible phases of the decision process, events, and interactions of persons involved in designing and implementing the IJV. The events in the survey form included the following topics: (1) when was first contact made to discuss the idea of the joint venture; (2) when was the first joint venture agreement signed by the participating organizations; (3) when was the joint venture registered with the Hungarian government; (4) when did production start-up occur; (5) when did the first domestic and export sales occur; (6) when, if ever, did the joint venture first result in a profitable return to the joint venture partners?

Questions of the phases in the decision process and the activities and interactions of persons included the following topics: (1) who first brought up the idea of forming the joint venture; (2) what were the events and reasons that led to the idea of forming an IJV; (3) what was decided at the time of the initial contact by the different organizations participating in the meeting; (4) what information was sought, if any, before and after the first meeting among the participants; (5) who, specifically, sought information related to the idea of forming an IJV; (6) who specifically was involved in the first contact and meeting among the IJV participants (names, titles, and office locations); (7) what information was learned, if any, while considering the idea of the IJV among the participating organizations; (8) what additional meetings were held during the discussions about forming the IJV, who attended each of these meetings, and what were the outcomes of each of these meetings; (9) what other IJVs or other forms of international business relationships were considered, if any, before or during the discussions about this specific joint venture; (10) was some type of process used to compare IJV alternatives, and if yes, please describe the process;

(11) what equity-share goal was sought by each participant in the IJV and why did each participant seek this particular equity share; (12) how, why, and what specific equity shares were agreed to among the participating organizations; (13) what facilitating organizations (e.g., legal, banking, trading companies, transportation, government) assisted in the design and creation of the IJV; (14) what organizational design was desired by each organization participating in the IJV; (15) what organizational design was decided upon for the IJV and how was this decision made; (16) what surprise or unplanned events occurred during the discussions leading to the IJV and how did these events affect the design of the IJV; and (17) what products, target markets and marketing strategies were discussed for the IJV and what decisions were made about these issues.

Implementation questions in the survey included the following topics: (1) what suppliers are being used and what supply problems are being experienced, if any; (2) what products are being manufactured and what manufacturing problems are being experienced, if any; (3) what domestic and export marketing channels are being used; (4) who are the senior managers, what organizations forming the IJV are represented by the senior managers, and how are the senior managers compensated; (5) how are the employees in the IJV organized and compensated; (6) what sales and profit levels are being achieved by the IJV in domestic and export markets.

Near the end of the first interview, each respondent was requested to estimate how much the joint venture enterprise met the expectations of the parent Hungarian enterprise. The respondent was asked to use a scale of zero to 100 in responding to this question. Using the same 100-point scale, each respondent was asked to estimate how much the joint venture met the expectations of the parent foreign enterprise. For each of these evaluation questions, each respondent was asked to explain his or her responses.

The National Environment and the Participating International Joint Ventures

Both of the IJVs studied were manufacturing enterprises located in Hungary. The design and implementation of IJVs located in Hungary were selected for study because the Hungarian Parliament passed a major revision in the country's IJV law that became effective in January 1989; the Hungarian IJV law is likely to be used as a model for revising IJV laws in other eastern European nations (cf. *The Economist,* 1989). At the start of the 1990s, the new law appears to include the most liberal IJV design and implementation regulations in Eastern Europe (cf. Holusha, 1989).

Here is how *The Economist* evaluated IJV environments in three Eastern European countries in August 1989.

> Getting western partners for joint ventures requires a mixture of generous terms and bold marketing. The Hungarians have so far been most energetic at this. The western partner can now buy up to 100% of a Hungarian company (though, if he does, it is no longer a joint venture); send his money home; get handsome tax breaks. The Hungarian Chamber of Commerce presses a list of attractive prospects on the passing journalist (anybody interested in goose-liver processing in Oroshaza?). Even so, Hungary has barely doubled the 150 joint ventures it already had in operation before the new law was introduced. [Quite an achievement in nine months time.] Yugoslavia and Poland have put the welcome mat out too; but Yugoslavia still has probably fewer than 400 joint ventures and Poland only 100 or so. The great majority, in all three countries, are small beer. (*The Economist,* 1989, p. 7)

If "small beer" IJVs are defined to include retailing enterprises with less than 20 employees and annual sales volume of less than $2 million, most (possibly more than 75%) IJVs in Eastern Europe are likely to have such characteristics. However, the new 1989 Hungarian IJV law is designed to attract large Western partners to participate in manufacturing IJV enterprises. The creation and implementation of large IJVs in the manufacturing sector are likely to have substantial ripple effects on increasing the sales and profits of domestic companies supplying these manufacturing IJVs. More importantly, many large state-owned Hungarian manufacturing enterprises face bankruptcy in 1990 and 1991; such threats will likely be reduced if the state-owned enterprises can be converted into IJVs with Western partners.

Consequently, the research opportunity was sought to examine, in-depth, the decision process in IJV design and implementation that involved large, state-owned Hungarian manufacturing enterprises and large Western manufacturing partners. The founding organizations for both of the IJVs examined fit this profile.

The first IJV was designed to manufacture and market a consumer durable[2] in Hungary, Western Europe, and less developed countries (LDCs). According to the Hungarian manufacturing VP in this new IJV, the Hungarian Government had completed plans in 1988 to close the prior enterprise's manufacturing operation before 1990 because of continued poor sales, losses and the lack of funds to continue government subsidies to pay the 450 employees. The employees had been informed that they would be unemployed sometime in 1989. However, a joint venture partner located in the U.S. was identified and the IJV agreement was signed in early 1989.

The second IJV included in the study is a first of two Hungarian-Japanese IJV, Polifoam (actual name). Polifoam manufactures polyethylene-based industrial and consumer products, such as insulation materials for building construction, insoles in shoe manufacturing, and camping mats. Polifoam was formed in 1984, started production in 1986, and reorganized to be qualified under the new Hungarian IJV law in 1989.

Presenting the details of the decision processes used in designing and implementing the two IJVs permits several comparisons and contrasts to be noted. While a large sample (n > 30) of case analyses is necessary before attempting some generalizations about IJV decision processes, single-case studies may be useful for developing insights for theory construction and for strategic management practices (Cyert, Simon, and Trow, 1956).

The details of the new Hungarian IJV law are presented in a flow diagram in Figure 11.1. Note in the first decision node that the new Hungarian IJV guarantees a positive response to the question of freedom to choose the conditions of cooperation among the founding organizations with respect to equity share (ownership percent),

---

2. The CEO of this IJV manufacturing a consumer durable requested that the firm not be identified because of some of the controversial issues raised about participating in the IJV; while the names of the firms have been changed, the decision process and events reported about this IJV have not been altered.

how costs are to be shared, and the management structure of the new IJV. The Hungarian 1989 IJV law is designed to permit the following flow of choices to occur among the decision nodes in Figure 11.1:

Page 1: 1-3-5-8-6
Page 2: 10-13-15-17-19
Page 3: 22-23-25-27-29.

While this planned flow through the decision process did occur for both IJVs examined in the study, serious problems occurred related to decision nodes 5, 23, and 25 in implementing the Hungarian-U.S. IJV. The two-to-three year agreed start-up period (delay) in the requirement of achieving a hard currency balance through sales to the West became a serious issue at the end of the first year of production (in December 1989). No hard currency sales occurred in 1989. In mid-December 1989 the National Bank of Hungary (one of the IJV partners) cancelled the IJV's line-of-credit (node 25) because of the failure to generate hard currency sales. A meeting was scheduled for late December among representatives of all the parent organizations to solve this problem.

With respect to node 23, the senior executive representing the U.S. founding organization was threatening to seek new suppliers and end purchase agreements with existing component suppliers because of failures to meet promised delivery dates and poor performance quality of the components. "That's impossible," "it's never been done," and disbelief were the initial reactions by the other partners and the existing suppliers. However, based on the possibility for such actions permitted by the affirmative answer to node 23 built into the IJV law, and the insistence of the U.S. partner, additional suppliers were added and the shares-of-purchase requirements awarded to the existing suppliers were reduced.

The Hungarian-Japanese IJV did not experience serious problems with respect to operating under the new Hungarian 1989 IJV law. The lack of problems is likely due to several reasons, including more cultural and manufacturing experience in Hungary. Polifoam had two-and-a-half years of manufacturing and marketing experience before 1989 and had been created in 1984. Substantial sales to customers in Western Europe and a hard currency bank balance in

FIGURE 11.1. Joint Venture Design Model

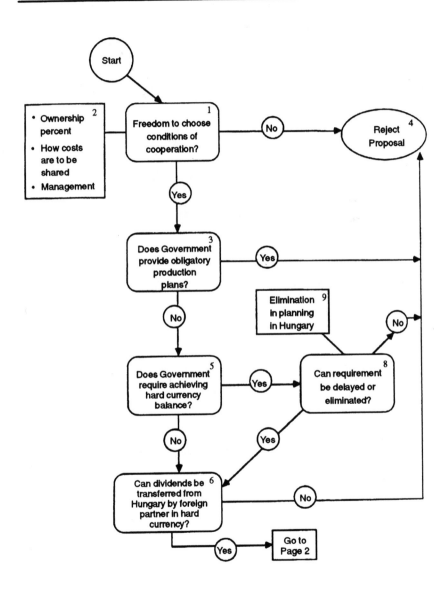

FIGURE 11.1 (continued)

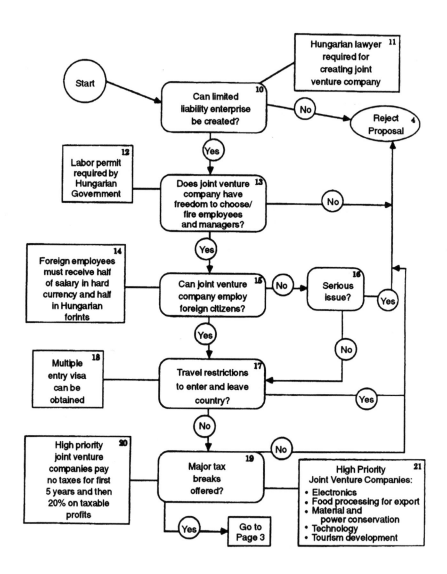

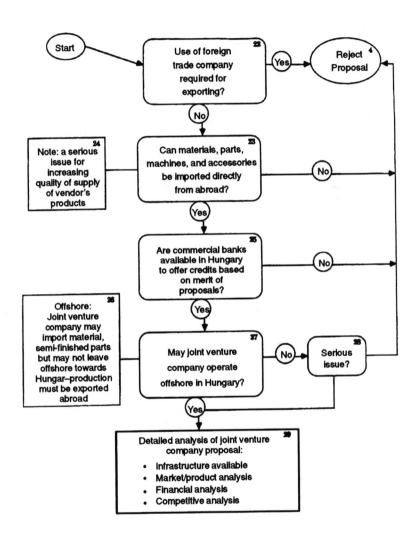

Hungary had been achieved in the first year, and every year, of manufacturing. Unlike the Hungarian-U.S. IJV, Polifoam did not require a substantial bank-supported line-of-credit for financing monthly operations.

The Hungarian 1989 IJV law does not solve several substantial weaknesses of operating an enterprise in Hungary. These weaknesses include: the nonconvertibility of Hungarian currency (Forints) into hard currencies; poor quality of raw materials and component parts; poor performance histories in meeting delivery schedules by suppliers; capital shortages; low performance standards for workers skilled only in using out-of-date technologies; financial accounting and bookkeeping systems noncomparable to Western systems; unmotivated managers using management tools that have not been changed since the 1950s; and the continued presence of a large, centralized bureaucracy that for more than 40 years, prior to 1989, had done the planning and controlled the decisions of all legal enterprises in the country (cf. Benedek, 1989).

Procedure

Two senior executives in each IJV participated individually in the first round of interviews. All the executives had been involved in designing and implementing the respective IJVs. In the Hungarian-U.S. IJV, the American senior executive was interviewed by the first author and the Hungarian senior executive was interviewed by the second author. The interviews were completed at the same time in separate offices. Each of the interviews was completed in two hours. The interviews were followed by a one-hour tour of the manufacturing plant. Follow-up interviews occurred at two- and three-week intervals with the same executives and one other executive (also Hungarian) at the manufacturing facility.

In the Hungarian-U.S. IJV, the American senior executive was not officially the CEO of the IJV. By remaining an employee of the U.S. parent enterprise, the American CEO was able to receive his entire salary in U.S. dollars and to avoid the new IJV law requirements that half the salary of foreign employees must be paid in hard currency (see node 14 in Figure 11.1).

In the Hungarian-Japanese IJV, the two senior executives interviewed were both Hungarians. One of these two executives was the official representative for the Japanese parent enterprise, Furukawa (this executive was fluent in English and was interviewed by the first author); no Japanese executive was employed or worked full-time in Hungary for Polifoam. The second executive was a former senior executive at the major Hungarian parent state-enterprise, Pannonplast. Both executives were full-time employees of Polifoam since the start-up of the IJV. One of the initial interviews lasted three hours and the other was completed in 90 minutes. Subsequent interviews occurred at other locations.

RESULTS

Details of the flow of activities, decisions, and interactions occurring in the design and implementation of the Hungarian-U.S. IJV are summarized in Figures 11.1, 11.2, and 11.3. While additional detail could have been used to depict many phases of the "realized strategy" (Mintzberg, 1988), the decision process used in designing and implementing the IJV may be described adequately in three distinct phases:

Phase 1: Solution-Opportunity Identification
Phase 2: Evaluation of Proposed IJV
Phase 3: Design and Implementation of IJV

Phase 1 in Figure 11.2 is described as a flow of events from boxes 1-3-5-7-9 with explanations and choice criteria appearing for each event (boxes 2-4-6-8-10). A flow of events, decisions, and interactions occurred in each phase of the decision process. However, for simplicity phase 1 is depicted as a series of events only (events appear as rectangles in the figures). Binary (yes/no) choice rules appear as rounded rectangles in Figures 11.3 A and B and other flow diagrams.

Phase 1 of the Hungarian-U.S. IJV: Solution-Identification

Similar to Bjorkman's (1989) main findings for FDIs, the emergence of a solution (the IJV opportunity) triggered the start of the

FIGURE 11.2. Solution-Opportunity Identification in Hungarian-U.S. Consumer Durable Manufacturing Enterprise

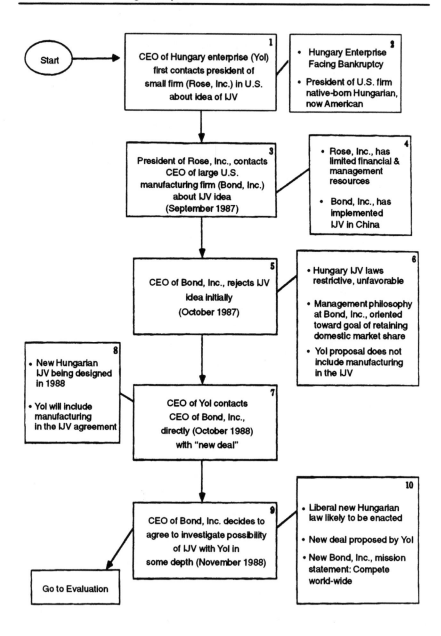

decision process that led eventually to the new Hungarian-U.S. enterprise. For the Hungarian enterprise Phase 1 would be labelled more appropriately as "crisis identification." In 1987 the Hungarian parent enterprise was experiencing substantial sales declines, net losses, and government threats of permanent closing.

Mintzberg, Raisinghani, and Theoret (1976) proposed three categories of decision-making processes along a continuum. At one extreme are opportunity decisions that are initiated on a purely voluntary basis to improve an already secure situation. At the other extreme are crisis decisions, where an organization is facing intense pressures that are forcing immediate action. Problem decisions are defined as those that fall between the two extremes. Mintzberg, Raisinghani, and Theoret (1976) propose that crisis decisions are typically triggered by single stimuli whereas problem and opportunity decisions typically require multiple stimuli before action is taken. The Hungarian-U.S. IJV decision process supports their proposition. Without the external threat of declaration of bankruptcy and plant closing triggering search activities for an IJV partner, most likely the Yol enterprise would have continued to exist with government subsidies covering annual operating losses. However, for Bond, Inc., the U.S. enterprise, several pieces had to come together before the proposed IJV was identified as a legitimate opportunity. Initially, Bond quickly rejected the idea of an IJV in Hungary (see box 6 in Figure 11.2).

Yol's initial proposal was to create a distribution-only IJV with Bond. The initial proposal did not include the ownership of the manufacturing operation by the IJV. In October 1988, one year after the initial proposal, a new IJV proposal was made by Yol that included the manufacturing facility as part of the IJV (box 8 in Figure 11.2). Yol would no longer be in existence as a separate and distinct enterprise; Yol would be absorbed by the new IJV, if the new IJV would be implemented. Note also in Figure 11.2 that the Bond's senior managers were influenced by the likely passage of the new Hungarian IJV law.

A third factor was part of the multiple-triggering cues influencing Bond. A major change in strategic management philosophy occurred at Bond between 1987 and 1988. Prior to 1988 Bond was focused on retaining domestic market share in the U.S. and increasing profits partly by reducing manufacturing costs by starting up foreign manufacturing plants in the Far East. Earlier in the 1980s Bond had started up a manufacturing facility with a Taiwan domestic manufacturer. In 1987 the Taiwan manufacturer entered the U.S. market as a new competitor with its own brand name, while at the same time continuing as Bond's manufacturing partner. These separate sequences of events led Bond to a dramatic change in strategic thinking in 1987 and a new strategic management philosophy in 1988: compete aggressively for market share on a world-wide basis. Gaining equity share and management control of non-US. based manufacturing and marketing enterprises was perceived by Bond's senior managers as a positive way to operationalize the new strategic management philosophy. Consequently, in November 1988 Bond agreed to investigate the possibility of an IJV with Yol (box 9 in Figure 11.2).

Note also at the start of Figure 11.2 that Yol's senior management initially contacted the president of a much smaller U.S. manufacturing enterprise, Rose, Inc. The cultural link between the CEOs at Yol and Rose was the key reason for this initial contact. Rose's CEO was a native-born Hungarian, spoke Hungarian fluently, and was now a successful executive in the U.S. in the same industry as Yol's CEO. This link was enough for Yol's CEO to initiate contact with Rose's CEO.

Systematic search for IJV partners in other countries or firms did not occur for either the Hungarian (Yol) or the U.S. (Bond) enterprise. Such a restricted search and evaluation decision process complements Bjorkman's results in his investigation of Finnish FDIs.

Phase 2 of the Hungarian-U.S. IJV: Evaluation

The senior executives at Bond used a series of conjunctive decision rules to evaluate the proposed Hungarian IJV. Three of these decision rules are summarized in Figure 11.3A.

Based on the firm's recent, perceived negative, experiences with the firm's Taiwanese manufacturing partner, Bond sought to control 51% of the voting equity shares, control of the CEO position, and authority to install its own financial accounting system in the proposed IJV (see box 2 and decision node 1 in Figure 11.3A). Having a domestic monopoly and favorable conditions for high sales and a

FIGURE 11.3A. Evaluation of Proposed Hungarian-U.S. Consumer Durable Manufacturing Enterprise

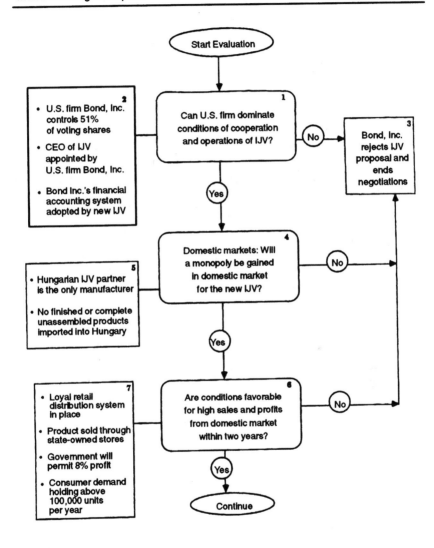

FIGURE 11.3B. Evaluation of Proposed Hungarian-U.S. Consumer Durable Manufacturing Enterprise

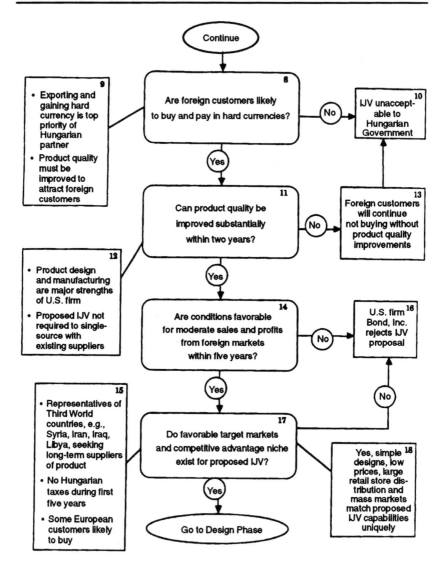

positive cash flow from marketing in Hungary only were also necessary but not sufficient conditions for evaluating the proposed IJV favorably by Bond (see nodes 4 and 6 in Figure 11.3A).

Bond's share of the financing requirements was less than half (45%) of the total equity raised for the new IJV (not included in the figures for the case). The National Bank of Hungary (NBH) agreed to become one of the IJV partners; the bank provided a 250 million (USD $3.5 million) line-of-credit for the new IJV. In comparison to the net worth of the former Hungarian manufacturing enterprise (as perceived by former Yol executives), the Hungarian managers in the new IJV commented several times during 1989 that Bond received extremely favorable terms in the IJV agreement. The American executive representing Bond in Hungary often responded to these statements that Bond was making additional financial commitments to the new IJV that included his presence and expertise, and long training programs in Hungary of manufacturing, engineering, and financial experts from Bond. Still, the perception was reported by both the Hungarian and American senior managers to be widespread among Hungarian managers in the IJV that the Hungarian government forced Yol to be sold cheap to a Western enterprise. During the fall 1989 and winter 1990, editorials on this question appeared in several of the leading newspapers in Budapest with respect to several Hungarian-Western IJVs.

Additional evaluation decision nodes appear in Figure 11.3B. Will the IJV generate hard currency sales (node 8 in Figure 11.3B)? This question was the most serious issue for the owner representatives of Yol, that is, government officials and the NBH. The principal reason for the Hungarian government and NBH approving of IJVs with Western partners is the generation of hard currency; these funds would become deposits in NBH and a portion of these funds could become part of Hungary's hard currency cash flow for paying for Western products.

The likelihood of generating hard currency would only be realized if product quality was improved substantially within two years (node 11 in Figure 11.3B). Such improvement was judged as likely by Bond and Yol senior executives for two principal reasons: (1) Bond's product design and manufacturing expertise and (2) the liberal terms of the managing of the new IJV (see node 12 in Figure

11.3B). Several favorable target markets and marketing conditions (nodes 15 and 18) led to the conclusion to advance to designing and implementing the IJV.

Phase 3 of the Hungarian-U.S. IJV: Design and Implementation

The actual design and implementation of the Hungarian-U.S. IJV is summarized in Figure 11.4. The 1989 Hungarian IJV law requires the parent firms to contract with a Hungarian legal expert to draft the IJV agreement (box 1 in Figure 11.4). Both the Hungarian and American executives interviewed reported that the legal expert contracted performed well in assisting in design and government approval of the IJV.

Because of the large monthly payroll and payments to suppliers, gaining a substantial line-of-credit from the NBH was important for implementing the IJV (boxes 3 and 4). In December 1989, eleven months after manufacturing had begun, a senior bank official of the NBH notified a Hungarian senior executive at the IJV that the line-of-credit was cancelled as of today (day of notification). The failure of the IJV to generate and deposit hard currency sales was given as the reason for the cancellation.

While meetings had occurred with prospective customers in Germany (FRG) and Greece, no hard currency sales actually had occurred in 1989. Domestic sales in Hungary had increased during the year to the point that the enterprise was breaking even by August and closed the year profitably. Hungarian and U.S. executives of the IJV were scheduled to meet with officials of the NBH in January when data collection on the IJV was ended.

The new employment agreement and supplier agreements (boxes 5 and 7) were sought by the U.S. IJV partner. Both the Hungarian and U.S. executives perceived the written, new employment agreement to have a substantial positive, motivational influence on employee performance in 1989. The former Yol employees had always received annual bonuses each December; they had been informed early in 1989 that the annual bonus was very unlikely in December. Employee bonuses were awarded in December but the bonuses were smaller than in previous years.

The threat of using new suppliers was not enough to gain on-time

FIGURE 11.4. Design/Implementation of Proposed Hungarian/U.S. Consumer Durable Manufacturing Enterprise

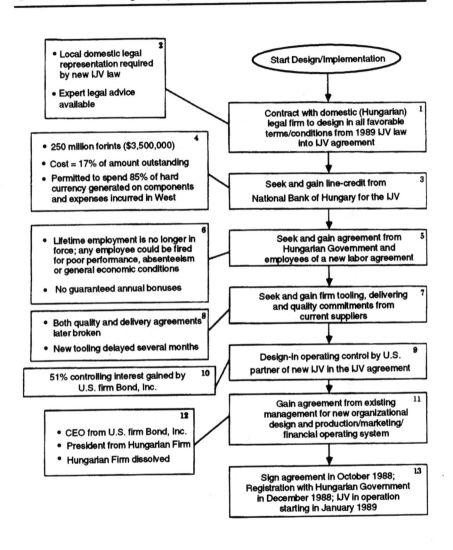

deliveries and higher quality from all existing suppliers for the new
IJV (box 8 in Figure 11.4). While the current suppliers were retained, agreements with new suppliers of components were signed
in the fall 1989.

The final terms of the agreement (boxes 9 and 11 in Figure 11.4)
included operational, management control by a Bond senior executive. The fact that this executive was not officially the IJV's CEO
(to avoid paying half his salary in Forints, see box 14, Figure 11.1)
is likely to have generated some resentment among the Hungarian
managers and IJV partners. This speculation is confirmed in a small
way by the bank's notifying the Hungarian senior executive but not
the American of the line-of-credit cancellation. The Hungarian senior executive then notified a senior executive at Bond's U.S. headquarters by fax. Bond's executive in Hungary was then notified by
telephone by an executive at the U.S. headquarters; he was as un-
happy with the use of this channel-of-communications as he was
with the cancellation notice.

Phase 1 of the Hungarian-Japanese IJV: Solution-Opportunity Identification

The initial steps in the decision-process of the Hungarian-Japanese IJV are depicted in Figure 11.5. The two enterprises most
involved in the decision process were Pannonplast in Hungary and
Furukawa in Japan. A senior Pannonplast executive who became
the CEO of the new IJV cited six reasons for first contacting the
Furukawa about exploring the possibility of an IJV. (1) Technical,
manufacturing know-how is one reason as shown in box 2 in Figure
11.5. (2) Pannonplast was aware that polyethylene-based products
were not being manufactured in any COMECON countries; a
manufacturing monopoly and a substantial distribution advantage
were possible for several Eastern European markets. (3) Pannonplast executives believed Pannonplast had the technical capability
for manufacturing high quality equal to the Japanese capabilities;
therefore, high profits were possible. (4) Pannonplast could gain
lots of useful information from Furukawa about product applications of polyethylene. (5) Pannonplast would learn Japanese organizational know-how and quality control methods. (6) Information
reciprocity might be possible: "we would provide information

FIGURE 11.5. Solution-Opportunity Identification in Hungarian-Japanese Industrial Manufacturing Enterprise

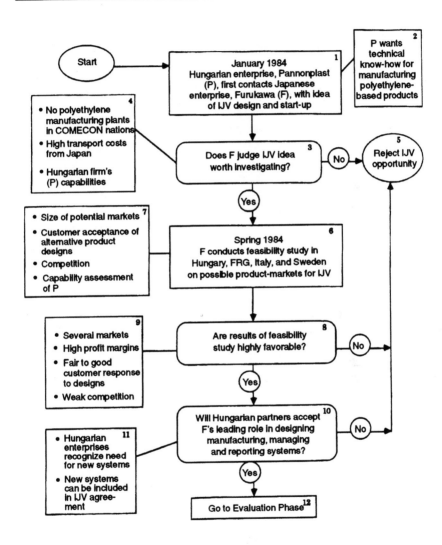

about domestic markets and the Japanese would provide results of technological developments."

The sixth reason ended up being included in the written IJV agreement. Furukawa agreed to provide the research results of technological developments in exchange for domestic market information. This agreement was made for a five-year period.

Furukawa's executives judged Pannonplast's IJV idea worthy enough of consideration (boxes 3 and 4 in Figure 11.5) to send three executives in March 1984 to direct a formal feasibility study on the technical and manufacturing capabilities of Pannonplast, competition, and market potential and product acceptance (boxes 6 and 7).

The favorable results of the feasibility study (box 9) and the desire of the potential Hungarian IJV partners to follow Furukawa's organizational and management leadership (boxes 10 and 11) led both Furukawa and Pannonplast to formally evaluate IJV designs.

Unlike the solution-opportunity identification for the Hungarian-U.S. IJV, both enterprises taking the leading role in the Hungarian-Japanese IJV appear to have perceived the IJV to be an opportunity not a crisis or problem situation. Compared to the Hungarian-U.S. IJV, the extreme positive and negative feelings felt by some Hungarian executives toward the U.S. enterprise (for being a savior and sinner by preventing bankruptcy and gaining control) were absent in the Hungarian-Japanese IJV.

Phase 2 of the Hungarian-Japanese IJV: Evaluation

The evaluation of the proposed Hungarian-Japanese IJV is summarized in Figure 11.6. Furukawa's executives wanted several enterprises to finance the IJV with Furukawa having a minority equity share (10%) in the new enterprise. The resulting equity share distribution appears in box 2. The reasons for seeking a minority share in the IJV are summarized in Figure 11.7 (box 2), the design of the IJV. The total start-up funding for the IJV was in Forints and the equivalent of $2.3 million (USD).

Furukawa's preference for a minority interest in the proposed IJV reflects Ohmae's (1989) theoretical comments on the "dangers of equity":

FIGURE 11.6. Evaluation Phase of Hungarian-Japanese IJV

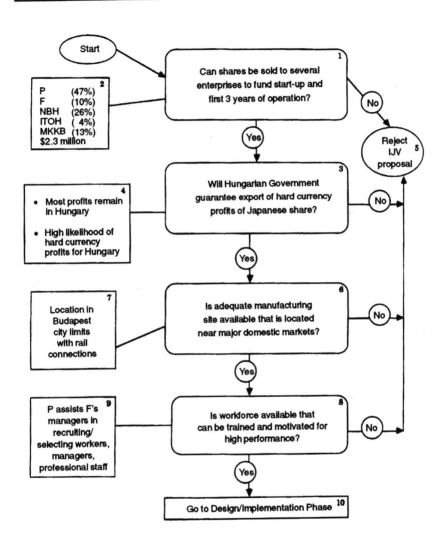

FIGURE 11.7. Design/Implementation of Hungarian-Japanese IJV

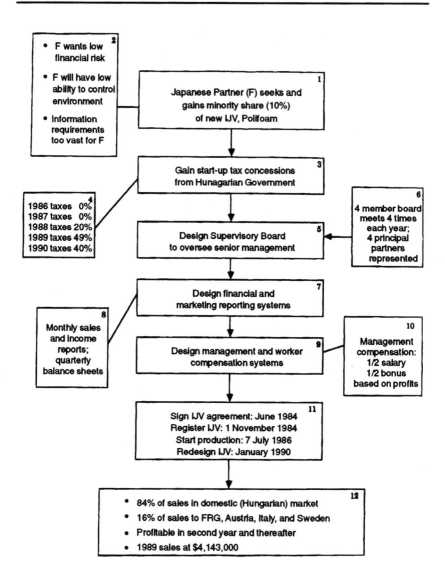

An emphasis on control through equity . . . immediately poisons the relationship. Instead of focusing on contribution to fixed costs, one company imperialistically tells the other, "Look, I've got a big equity stake in you. You don't give me all the dividends I want, so get busy and distribute my product. I'm not going to distribute yours, though. Remember, you work for me." (p. 149)

Ohmae further comments that equity by itself is not the problem in building successful alliances. "In Japan, we have a lot of 'group companies,' known as *keiretsu*, where an equity stake of, say, three percent to five percent keeps both partners interested in each other's welfare without threatening either's autonomy. Stopping that far short of a controlling position keeps the equity holder from treating the other company as if it were a subsidiary. Small equity investments like these may be the way to go" (p. 149).

The evaluation of the IJV proposal by Furukawa took place before the 1989 IJV law. Thus, Furukawa sought and gained guarantees from the Hungarian government in 1984 that Furukawa's share of hard currency profits could be taken to Japan (box 3 in Figure 11.3). The Hungarian government (via its bank representatives at NBH) quickly agreed to this question since most hard currency profits would remain in Hungary (box 4) because Furukawa would have only a 10% equity share.

In redesigning the Hungarian-Japanese IJV in 1989, the issue was raised of increasing Furukawa's equity-share from 10% to 31%. Under the new 1989 Hungarian IJV law a minimum of 31% equity share had to be owned by a foreign IJV partner for the IJV to qualify for the special low tax rates (see box 20 in Figure 11.1). However, the Furukawa executives did not want to consider an increased equity share; they preferred for Furukawa to maintain a 10% equity share.

The high quality of the proposed manufacturing location for the new IJV (boxes 6 and 7) and Pannonplast's assistance in recruiting and training a workforce, engineers, and managers (boxes 8 and 9), led to the design phase for the new IJV.

Phase 3 of the Hungarian-Japanese IJV:
Design and Implementation

Details of the design and implementation of Hungarian-Japanese
IJV are summarized in Figure 11.7. In designing the new IJV the
founding partners did seek and were granted start-up tax concessions from the Hungarian government (box 4 in Figure 11.7). Since
the start-up was planned three years before the enactment of the
1989 IJV law, the application and granting of tax concessions was a
15-month process.

The IJV founding partners designed a senior management board
into the IJV, the board to meet four times annually to review performance and plan manufacturing, financial, and marketing decisions
(boxes 5 and 6 in Figure 11.7). All founders of the new IJV agreed
to adopt Western financial and marketing reporting systems to include monthly sales and income reports (boxes 7 and 8).

The following compensation system was designed for the Hungarian-Japanese IJV (see boxes 9 and 10). All managers, including
the CEO, are paid in Hungarian currency. Given that substantial
profits are achieved, all managers receive substantial annual bonuses. The amount of the bonuses could equal the managers' base
salary depending on profit performance. Factory workers would
receive 90% of their total compensation in salaries but annual bonuses would be given based on profits of the enterprise.

A new manufacturing plant needed to be built before production
was started. The planning and construction of the new manufacturing facility were completed in 19 months. Production started in July
1986. Legal work was completed in January 1990 to enable the JV
to meet the requirements of the new Hungarian IJV law (box 11).

The results of the IJV include sales of 159 million and profits of
27 million Forints in the first calendar year of operation (1987).
Sales in 1988 were 233 million and profits of 74 million Forints.
The sales in 1989 were 290 million and profits of 76 million Forints. Approximately 84% of both sales and profits came from
domestic markets and 16% from Western European customers in
1989 (box 12).

The senior executives interviewed at Polifoam reported that Furukawa would be unlikely to assign 100 points (the top score on the

0 to 100 scale) in evaluating the IJV. The IJV CEO explained that the Furukawa executives believed that sales had grown too fast relative to profits and the sales growth planned for the IJV; the Furukawa executives had preferred and expected sales to be at 60% to 70% of production capacity instead of the more than 90% actual level by the end of the third year of operation.

Summarizing the Two IJVs

Table 11.1 is a summary of some of the events and characteristics occurring in the decision processes for the two IJVs. The two IJVs represent two different industries and the value of directly comparing the two is limited. Also the Hungarian-Japanese IJV has been operating for more years than the Hungarian-U.S. IJV. During 1989 the Hungarian-U.S. IJV was in the process of transforming the manufacturing plant of the former Yol enterprise. "My main job is to keep the lid on, keep the plant running while solving delivery problems, quality problems, training workers, finding customers, and installing new accounting and financial systems," was a comment made during several interviews by the American executive representing Bond. While the Hungarian-Japanese IJV was experiencing difficulties, the magnitude was less severe and more technical in nature.

Given these cautions and observations, the profile of Hungarian-Japanese IJV is more favorable than the profile of Hungarian-U.S. IJV in Table 11.1 in terms of problems, performance, and evaluation ratings.

Row 15 of the table presents the ratings for the IJV given by the respective Hungarian and foreign representatives interviewed in the study. For the Hungarian-U.S. IJV the Hungarian senior executive assigned a rating of 75 in evaluating how the IJV enterprise met the expectations of the Hungarian partners; the failure to gain hard currency sales was the reason offered for the rating of 75 versus a higher rating. (This rating was given before the NBH had cancelled the IJV's line-of-credit.) The American executive representing Bond assigned a rating of 80 to the IJV in meeting Bond's expectation. "Delays in receiving tooling and component parts," was the first reason offered for this rating versus a higher rating.

"100% +" was the expression used by the CEO in evaluating

TABLE 11.1. Comparisons of Hungarian-United States and Hungarian-Japanese IJV Design Characteristics

Characteristics	Hungarian-U.S. IJV	Hungarian-Japanese IJV
1. IJV has monopoly in Hungary	Yes	Yes
2. Share of IJV controlled by foreign partner	51%	10%
3. Product-market feasibility study done before IJV agreement signed	No	Yes
4. Complex supply requirement of components and raw materials	Yes	No
5. Serious supplier quality problems	Yes	No
6. Production/capacity ratio	60%	90%
7. Plan to increase capacity in 1990	Yes	No
8. Number of customers in Western Europe	0	14
9. Now earning hard currency	No	Yes
10. Prospects of earning hard currency	Low/Moderate	High
11. Net profit/sales ratio	1%	26%
12. Number of employees, managers, professionals	450	80
13. High sales growth forecasts by IJV	No	Yes
14. Operating now under new Hungarian IJV law	Yes	Yes
15. Level IJV has met expectations of Hungarian/foreign partners (on a 0-100 scale)	75/80	100/94

Polifoam from the viewpoint of the Hungarian partners. The current situation (January 1989) of "very small unused capacity" was the only reason given for the 94 rating assigned that Furukawa would assign as reported by the Hungarian executive representing Furukawa.

STRATEGIC MANAGEMENT IMPLICATIONS

Ohmae (1989) suggests that good combinations in strategic alliances are the exception, not the rule.

Two corporate cultures rarely mesh well or smoothly. In the academic world, there is a discipline devoted to the study of interpersonal relationships. To my knowledge, however, there is not even one scholar who specializes in the study of *intercompany* relationships. This is a serious omission, given the importance of joint ventures and alliances in today's competitive environment. We need to know much more than we do about what makes effective corporate relationships work. (Ohmae, 1989, p. 154)

Understanding intercompany relationships does likely involve microanalytical detail which Kogut (1988, p. 329) emphasizes is difficult to acquire for one firm, not to mention for a cross-section of joint ventures. Thus, the use of case studies of industries or a few IJVs may be helpful in learning intercompany relationships and building theoretical propositions grounded in reality.

One of several limitations in the study reported in the present article is that most of the data were gathered *ex post* through multiple interviews with only a few of the persons involved in the actual decision processes. Extensive interviews through time are possible in joint venture research; for example, Shortnell and Zajac (1988) report that teams of two individuals made annual visits to each of 13 internal corporate joint ventures over a period of four to five years. Similar research is now being planned by the authors of the present article along with colleagues at the University of Lodz, Poland, and the University of Innsbruck, Austria. Our plan is to study IJVs involving Western partners and Polish or Hungarian enterprises

from the time the agreement is registered with the national government or before and up to one year following manufacturing or
retailing by the IJV. Six additional IJVs have agreed to participate in
this study in Hungary by February 1990. Attempts to contact IJVs
planned for Poland to participate in the study started in February
1990.[3]

A second limitation is the two-case sample size. Though single-
and limited multiple-case research studies on decision processes
have been reported in the literature (e.g., Cyert, Simon, and Trow,
1956; Bettman, 1970; Pettigrew, 1975; Corey, 1978; Burgelman,
1985; Moller, 1986; Shortnell and Zajac, 1988; Bjorkman, 1989),
larger case sample research studies combined with other survey
research methods (cf. Shortnell and Zajac, 1988) are needed. The
justification for the present article is the belief that microanalytic
detail is needed on the emerging decision processes involving intercompany relationships if we are to understand such relationships
and construct relevant behavior-based theories of IJV decision processes. However, the use of DSA combined with document analysis
and annual interview periods for two to four years (conducted by
teams of researchers in several countries) is recommended. From
such joint research ventures fairly large samples of case analysis
(n > 30) should be available for formal testing of hypotheses.

A few theoretical propositions for strategic management are supported by the observations reported for the two IJVs. First, different
enterprises participating in designing the same IJV may be working
from opposite ends of Mintzberg, Raisinghani, and Theoret's (1976)
continuum of decision-process categories. The solution-opportunity
identification phase for the U.S. enterprise, Bond, was the solution-
crises identification phase for the Hungarian enterprise, Yol. In the
other case, executives at both Furukawa and Pannonplast perceived
the possible IJV as a solution-opportunity.

Second, the first scenario of combining the two extremes of the

---

3. In 1990 Tomasz Domanski and Elisabeth Guzek, Department of Marketing
and Market Research, University of Lodz, Poland, are directing the research project
in Poland. The semi-structured questionnaire and the use of the DSA and document
analysis reported in the present chapter are being used for data collection from the
IJVs in Poland.

proposed decision process continuum among two or more enterprises is more likely to result in lower performance, poor communications, and more failures compared to the second scenario. While appearing obvious, such a proposition may be a useful warning that the super-good deal for a Western partner may turn bad if the Eastern European partner feels the benefits of the IJV are mainly one-sided. Also, the extent (e.g., the variance in performance explained) that this proposition is supported in practice still needs to be learned.

Third, the equity share held by the foreign IJV partner is likely, in large part, to be a function of the strategic management orientation of the foreign partner (also cf. Stopford and Wells, 1972; Kogut, 1988; Ohmae, 1989). After perceiving themselves to be burned badly by having a current Taiwan supplier become a competitor in the U.S. domestic market, Bond sought and gained 51% equity-share control of the reported Hungarian-U.S. IJV. In the second case, the strategic management orientation of Furukawa was *neither* to seek *nor* accept a dominant equity share in the Hungarian-Japanese IJV.

No one form of equity-sharing is likely to be always the most appropriate for IJVs. The "shared management" approach advocated by Ohmae (1989) for some strategic alliances has been found by other researchers (cf. Killing, 1983; Hansen, 1989) as more often resulting in failure compared to the "dominant parent" IJVs. In a dominant parent IJV one of the parent enterprises manages the IJV similar to a wholly-owned subsidiary. In shared management ventures both parents manage the enterprise (cf. Hansen, 1989). On this issue of equity-share association with performance, Franko (1989) found no significant impact on performance of minority versus 50-50 IJV ownership among U.S. multinationals participating in IJVs.

Finally, the results for the two case studies may be helpful for extending Kogut's (1988) theoretical observations on the motivations for IJVs. Kogut proposes three sometimes complementary theoretical motivations for joint ventures. First, a transaction cost theory which posits that firms transact by the mode which minimizes the sum of production and transaction costs. Second, strategic behavior posits that firms transact by the mode which maximizes profits through improving a firm's competitive position vis-à-vis rivals. Third, organizational knowledge posits that one or both firms desire to acquire the other's organizational know-how; or one firm wishes to maintain an organizational capability while benefitting from another firm's current knowledge or cost advantage.

In the first case, the strategic behavior rationale appears to dominate Bond's approach to the IJV decision process: maximizing profits and controlling competition world-wide were stated strategic management goals for Bond. Transaction cost theory may be the rationale most appropriate for Yol's motivations for entering the IJV decision process. Yol wanted help in minimizing production and transaction costs; drastic reductions in transaction costs coupled with increases in revenues were needed for Yol to survive in some form. Thus, for the same IJV, different theoretical explanations may be applicable for explaining the IJV motivations for two or more enterprises from different nations.

For the Hungarian-Japanese IJV, the organizational knowledge and learning rationale proposed by Kogut (1988) for motivating joint ventures was observed for both Furukawa and Pannonplast. The representatives of both firms referred to the organizational expertise of the other firms in different spheres (Furukawa's technical and organizational design expertise were mentioned by Pannonplast's representative and domestic and Eastern European market knowledge was mentioned by Furukawa's representative) as motivations for considering the IJV. Transaction cost and strategic behavior explanations were complementary explanations for the Hungarian-Japanese IJV. Possibly, observations of mutual respect jointly displayed by both domestic and foreign partners through organizational knowledge and learning motivations increases the likelihood of success and high performance for the JV.

BIBLIOGRAPHY

Aharioni, Y. 1977. *Markets, Planning and Development,* Cambridge, Massachusetts: Ballinger.

Benedek, Thomas. 1989. "Joint ventures in Eastern Europe," Institute for Industrial Economics, Budapest.

Bettman, James R. August 1970. "Information Processing Models of Consumer Behavior," *Journal of Marketing Research,* 7, pp. 370-376.

Bjorkman, Ingmar. 1989. *Foreign Direct Investments: An Empirical Analysis of Decision Making in Seven Finnish Firms*, Helsinki: The Swedish School of Economics and Business Administration.

Burgelman, R. A. 1985. "Managing the New Venture Division-Research Findings and Implications for Strategic Management," *Strategic Management Journal*, 5, pp. 241-264.

Cohen, Michael D., James G. March, and Johan P. Olsen. 1972. "A Garbage Can Model of Organizational Choice," *Administrative Science Quarterly*, 17, pp. 1-25.

Corey, E. Raymond. 1978. *Procurement Management: Strategy, Organization, and Decision Making*, Boston: CBI Publishing.

Cyert, Richard M., Herbert A. Simon, and D. B. Trow. 1956. "Observation of a Business Decision," *Journal of Business*, 29, pp. 237-248.

Dean, Richard. Interview in Bill Keller. 'Capitalism: Big Macs in Moscow,' *The Times-Picayune*, New Orleans, January 28, 1990, p. A-18.

Denzin, Norman K. 1978. *The Research Act*, 2nd ed., New York: McGraw-Hill.

Dyson, Esther. "High Risks, Distant Payoffs," *Forbes*, 144, December 11, 1989, pp. 114-116, ff.

Franko, Lawrence G. Spring, 1989. "Use of Minority and 50-50 Joint Ventures by United States Multinationals During the 1970s: The Interaction of Host Country Policies and Corporate Strategies," *Journal of International Business Studies*, 20, 19-40.

Hansen, S. O. 1989. "The Pros and Cons of Concluding a Joint Venture," in *East-West Joint Ventures: Incentives and Disincentives*, ed. by S. O. Hansen and U. Kivikari, Institute for East-West Trade, Turku School of Economics and Business Administration, Turku, Finland, pp. 3-20.

Holusha, John. "Eastern Europe: Its Lure and Hurdles," *The New York Times*, December 18, 1989, pp. 25, 30.

Howard, John A., James Hulbert, and John U. Farley. April 1975. "Organizational Analysis and Information-Systems Design: A Decision-Process Perspective," *Journal of Business Research*, 3, pp. 133-148.

Hulbert, James M. 1981. "Descriptive models of marketing decisions," in *Marketing Decision Models*, ed. by Randall L. Schultz and Andris A. Zoltners, North Holland, pp. 19-54.

Hulbert, James M., John U. Farley, and John A. Howard. 1972. "Information Processing and Decision Making in Marketing Organizations," *Journal of Marketing Research*, 9, pp. 75-77.

Hume, Scott. 'How Big Mac Made It to Moscow,' *Advertising Age*, 61, January 22, 1990, pp. 16, 51.

Jick, Todd D. December 1979. "Mixing Qualitative and Quantitative Methods: Triangulation in Action," *Administrative Science Quarterly*, 24, pp. 602-611.

Keller, R. "Capitalism: Big Macs in Moscow," *The New York Times*, in the *Times-Picayune*, New Orleans, January 28, 1990, p. A-18.

Kelly, M. W. 1981. *Foreign Investment Evaluation Practices of U.S. Multinational Corporations*, Ann Arbor, Michigan: UMI Research Press.

Killing, P. 1983. "How to Make a Joint Global Venture Work," in *Managing Effectively in the World Marketplace*, ed. by D. N. Dickson, Wiley, New York.

Kogut, Bruce. 1988. "Joint Ventures: Theoretical and Empirical Perspectives," *Strategic Management Journal*, 9, pp. 319-332.

March, James G. 1981. "Decisions in Organizations and Theories of Choice," in *Assessing Organizational Design and Performance*, ed. by Andrew Van de Ven and William Joyce, New York: Wiley Interscience.

Mintzberg, Henry, Duru Raisinghani, and Andre Theoret. June 1976. "The Structure of 'Unstructured' Decision Processes," *Administrative Science Quarterly*, 21, pp. 246-275.

Mintzberg, Henry. December 1979. "An Emerging Strategy of 'Direct' Research," *Administrative Science Quarterly*, 24, pp. 582-590.

Mintzberg, Henry. Fall 1988. "The Strategy Concept I: Five Ps for Strategy," *California Management Review*, 30, pp. 12-27.

Moller, K. E. 1986. "Buying Behavior of Industrial Components: Inductive Approach for Descriptive Model Building," in *Research in International Marketing*, ed. by P. W. Turnbull and S. J. Paliwoda, Kent, U.K., Croom-Helm.

Ohmae, Kenichi. March-April 1989. "The Global Logic of Strategic Alliances," *Harvard Business Review*, 67, pp. 143-154.

Pettigrew, Andrew. May 1975. "The Industrial Purchasing Decision as a Political Process," *European Journal of Marketing*, 18, pp. 133-145.

Shortnell, Stephen M. and E. J. Zajac. 1988. "Internal Corporate Joint Ventures: Development Processes and Performance Outcomes," *Strategic Management Journal*, 9, pp. 527-542.

Stopford, M. and L. Wells. 1972. *Managing the Multinational Enterprise*, Basic Books, New York.

The Economist, "Eastern Europe Survey," August 12, 1989, Special Section.

Witte, Erhard. 1972. "Field Research on Complex Decision Making Processes— The Phase Theorem," *International Studies of Management and Organizations*, 2, 123-132.

SECTION IV.
EUROPEAN MARKETING:
WHAT IS HAPPENING AFTER 1992?

Chapter 12

Fortress Europe:
Which Industries Are Most Vulnerable?

Trina L. Larsen
Robert T. Green

The impending completion of the European Community's (EC) internal market has serious implications for international marketers. The EC's internal market barriers are scheduled to be removed by 1992. The existing market barriers include tariffs and quantitative restrictions, customs delays and related administrative burdens, governmental procurement procedures, and differences in technical regulations. The removal of these barriers will greatly facilitate the marketing of products within the EC.

The completion of the integration of the internal market in the EC will present opportunities for both EC and non-EC firms. Although a focus is often directed toward the 320 million consumers which will make up the newly integrated market, the direct benefits of the integration of the EC will arise from supply-side rather than demand-side effects (Quelch, Buzzell, and Salama, 1990; Delachaux, 1990). The removal of internal barriers will lower costs, with subsequent increases in competition and the exploitation of economies of scale.

International marketers will also be faced with a potential threat, however, that arises from uncertainty regarding the erection of "Fortress Europe." This term refers to the fear that an integrated EC will erect new barriers to the entry of its market by non-EC nations at the same time it is dismantling its internal barriers. The fear that protectionism will increase has been expressed by external as well as internal sources (Henderson, 1989; Morrison, 1989). For instance, a Conference Board survey found that protectionist fears were the overwhelming concern of most European executives, due to the uncertainty regarding the goals of integration (Morrison, 1989). While a goal of the EC integration is an increase in competition, it is not entirely clear if this competition is to include firms from non-EC nations, or if it is to be focused primarily on increasing competition among EC firms. Is the integration of the internal market designed to benefit European consumers or European producers? If the goal is to benefit the latter, the events leading up to 1992 may result in an increase in EC protectionism (Quelch, Buzzell, and Salama, 1990).

While acknowledging that the further integration of the EC will generally enhance opportunities to internal marketers due to the eradication of barriers within the mammoth EC marketplace, the erection of external trade barriers would negatively affect the trade of specific types of products. To the extent that "Fortress Europe" is a real threat, it would be useful for international marketers to know which products would be most threatened by its existence. The study reported in this paper represents an attempt to identify those products which are most vulnerable to this possibility and to discuss the implications for international marketers of these vulnerable products.

BACKGROUND

The integration of the EC's internal market is the culmination of a process that began in 1957 with the signing of the Treaty of Rome. At that point the ultimate goal of economic integration was to be the political union of member countries, yet immediate benefits from the establishment of a customs union were expected. The immediate benefits were perceived to be an enlarged market, greater mobility for workers and professionals, and the best quality products at the lowest prices for consumers (Shanks and Lambert, 1962).

With minor differences, these are generally similar to the benefits that are predicted to arise from the events scheduled for 1992. The earlier benefits were primarily directed toward improving the standard of living of the EC population, while the effects of the creation of a true European internal market in 1992 are most often discussed in terms of the competition and efficiency of firms. A 1988 report commissioned by the EC predicted that the effects of the 1992 program would be lower costs and prices, increased investment and improved competitiveness (Cecchini, 1988). The four principal types of effects of 1992 identified by the Directorate-General for Economic and Financial Affairs of the Commission of the European Communities are:

i. a significant reduction in costs due to a better exploitation of several kinds of economies of scale associated with the size of production units and enterprises;
ii. an improved efficiency in enterprises, a rationalization of industrial structures and a setting of prices closer to costs of production, all resulting from more competitive markets;
iii. adjustments between industries on the basis of a fuller play of comparative advantages in an integrated market;
iv. a flow of innovations, new processes and new products, stimulated by the dynamics of the internal market. (*European Economy*, 1988, p. 17)

The Directorate-General's report concentrates on the effects of integration on European firms. But non-EC firms must be concerned with the implications for them, especially for those firms primarily involved in exporting to the EC.

In the years immediately following European integration efforts (the 1960s), EC imports experienced a large shift away from the U.S. and non-member European countries and toward EC member countries (Green and Larsen, 1985). It is reasonable to expect a similar effect in the years immediately following 1992.

While EC nations' imports shifted back toward the U.S. and non-member countries in the late 1970s and early 1980s (20 years after the initial integration efforts), the EC response to that point was not to applaud the increase in competition from imports, but to call for increased protectionism (Ziebura, 1983, p. 130; Page, 1981, p. 17).

EC officials claim that integration of its internal market will not harm other nations' exports to the Community. On the contrary, they expect faster economic growth that will create a greater demand for imports, actually increasing imports by seven percent as a result of the unified market (Lublin, 1989). These officials cite the

EC's longstanding commitment to open trade and maintain that this commitment will be bolstered as its market becomes the largest in the industrialized world (Lublin, 1989). It is suggested that uniform standards and streamlined customs requirements will be of great benefit to non-EC as well as EC firms.

Many others, however, remain skeptical of these assurances. For instance, Henderson (1989) argues that much depends on the ability and willingness of EC nations to cooperate and a sustained EC commitment to trade liberalization. Citing contradictory public statements by Mr. William de Clerq, then the EC's Commissioner for External Relations, he states that the Cecchini Report paints too rosy of a picture regarding the post-integration situation. While restating the EC's commitment to open trade, Mr. de Clerq emphasized EC reciprocity, which Henderson notes is not "in and of itself a liberal notion, and stricter notions of reciprocity–i.e., involving an exact matching of advantages at each single bilateral move towards liberalization–could amount to placing restrictive conditions on the liberalization process" (Henderson, 1989, p. 11).

The focus remains on uncertainty, as divisions within the EC and within the European Commission itself remain regarding the goals of integration and the commitment to free trade. These divisions were visible in the shift in the EC's interpretation of the policy of reciprocity with respect to the financial sector. "In the middle of 1988 it was taken to mean 'equal access on equal terms.' By mid-1989 the Commission line had softened considerably, and it was proposing to take action only where equivalent treatment of EC and domestic institutions was not available or where it appears that credit institutions of the Community do not enjoy national situations in a third country,' with the latter case being sufficient grounds for action against subsidiaries controlled from the third country in question" (Quelch, Buzzell, and Salama, 1989, p. 52). Additionally, anti-dumping regulations have been written in such a way that the EC may be able to bring dumping charges against virtually any product, claiming that it is being sold at less than cost (Nelson, 1989).

The auto industry is another area where "Fortress Europe" is a possibility due to divisions within the EC (Browning, 1989). European automobile companies are currently highly protected (by subsidies, tariffs and quotas), yet the extent of the protection differs. Five of the 12 EC nations have restrictions on Japanese automobile imports; for example, Italy maintains a quota of 3,000 cars, France a quota of 3%, the United Kingdom a quota of 11% and Germany has no quota at all (Morrison, 1989; Quelch, Buzzell, and Salama, 1989). Executives from Italian and French automobile manufacturers have called for protection from future imports (Morrison, 1989; "Renault . . .", 1988). In face, EC officials are not discussing dismantling automobile import barriers completely, but rather moving to transitional protection (Revsin, 1988). "Transitional protection" will also be provided for the textile and footwear industries (Riemer, 1988).

There is also uncertainty about how potential protectionism would affect imports from various sources. Many EC-based multinationals have global subsidiaries. How would protectionism affect their intra-firm trade? And the attitude toward EC imports from LDCs, the U.S., and Japan differs. While some sources worry that by more aggressively marketing to the EC, it may become an arena for the U.S. and Japan to settle their trade dispute (Morrison, 1989), in general, protectionism against Japanese imports seems to be more acceptable (Quelch, Buzzell, and Salama, 1990; Franko, 1990). Yet, how would protectionist policies against Japanese imports differentiate between imports from Japanese companies that originate in Japan versus imports from Japanese companies that originate in their subsidiaries in the United States? In 1989 the Commission decided to impose anti-dumping duties on Ricoh photocopiers made in the Japanese company's U.S. subsidiary (Quelch, Buzzell, and Salama, 1990). Other industries could potentially face similar action in the future. Once again, the primary concern revolves around uncertainty.

One response by firms to this uncertainty has been an increase in mergers, acquisitions, restructurings, and joint ventures (Franko, 1990). In 1987 U.S. foreign direct investment to the EC was growing at an annual rate of 24%; Japanese foreign direct investment to the EC was growing at a rate of 90% (Quelch, Buzzell, and Salama, 1990). In fact, given that one goal of the 1992 plan is to alter companies' attitudes toward the EC (that is to psychologically change the perception of the EC to a more "European" approach as opposed to a collection of individual nations set in Europe), non-EC firms may be in a better position to capitalize on the integration changes. For example, Americans already tend to think about Europe as a single entity; more so than their European counterparts (Quelch, Buzzell, and Salama, 1990).

Foreign direct investment and alliances are important alternatives for firms' EC market entry, but it may not be a viable alternative for all firms or for 100% of a firm's entry. Thus, though it is impossible to predict whether or to what extent "Fortress Europe" will materialize, firms currently or considering exporting to the EC should have some idea of the products that will be most vulnerable. The purpose of this study is to identify those products which appear to have the greatest vulnerability to the erection of "Fortress Europe."

METHODOLOGY

It is likely that the products most vulnerable to the erection of "Fortress Europe" are (1) found in industries strongly entrenched in Europe; (2) substantially traded among EC nations; and (3) in product categories characterized by high trade growth in the EC. Rapidly growing products would be likely targets for competition from non-EC companies, and the existence of established and active EC companies would present vested interests that could advocate protection from non-EC competition (and perhaps the economic power to elicit it). The automobile industry would be an example of such an industry. The methodology employed in the present study was devised to identify products that possess these characteristics.

Given that the purpose of this study is to identify export industries which are most vulnerable to the erection of "Fortress Europe," international trade statistics are utilized. While other factors, such as foreign direct investment and alliances, will mitigate the problems presented to firms by "Fortress Europe," the focus of this study remains on trade.

Import data for the 12 member nations of the EC were gathered for two years: 1985 and 1987. The data were obtained from the United Nations and consisted specifically of the value of imports each EC nation obtained from all of the individual nations of the world. Data from 1987 were employed because this was the most recent year for which U.N. trade data were available at the time of the study. The selection of 1985 was based on the desire to examine relatively recent trends, in order to minimize the identification of products whose major growth had occurred at an earlier period. While a ten year time span could have been used, the magnitude of the changes over the period would have obscured more recent trends which are of greater interest, since the White Paper on Completing the Internal Market was published and endorsed in 1985, and was reaffirmed by the Single European Act in 1987.

The analysis was restricted to the import of manufactured product categories, classified at the fairly disaggregated four-digit Standard International Trade Classification (SITC) level. An advantage of using a disaggregated approach is that the analysis is more product specific, thus increasing the relevance of the results. However, it yields an unwieldy number of individual product categories, many of which account for a relatively insignificant amount of EC imports. In order to reduce the number of product categories and to eliminate product categories with relatively insignificant amounts of EC imports, the study employed only product categories accounting for EC imports of $500 million or more in either 1985 or 1987. Thus, the analysis is restricted to product categories accounting for a relatively large volume of annual EC imports. These categories would be more likely to attract industry and government attention, and would thus be more vulnerable to protectionist sentiment. The analysis began with 385 product categories, and at this stage 221 were eliminated. Thus, 164 manufactured product categories remained. The large majority of EC manufactured imports originates in developed nations.

Product categories for which there is significant foreign (non-EC) import competition were then identified by calculating the ratio of the value of within-EC imports to the value of non-EC imports for each of the 164 product categories. A high ratio indicates a relatively minor amount of non-EC competition for EC imports, while a low ratio indicates a relatively large non-EC presence. The median ratio was 2.32, and all 82 product categories equal to or less than 2.32 were extracted for further analysis. In 1987, these 82 manufacturing product categories accounted for 38.0% of EC imports from within the EC, and for 63.1% of EC imports from non-EC sources. These are the product categories for which non-EC penetration in the EC market is relatively high, and they would therefore be more vulnerable to protectionist sentiment than product categories for which there is a relatively minor amount of competition from non-EC sources.

Next, the average growth rate of both within-EC and non-EC import growth was computed for each of the 82 product categories. Based on the result of these computations, products were divided into "Low Growth" and "High Growth" categories. The Low Growth/High Growth cut-offs differed for non-EC imports and within-EC imports, due primarily to the impact that currency fluctuations occurring during the 1985-1987 period were having on the value of non-EC imports. The average annual growth rate employed as the cut-off between the high and low growth products was 40% for within-EC imports and 50% for non-EC imports. The product categories were then divided into four groups which correspond to the four quadrants of the matrix in Figure 12.1. The specific product categories located in each of these quadrants are presented in Tables 12.1 and 12.2, and the results are discussed below.

Product categories experiencing low within-EC import growth and low non-EC import growth would not seem likely to be candidates for protectionist measures. Similarly, product categories in which there is high within-EC import growth and low non-EC import growth would not be particularly strong candidates for protectionist measures; product categories in this quadrant are from EC industries which are already extremely competitive.

However, products located in the other two quadrants appear vulnerable to potential protectionism, especially those located in the high non-EC import growth/high within-EC import growth quadrant. In this quadrant the import growth of the product categories is booming in general, and it would seem likely that the EC nations would have a substantial interest in restricting the competitiveness of products from non-EC nations in order to permit EC firms to capture the market in these rapidly growing categories. Also, the product categories in the low within-EC/high non-EC import share quadrant may be relatively strong candidates for protectionist measures. The argument for protectionism in this quadrant would paral-

FIGURE 12.1. Non-EC Import Growth

Within EC Import Growth		High	Low
	High	Low Vulnerability	High Vulnerability
	Low	Low Vulnerability	High Vulnerability

lel the infant industry argument for trade restrictions. In this case, imports from outside of the EC are growing rapidly, yet imports from other EC nations are not currently competitive. Thus there may be an incentive to erect barriers to non-EC imports in order to increase the competitiveness of EC firms, since these markets appear to represent areas of substantial opportunity.

FINDINGS

Low Vulnerability Products

The products listed in the upper portion of Table 12.1 represent those which exhibit low within-EC import growth and low non-EC import growth. Thus, they would be considered to be relatively low vulnerability candidates for protectionism by a unified EC market. One general feature of these products, supportive of the low vulnerability expectation, is that they mostly represent mature industries (e.g., paperboard, cotton fabric, woven cotton, leather). With few exceptions, they are generally low technology products and are not industries likely to command significant official attention for future growth targeting.

TABLE 12.1. Low Vulnerability Products

Section 1

Low Within EC Growth and Low Non-EC Growth Quadrant

SITC#	Product Category	Within EC Growth	Non-EC Growth
6413	Kraft, Paper, Paperboard	41.1	38.3
6821	Copper, Alloys, Unwrought	17.7	3.6
6715	Other Ferro-Alloys	−4.8	3.3
7114	Aircraft Eng., incl. jet	37.3	27.4
6521	Grey Woven Cotton Fabric	29.3	14.3
7293	Microelectronics	34.1	33.6
7341	Aircraft, Heavier than Air	13.4	13.2
6119	Leather, nes.*	23.5	29.3
6814	Alum. Alloys Unwrought	19.7	19.1
5413	Antibiotics	23.5	20.9
7149	Office Mach, nes.*	49.9	33.9
5136	Unorganic Bases, etc., nes.*	34.0	25.6
5619	Fertilizer, nes.*	22.1	18.4
5133	Inorganic Acids, etc.	36.0	33.4
6741	Iron, Steel, Heavy Plate, etc.	26.0	10.2
8624	Photo Film, exl., Dev. Cinema	38.6	28.1
6535	Woven Synth. Fabrics	30.8	39.4

6522	Woven Cotton, Bleached, etc.	38.4	38.9
7197	Ball Roll, etc. Bearings	45.5	20.2
6785	Iron, Steel, Tube Fittings	42.2	36.1
5611	Chem. Nitrogeneous Fertilizer	18.6	36.0
6782	Iron, Steel, Tube Seamless, nes.*	25.7	16.8
5142	Metal Compound of Inorg.	38.2	21.0

Section 2
High Within EC Growth and Low Non-EC Growth

8619	Measuring Cntrlling. Instr.	52.1	29.1
7353	Ships and Boats Non-air	98.4	23.1
7349	Aircraft Parts, etc.	87.0	-18.5
7222	Switchgear etc.	53.2	31.4
8921	Printed Books, Globes	52.3	31.0
6942	Steel, Copper, Nuts, Bolts, etc.	52.4	38.4
6314	Improved Reconstit., Wood	60.2	38.9
7231	Insulated Wire, Cable	52.8	39.9
6299	Oth. Rubber, Articles, nes.*	53.5	34.9
6411	Newsprint, Paper	70.9	9.7
7142	Acct. Mach., Computers	59.6	36.3
8911	Snd. Recorders, Phonogr. Parts	67.4	39.2
8611	Opitcal Elements	57.3	39.6
7295	Elec. Measuring Contrl. Equip.	58.1	34.1
8616	Photographic Equip. nes.*	89.3	31.8

* nes. = not elsewhere specified

277

TABLE 12.2. High Vulnerability Products

Section 1
Low Within EC Growth and High Non-EC Growth

SITC#	Product Category	Within EC Growth	Non-EC Growth
8413	Leather, Clothes, Accessories	38.0	69.6
8614	Cameras Still, Flash App.	48.7	63.9
8310	Travel Goods, Handbags	41.7	69.4
6114	Leather Bovine nes. equine*	32.8	45.0
7143	Statistical Machines	48.4	49.3
6415	Paper, etc., in Bulk nes.*	43.7	47.8
8412	Textile Clothing, Access., Non-knit	49.7	55.4
6952	Tools nes.*	44.8	41.2
6569	Other Textile Prods.	35.9	66.9
7291	Batteries, Accumulators	48.2	52.1
7250	Domestic Electrical Equip.	48.9	69.6
8510	Footwear	41.9	52.9

Section 2
High Within EC Growth and High Non-EC Growth

SITC#	Product Category	Within EC Growth	Non-EC Growth
6575	Carpets, Knotted, etc.	61.2	48.4
6312	Plywood	50.6	43.9
7329	Motorcycles, etc., Parts	75.0	64.8
7242	Radio Broadcast Receivers	61.6	67.7
8944	Outdoor Sport Goods nes.*	57.6	53.9

8942	Toys, Indoor Games	52.6	73.6
7249	Telecomm. Equip. nes.*	70.1	60.5
8411	Textile Clothes, Not Knit	57.6	57.3
6412	Other Printing Paper nes.*	61.9	79.9
7151	Mach. Tools for Metals	66.4	45.6
7296	Electro. and Mech Handtools	55.2	59.2
8617	Medical Instr. nes.*	61.4	46.3
7221	Elec. Power Mach.	61.3	40.2
6324	Building Woodwork, Prefabs	54.0	59.4
6419	Oth. Paper, etc., nes., Bulk*	50.3	49.0
8912	Snd. Recording Tapes, Discs	68.3	50.8
7241	Television Receivers	69.0	84.0
7181	Paper, etc., Mill Mach.	60.0	69.7
5128	Or.-inorg. Compounds, etc.	58.1	63.7
5310	Synth. Dye, Nat., Indigo, Lakes	60.5	54.0
7331	Bicycles, Non-motor Parts	51.7	84.1
7115	Piston Engines, Non-air	51.4	47.4
7195	Powered Tools nes.*	65.7	41.5
7198	Oth. Mach., Non-elec.	67.4	40.8
7184	Constr., Mining, Mach. nes.*	53.1	64.1
7182	Printing, Binding Mach.	91.0	64.1
7193	Mechanical Handing Equip.	65.0	42.2
6972	Base Metal Domestic Utensils	57.8	52.3
7171	Textile Machinery	68.4	41.5
5124	Aldehyde, etc., Fnct. Cmpds.	64.5	65.9
5417	Medicaments	54.3	55.2

* nes. = Not elsewhere specified

Office machines and microelectronics are also identified in Table 12.1 as areas characterized by low import growth both from within and outside the EC. These product categories are from industries in which individual EC nations have been attempting to develop technological expertise, and have therefore been exhibiting low growth of imports from within-EC sources as well as from non-EC sources. The completion of the integration of the internal EC market will force these nations to open up trade among themselves, but may not go so far as to drop restrictions to imports from outside the Community, since further development of these industries is sought. Thus, these product categories are unlikely to experience an increase in barriers, because they are already receiving protection from outside imports.

A major exception to the analysis presented above with regard to low-growth imports is aircraft. One possible explanation for the positioning of this important product category in the low/low quadrant relates to the high year to year volatility that occurs in aircraft imports. The extremely high unit value of aircraft fosters large swings in annual imports, and 1985 and 1987 may have been years in which these imports were relatively static.

The products listed in the lower portion of Table 12.1 represent those which exhibit high within-EC import growth and low non-EC import growth. These would be products for which EC firms are already in a strong competitive position relative to outside firms and are therefore low vulnerability candidates for protectionism by a unified EC marketplace.

There are three general features that characterize the products contained in the high within-EC/low non-EC import growth category. First, there are product categories from industries that are already receiving protection: aircraft parts, ship-building, and computers. While these products may continue to be protected from outside imports, new demands for increased protection would not be expected. Second, the product categories tend to be located in industries in which EC firms have a well-established, strong competitive advantage (e.g., electrical measuring equipment, photographic equipment, and optical elements.) These products are competitive globally and would not require protection to remain competitive in the EC market, in which their internal trade is already increasing. Third, this category contains many products for which geographic proximity plays a large role in determining relative import competitiveness, and thus they would not be especially threatened by imports from outside of the EC. Examples of these product categories would be books, and nuts and bolts. Since import competition would not be expected to be particularly fierce due to the nature of these products, they would not be expected to be strong candidates for new calls for protectionism.

High Vulnerability Products

Product categories identified as having a high vulnerability to the imposition of higher EC trade barriers are presented in Table 12.2 The products listed in the upper portion of Table 12.2 represent those which exhibit low within-EC import growth and high non-EC import growth. They would be considered relatively high vulnerability candidates for increased protectionism because a reduction in outside competition could mean increased opportunities for EC firms.

The key feature of the products contained in the low within-EC/ high non-EC quadrant is that they are all from industries which have been traditionally strong in the EC (e.g., leather clothes, tools, textiles, footwear) but in which EC firms are losing competitiveness. When combined with the flourishing internal demand for these products, the decrease in EC competitiveness would support the expectation of increased demands for protectionism. Additionally, some individual EC nations' exports are especially concentrated in these industries (e.g., Spain and Italy). It would be expected that these countries would apply pressure to protect products vital to their national economic interest. Thus, these products could be especially vulnerable to the erection of a "Fortress Europe."

The products listed in the lower portion of Table 12.2 represent those which exhibit high within-EC import growth and high non-EC import growth. The industries represented by the products would be considered the battleground industries for the immediate future. EC demand for these products is flourishing from virtually all sources of imports. Many are high technology industries (e.g., telecommunications and medical instruments) which represent the basis for future EC economic ascendancy. Other product categories represent key industries in individual EC nations (e.g., machine tools in Germany). In general, the product categories in this high/ high quadrant are all strong EC industries which represent present and future overall competitiveness for the EC and which face strong global competition. One way to facilitate future competitiveness and gain market share in these battleground industries would be to protect them from outside competition. Thus these product categories appear vulnerable to the prospect of increased calls for protectionism and the erection of "Fortress Europe."

LIMITATIONS

The preceding findings should be interpreted within the context of the study's limitations, a number of which are related to the variables considered. The purpose of this study was to identify non-EC export industries that may be vulnerable to the potential adverse effects of the completion of the internal market in the EC. In doing so it considers international trade flows from within and outside the EC without incorporating other factors such as foreign direct investment. An underlying assumption is that trade and foreign direct investment are substitutes for one another, where under some circumstances trade and foreign direct investment may be complementary. That is, in the absence of barriers, foreign direct investment may stimulate subsequent intra-firm trade. Additionally the issue of trade creation versus trade diversion is not addressed. Also, the study analyzes EC and non-EC trade. It does not differentiate among the source nations of non-EC exports to the EC. A further limitation is related to the short time frame used; a factor that places limitations on the extent to which the findings can be viewed as definitive.

DISCUSSION

This study has represented an attempt to project the product categories for which EC barriers are most likely to be erected in conjunction with the formation of an integrated market. It has been postulated that the most vulnerable products will share two characteristics: (1) they will be products for which the volume of EC imports is large (operationally, $500 million); and (2) the EC demand for imports of the products from outside the Community is expanding at a rapid pace. Product categories characterized by small import volumes are not likely to have economic or the associated political power to achieve protection (although exceptions undoubtedly exist). Similarly, protection is unlikely to be granted to product categories for which imports from outside the EC are not exhibiting rapid growth, since they do not represent a threat to EC businesses.

The employment of the preceding criteria has yielded a list of vulnerable product categories that share certain characteristics. First, there are products which represent major industries in individual EC countries, but which may not be competitive by world standards. The textile industry is illustrative of this situation, since it is a prominent industry in individual EC nations, although not necessarily competitive with imports from such low-cost producers as China, Korea or Brazil. For such products there is likely to be substantial lobbying for the imposition of EC trade barriers, since domestic industries will be either jeopardized or deprived of a major share of the expanding EC market. These products are often currently protected in their home EC nation, but not in other EC nations. The expansion of protection to include all EC nations could therefore have a serious impact on non-EC producers.

The second commonly found feature of high vulnerability product categories is that several are in technology-intensive industries that many consider critical for future industrial competitiveness. Examples of such product categories include machine tools, advanced telecommunications equipment, televisions, recording equipment, and biotechnology. All of these product categories exhibit very high import growth among EC nations, from sources both inside and outside the Community. Will EC producers of such products be content to continue to share the market with foreign competitors? Will the EC believe that it is in the Community's interest to enhance the development of these industries by providing increased protection for EC producers? The answers to these questions will have serious consequences for non-EC firms currently exporting to the EC.

The study's findings indicated some "low-vulnerability" products that qualify as technology intensive, or as strong national industries that are not necessarily competitive on an international scale, or both. Examples of the former include aircraft and computers; examples of the latter include ships and steel. In most cases, these industries are already receiving a degree of protection that discourages outside imports, and it is unlikely that this protection will intensify as EC integration progresses.

CONCLUSION

How should companies in high-vulnerability industries react to this situation? From a tactical standpoint, these companies should consider strong lobbying efforts. Strategically, however, the reaction needs to consider the long-term implications associated with the potential loss of a share of the EC market if the possibility of increased barriers is realized. Non-EC companies currently involved in exportation of high-vulnerability goods to the Community are the ones that need to give the most attention to an increased manufacturing presence within the EC. They are also the firms that should most vigorously pursue the establishment of strategic alliances with EC firms that could assist in overcoming the imposition of new barriers.

This study has attempted to identify products that are most vulnerable to the erection of barriers in conjunction with "Fortress Europe." This identification is necessarily speculative and based on assumptions that may not be borne out as European integration unfolds. After all, EC officials are constantly deriding those who express concern over "Fortress Europe." Perhaps the EC will remain as open to trade from the outside as is historically the case. It is not possible for firms that are heavily involved in exports to the EC to be assured by such statements, however. They must plan for the possibility that new barriers will arise, and that their EC markets could be affected. This study has been an attempt to indicate those products most likely to be impacted by this eventuality.

Future research should attempt to assess the effects of factors other than trade. Additionally, further analyses are necessary to update the study, and to further examine the effects of economic integration in the EC throughout the period leading up to 1992 and thereafter. Economic integration is becoming increasingly important in the global marketplace as the world breaks down into three major economic blocks–Europe, the Americas, and the Asian nations (Ohmae, 1985).

BIBLIOGRAPHY

Browning, E.S. "Hills Hopes Talks Will Prevent a Protectionist 'Fortress Europe.'" *Wall Street Journal*, September 12, 1989, p. A21.

Cecchini, Paolo, with Catinat, Michael and Jacquemin, Alexis. 1988. *The European Challenge of 1992*, Aldershot: Wildwood House.

Delachaux, Francois. January/February, 1990. "The Effects of 1992 on European Business," *Business Horizons*, pp. 33-36.

European Economy: The Economics of 1992. 1988. Belgium: Commission of the European Communities, Directorate-General for Economic and Financial Affairs.

Franko, Lawrence G. 1990. "Europe 1992: The Impact of Global Corporate Competition and Multinational Corporate Strategy," *European Business Journal*, pp. 23-32.

Green, Robert and Larsen, Trina. 1985. "Evolution Toward Protectionism in the EC: An Empirical Study." *Management International Review*, 25, pp. 5-16.

Henderson, David. 1989. *1992: The External Dimension*, New York and London: Group of 30.

Lublin, Joann S. "Japanese Increasingly View Takeovers as Faster, Cheaper Way to Enter Europe." *Wall Street Journal*, July 12, 1989, p. A12.

Morrison, Catherine. 1989. *1992: Leading Issues for European Companies*, New York: The Conference Board.

Nelson, Mark M. "U.S. Is Wary of EC Import Regulations." *Wall Street Journal*, June 29, 1989, p. A1.

_____ . "Some Support in EC is Seen for TV Quotas." *Wall Street Journal*, July 10, 1989, p. B1.

Ohmae, Kenichi. 1985. *Triad Power*, New York: The Free Press.

Page, S.A.B. September, 1981. "The Revival of Protectionism and its Consequences for Europe." *Journal of Common Market Studies*.

Quelch, John A., Buzzell, Robert D., and Salama, Eric R. 1990. *The Marketing Challenge of 1992*, Reading, MA: Addison-Wesley Publishing Company.

"Renault Chief Urges Protection," *Financial Times*, March 25, 1988.

Revsin, Philip. "United Front: Europe Will Become Economic Superpower as Barriers Crumble." *Wall Street Journal*, December 29, 1988, p. A1.

_____. "Brussels Babel: European Bureaucrats Are Writing the Rules Americans Will Live By." *Wall Street Journal*, May 17, 1989, p. A1.

Riemer, Blanca. "Laying the Foundation for a Great Wall of Europe." *Business Week*, August 1, 1988, pp. 40-41.

Shanks, Michael and Lambert, John. 1962. *The Common Market Today and Tomorrow*, New York: Praeger.

Ziebura, Gilbert. 1983. "Internationalization of Capital, International Division of Labor and the Role of the European Community," in, Tsoukalis, Loukas, ed., *The European Community: Past, Present and Future*, Great Britain: Basil Blackwell.

Chapter 13

A Normative Framework for Assessing Marketing Strategy Implications of Europe 1992

Subhash C. Jain
John K. Ryans, Jr.

The European Community (EC) has embarked on an ambitious program to eliminate all remaining barriers to a true common market by the year 1992. In principle, the 12-member EC is already a single market. No national tariffs or import quotas remain, and the member nations abide by a common agricultural policy of price supports and production management. In industry, European nations have ceded substantial sovereignty to the Community. Steps have even been taken to begin to put the ECU (European Currency) into the consumer's hand.

But a variety of non-tariff barriers have continued to make the Community a less-than-fully-common market. These include differing national standards, expensive and time-consuming customs formalities, insulated capital markets, restrictive government procurement practices, barriers to services, and other restrictions. These barriers have kept the EC member countries as separate national markets. For example, it is almost impossible for German companies to sell phones to the French telecommunications monopoly, or for the Dutch to market life insurance in Britain.

The EC is determined to emerge at the end of 1992 as a single market with freedom of movement for goods, services, people, and capital. If the program succeeds, the EC will develop into a $4

This chapter was originally published in *Journal of Euromarketing*, Vol. 1(1/2) 1991.

trillion market of 320 million people (U.S. Department of Commerce, 1989). Such a 12-country amalgamation will bring the EC to a competitive level with Japan and the new U.S./Canadian axis and move the world marketplace closer to the Global Triad envisioned by Ohmae (1985). The resultant evolution toward three giant markets offers a significant challenge to both international market planners and academic researchers.

As the European partners were moving resolutely toward effecting the 1992 mandate, they were presented an additional challenge in mid-to-late 1989 with the "freeing" of Eastern Europe. Early forecasters saw Eastern Europe's rapid market economy evolution as a major impediment or even a prohibiting force in achieving European Community 1992. However, with West Germany's rapid and peaceful assimilation of East Germany and the political/economic strides by other former Eastern Block countries, from a marketer's point-of view, in fact, these new Eastern European players have simply made the overall market larger and have increased his or her strategy alternatives. To illustrate the latter, the special EC status of the Polands, Hungarys, etc., makes entry through one of these routes a viable alternative.

Considering the marketing implications of the EC alone, of course, poses a significant theoretical and conceptual challenge to researchers. In fact, a testable theoretical construct to better understand global marketing may well develop incrementally with the EC providing the first step. In this article, the authors will seek to identify the factors that need to be included in a normative model for marketing in the EC (and ultimately, a global market). Next, these factors will be arranged in a form that permits developing a series of testable research questions. Finally, a future research agenda on this global marketing issue will be proposed.

EUROPE 1992 AND MARKETING

Europe 1992 appears to offer an exciting new era of Europe-wide marketing. According to a Booz Allen and Hamilton survey, for example, a large majority of European CEOs believed they would change their management of marketing and sales more than any other function because of the harmonization (Harris, 1988). Similarly, a survey of 1200 chief executive officers of U.S. companies by the Bank of Boston showed that the majority of the respondents will change their marketing strategies as a result of the creation of Europe 1992 (Howell, 1989).

Major marketing concern vis-à-vis Europe 1992 revolves around the development of a realistic pan-European market (Onto, 1988; Ryans and Rau, 1990; Toman, 1989; and Vandermerwe and L'Huillier, 1989). Specifically, the following questions become relevant: (a) Does European unification make developing a Euro-brand a viable strategy to pursue? (b) Does a standardized marketing program after 1992 appear possible? (c) Does the marketing organization need to be structured differently in response to the Europe 1992 program?

The standardization issue itself, of course, is hardly new for marketers. Whether to standardize or customize all or part of their marketing effort has been a vexing question with which international marketers have wrestled since the 1960s. Interest in the international issue again revived in the mid-1980s. This is attributed to Levitt (1983), who argued that the worldwide marketplace has become so homogenized that multinational corporations can market standardized products and services. Since then a number of papers have been published on the subject. Walters (1986) presented an overview and evaluation of the standardization debate and provided evidence on corporate implementation of standardization strategies. Quelch and Hoff (1986) presented a framework for implementing a global approach to fit each business. Wind and Douglas (1986) outlined the internal and external factors that impinge on the standardization issue. Jain (1989) examined factors that affect marketing program standardization and established a research agenda on the standardization issue.

As Europe moves toward unity in 1992, the standardization issue becomes significant afresh. The feasibility of standardized marketing globally has often been questioned due to the existence of economic, cultural, political, and legal differences among nations. The EC market, however, is much smaller and relatively homogeneous, at least economically, when considered in the context of the entire world. In addition, with the implementation of the 1992 program, to some extent political and legal barriers that prevent marketing standardization within a regional context will be reduced.

Then, the question is: Can standardized marketing be practiced in the emerging Europe? The European situation puts the concept of standardization of international marketing strategy to a regional test. Already, in fact, the increase in European-wide satellite TV has begun to attract regional advertising (Howard and Ryans, 1989). However, if marketing standardization does not work in the post-1992 EC, it will be naive to expect its application to the world-wide marketplace.

The examination of the standardization issue with reference to Europe is important from another perspective as well. International experts (Kelly, 1988; Laird and Yeats, 1988) predict that in 25 years or so, there will be four/five major market groups worldwide such as North American market, Pacific-region market, Indian Ocean market, Mideast market, and Latin American market. The EC experience on standardization will be useful in formulating marketing strategy for other regional markets.

ASSESSING MARKETING STRATEGY IMPLICATIONS

Essentially, the events surrounding EC-92 and especially the economies of scale in marketing activities it implies, offer an unprecedented opportunity to begin to study the standardization issue and to consider the whole marketing strategy area within a regional context. Figure 13.1 offers a suggested framework for assessing marketing strategy implications of Europe 1992. There are four key imperatives that affect marketing strategy in a regional economy. These are: customer factors, business factors, corporate factors, and political factors. The first two, i.e., customer factors and business factors, combine to determine the potential of EC-wide marketing. The remaining two factors capture the readiness of the firm to adapt to 1992. The potential and readiness together ascertain the strategic thrust of the business. The marketing implications result from the strategic thrust of the business. Different variables under the four factors which influence the strategic thrust are given in Table 13.1. In the following section, each of the four factors is considered individually.

Customer Factors

The customer factors may be the single most important factor that affects the decision on EC-wide marketing (Britt, 1974; Keegan, 1969). As political and economic boundaries fall, some of the social and cultural ones may get reinforced. Just as the Americans tend to remember their ancestry because they are afraid of becoming too homogenized, there might well be a nostalgic strengthening of national ties among the Europeans. Since business-to-business marketing has been felt to be less culturally sensitive than consumer marketing, it is the latter that receives most of the concern. And, even with the latter, there is growing evidence that Europeans are starting to be less culturally heterogeneous (Peebles and Ryans, 1990). Confounding the cultural impact even more, however, is the fact that the Europe 1992 program focuses on supply rather than demand. It will make individual country markets more accessible, not more identical. Thus the established cultural, historical, institutional, and typological differences among the EC nations will undoubtedly continue to operate beyond 1992.

As noted in Table 13.1, the buyer factors involve a number of sub-factors or considerations. One is *usage patterns*. If the way the product is used or consumed is based on some cultural dimensions rather than the functional ones, it may be more difficult to Europeanize (Kotler, 1986). Consider the example of washing machines. It does not matter how they clean, Britishers prefer front loaders while the French want top loaders. Germans like lots of different settings and high spin speeds while Italians favor a slower speed (Toman, 1989). Similarly, if the customers have diverse interests that cannot be rationally supported, standardization would be difficult (Vandermerwe and L'Huillier, 1989). It will be a long time, for instance, before the French allow themselves to drink the instant coffee Britons adore. In brief, if the use of a product is based on common preferences region wide, it has the potential to be standardized.

Product image is another consideration. If the image of a product is strictly local or national, it may be more difficult to market it region-wide. *IBM* has a reputation that seems to precede its entry in business and consumer markets, while *Coca-Cola* and *Pepsi-Cola* have gained global images. *Levis* stand for comfort and good looks

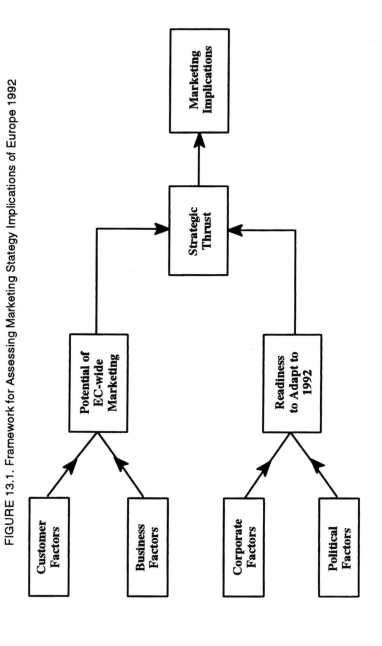

FIGURE 13.1. Framework for Assessing Marketing Stategy Implications of Europe 1992

292

and prior to *glasnost* had often been an interesting barter item in the Soviet Union; Soviet citizens often traded almost anything for a pair of *Levis* jeans. But such an image takes a long time and a tremendous investment to get established (Ohmae, 1985; Kirkland, 1988). Often, different national markets for a given product are in different *stages of market development*. However, if a mass market has evolved region-wide, the product can be marketed in its standardized form. If the *product specifications* that people value vary from nation to nation, acceptance of standardized products would be adversely affected (Boddewyn and Falco, 1988). This is a particular concern for business markets that typically rely on specifications other than emotional factors. Thus, the changes in standards that are underway in virtually every market category in the EC may provide special non-tariff barriers for many producers from outside the market. Further, products with high *national identification* may not be acceptable throughout the EC. For the Germans the "good" beer is non-pasteurized and therefore, imported beer is often out of the question. Similarly, oily Italian mayonnaise does not interest the Dutch who like it creamy (Browning, 1989). EC-wide standardization is more feasible for products for which the *communication process* involves high symbolic message and low language content. This way the impact of cultural differences vis-à-vis language differences is minimized. Finally, *customer loyalty* to their local brands discourages EC-wide marketing (Reshaping Europe, 1988).

As a result of Europe 1992, many industries are restructuring, leading to industry concentration. To illustrate, Maytag's acquisition of Hoover in the U.S. was driven by the former's desire to participate in the new European market. Such concentration reduces the number but not necessarily the level of market costs as companies vie for market share. While this will be discussed further under business factors, such concentration also implies *concentration among customers*, which is especially an issue for the business buyers. The shift to fewer, larger business customers may result in more customization than standardization, since each customer could want his or her needs to be met more precisely.

Products permitting market *segmentation* based on lifestyle or demographic differences across the new European market provide a better opportunity for standardization than those where the market

TABLE 13.1. Factors Determining Europe 1992's Effect on Marketing

1. Customer Factors

a. Usage patterns (culturally vs. functionally defined; diverse interest between users vs. concentration and/or networking of users; reflect traditional vs. new habits).
b. Product images (local vs. national vs. global market).
c. Market development (local vs. concentrated vs. mass market).
d. Product specifications (local vs. uniform).
e. National identification (high vs. low).
f. Communication process (high vs. low language content).
g. Customer loyalty (high vs. low).
h. Customer concentration (high vs. low).
i. Segmentation criterion (geographic vs. Pan-European lifestyle).
j. Parallel importing (low vs. high).

2. Business Factors

a. Scale economies (personal contact with customer necessary vs. mass communication possible; strong distribution outlets with resistance to change vs. integrated distribution network; complex channels with multiple layers vs. simple channels; labor intensive manufacturing with high variable cost vs. asset intensive with high fixed cost; low value added vs. high value added product; local sourcing vs. global sourcing; difficult to transport vs. easily transportable; stable technology vs. short life cycle; easily acquired technology vs. protected/proprietary technology; low vs. high R & D content).
b. Nature of product (tailor-made vs. commodity-like; old vs. new product).

c. Excess to distribution (local vs. universal).
d. Profit economics (cost-benefit relationship of EC-wide marketing).
e. Competitive advantage (low vs. high).
f. Product benefits (local vs. universal).
g. Industry concentration (low vs. high).
h. Emergence of new channels (low vs. high).
i. Availability of media (low vs. high).
j. Development of new media (low vs. high).

3. Corporate Factors

a. Managerial talent (country-oriented management vs. multinational experience).
b. Management orientation (risk averse bureaucrats vs. professionals).
c. Financial resources (weak vs. strong).
d. Access to outside funding (narrow/illiquid financial market vs. easy access to capital).
e. Existing commitments (low vs. high commitments to labor, stockholders, third parties).

4. Political Factors

a. Product standards (national vs. EC).
b. Media standards (national vs. EC).
c. National interest (low vs. high stakes in business because of national security or trade balances, etc.).
d. Political importance (low vs. high).
e. "Fortress Europe" mentality (high vs. low).

is segmented geographically. According to Quelch and Buzzell (1989), lifestyle segmentation is likely to become more important as EC customers begin to adopt similar behavior patterns as a result of the 1992 program. And, Walsh (1990) looks to age group differences as an important basis for segmentation in Europe. Using standardized marketing research tools, it may be possible to identify Pan-European consumer segments, which can be served with a standardized marketing program; i.e., selling standardized Euro-brands employing common positioning strategy and package design (Peebles and Ryans, 1990). Again, this is not necessarily a new concept, but is one that will be facilitated by the EC's common marketing rules. The young, the affluent and the mobile are examples of such segments. Many retailers, for example Benetton and Ikea, are serving similar consumer segments in different EC countries with a common brand name and marketing program.

With the implementation of the Europe 1992 program, border crossings should become simple and efficient. As a result, *parallel importing* could increase, although many companies are presently working hard to rationalize their distribution channels. Where parallel marketing is possible, this will make it difficult for manufacturers to charge different prices for the same product among the EC countries. For products where parallel importing is expected to be high, it will be beneficial to pursue standardized marketing.

Business Factors

The business factors deal with the economies of pursuing EC-wide common marketing strategies. The strongest case for standardized marketing strategies throughout the EC can be made based on *economies of marketing scale*. With the elimination of physical, technical and fiscal barriers, economists often think in terms of world scale plants that can manufacture standardized products at substantial savings (McClenahen and Moskal, 1989). Such savings occur due to factors such as longer and more efficient production runs of standardized products, the need for fewer stockkeeping units, a decrease in sales forecast errors, and the feasibility of doing more reliable production and logistics planning. Similarly, faster and reliable transportation of goods across country borders should make it feasible to consolidate warehouses and thus reduce distribution-related investments in the EC while improving customer service. For example, by 1992, Philips expects to save $300 million annually by reducing clerical staff, closing warehouses and cutting inventories (Tully, 1989). Similarly, Avery International Europe has cut the number of distribution warehouses from one for each country to five regional warehouses, and plans to provide the product to the customer anywhere in Europe within 24 hours (Higgins and Santalainen, 1989). Standardization will be particularly relevant for products requiring global sourcing, that are based on high R&D content, and are easy to transport across borders.

However, the largest immediate scale economies for many concerns lie with marketing. Elimination of border controls should result in cost savings in logistics and transportation. Similarly, with the relaxation of restrictions on TV advertising, economies of scale should be achievable in the promotion area. Growing recognition of the importance of satellite television as a border-crossing promotional medium should further help in undertaking EC-wide advertising efficiently (Howard and Ryans, 1989).

Studies on the subject show that standardization varies with the *nature of the product*. For example, standardization is more feasible for industrial goods than for consumer goods (Baker 1977; Boddewyn, Soehl, and Picard 1986). Further, standardization may work better for products new to the region than extending a national product to the entire region. New products representing innovative technologies may not face cultural barriers. For a variety of reasons, new products are expected to play a prominent role in the EC marketing programs. To become globally competitive the EC companies are likely to spend more on R&D to seek innovations resulting in new products. Further, companies entering the EC-wide market for the first time will find it easy to do so through new brands, designs or models. New products may make it easy to get distributors and to induce customers to switch suppliers (Quelch, Buzzell, and Salama, 1990). In addition, exporting a *strong* national brand to countries where it has been sold should be easier than a *weak* brand.

Access to distribution channels throughout the EC will be an important factor in opting for standardization. Traditionally, retailing in the EC has been fragmented and national in scope. But with the Europe 1992 program, large retailing organizations, with operations spread throughout the 12-nation area, can be expected to emerge (Cecchini, 1988). Some leading retailers, such as U.K.'s Marks & Spencer, already have an EC 92 agenda in place and are working toward it. This shift in the retailing sector, along with other middleman changes, will provide greater clout to retailers, wholesalers and agents, which, in turn, could mean greater pressure on margins and reduced power for the manufacturers (Ryans and Rau, 1990). Thus, unless a firm already has a well-formed 12-country distribution in place, access to distribution channels could be trouble-some, especially for latecomers, or for small and medium-sized producers (Mitchell, 1989).

Ultimately the decision on EC-wide marketing will be based on *profit economics*; i.e., the cost-benefit relationship of following a nation-by-nation approach versus standardization. However, the cost-benefit relationship is relevant only in the long run (Hamel, 1988). In the short-term, even with standardization, costs are likely to rise. To illustrate, prices may have to be cut to build market share, distributors may have to be provided increased promotional allowances and so on.

Europe 1992 will call into question the long-established cost and value relationships between companies, their customers, and their competitors. This could produce intense price competition in many businesses affecting the profit economics. At the same time competition will become tougher, as has already been seen in autos, white goods and tires. Standardization of marketing strategy will have to be viewed in light of such an environment. A Volkswagen Golf before taxes is 55% more expensive in Britain than in Denmark and 29% more expensive in Ireland than in Greece. A brand of chocolate bar is sold for 26% less in Belgium than in France and Germany and another for 14% less in Germany than in France (Friberg, 1989). Price differentials of this magnitude could not be sustained in a unified market even if desired by a firm, as an enormous gray or parallel market would evolve. In such a situation, in fact, a standardized product for the entire EC market may not be economically a sound decision.

Relatively, a company with a sizable *competitive advantage* will find it more feasible to pursue EC-wide marketing (Murray, 1989). The competitive advantage may consist of established brand name, weak rivals, barriers in segmenting the market, insulation against new entries, or guaranteed access to markets. Take the former, those brands in lead recognition and image positions across Europe may find their task somewhat easier.

Further, brands that provide rational, logical *product benefits* instead of purely emotional appeal offer a better opportunity for EC-wide marketing (Schultz, 1989). The focus on product benefits helps in avoiding local lifestyle differences (Vandermerwe and L'Huillier, 1989). Toman (1989) notes that a "natural" image appeals to Europe's growing band of environmentally concerned consumers, especially if the message is simple and visual. For example, Swiss Milka milk-chocolate candy bars are being successfully promoted across Europe with TV commercials showing a cow moving in a mountain meadow. The desirability of freshness and natural food sources are well appreciated Europe-wide.

The Europe 1992 program has triggered a wave of *industry concentration*. Through mergers, acquisitions, and formation of strategic alliances, companies in many industries are consolidating their position to achieve scale economies, broader distribution or even merely to become major players. In the food industry, for example, France's BSN, a major producer of food and drinks, has bought eight other European food companies since 1986, including Nabisco's European business. Pirelli, the Italian company, has bought the U.K.-based tire company; the U.S.-based Sara Lee has acquired AKLO's consumer products division and Dutch coffee producer Van Neile; and the list goes on. Standardization of marketing strategy throughout the EC appears more likely in the case of industries with high concentration. With a world-scale plant and a large market share, a new or acquired company in a highly concentrated industry will be motivated to manufacture and sell standardized products at lower prices.

The 1992 program has also triggered the *emergence of new types of channels* in the EC, such as Pan-European franchising, direct mail, telemarketing, and other nontraditional distribution channels (Quelch, Buzzell and Salama, 1990). Again, standardized EC-wide marketing may be more likely for products that can be distributed through these new types of channels, which stretch well beyond national borders.

Currently, in most EC countries, television advertising is expensive and somewhat limited in availability. And, most non-business publications' coverage is limited along national or language boundaries. However, partially driven by EC 92 and partially by technology, new community-wide advertising alternatives are now (or shortly will be) available. Presently, the Super Station, satellite television, claims 20 million households and spans the EC, as do several other satellite stations. Companies such as Goodyear International, Coca-Cola, Kawasaki, and Opel are already employing Pan-European advertising via this medium. In addition, *The European*, called Europe's first national newspaper, offers a new weekly alternative and likely serves as the forerunner for new trans-Europe print media. Such media will facilitate a standardized European marketing strategy.

Corporate Factors

Examined in this section are the company-related factors that create conditions for successful implementation of EC-wide marketing. Standardization across the 12-nation Community requires sufficient *managerial talent* capable of handling business *for the entire region* (Caulkin, 1988; Higgins and Santalainen, 1989; McClenahen and Moskal, 1989). If the managers have essentially grown up in a single country rather than having multinational experience, it will be difficult for the firm to adopt an EC-wide perspective (Murray, 1989; Ohmae, 1985).

Another relevant factor here is *management orientation* (Mitchell, 1989). It comprises such considerations as managers' attitudes toward foreigners and overseas environments, their willingness to take risks and seek growth in unfamiliar circumstances, and their ability to make compromises to accommodate foreign viewpoints (Pearce and Roth, 1988; Hunsicker, 1989). Three primary orientations toward building multinational enterprises may be considered: ethnocentric (home-country-oriented), polycentric (host-country-oriented), or geocentric (world-oriented). Standardization is most feasible if the orientation is geocentric. Geocentric orientation provides flexibility sufficient to exploit standardization opportunities as they emerge and to react to unanticipated problems within the context of the overall corporate interest (Simmonds, 1985; Quelch and Hoff, 1986).

To position itself to effectively compete in the EC market, a firm requires substantial *financial resources*; for example, to develop and fully exploit distribution channels. A financially weak organization will have to put aside the adoption of an EC-wide posture. Related to corporate financial resources is the matter of *access to outside funding*. If the financial markets are relatively opened rather than closed to the firm, standardization would be easier to accomplish.

Finally, a firm's *existing commitments* may prevent it from seeking EC-wide markets with a common marketing program. These commitments comprise specialized assets (i.e., assets highly specialized to the particular business or location); fixed costs of changing existing perspectives (i.e., fixed costs involved in developing an EC-wide standardized marketing program; such as settlement with existing distributors, maintaining service capabilities, etc.); and strategic inter-relationships (i.e., interrelationships among different parts of the firm in terms of image, marketing ability, and shared facilities) (Porter, 1980; Harrigan, 1980). To illustrate the former, many U.S. firms transferred production outside their North American home in response to the "Superdollar" of the early to mid-'80s. This commitment of resources may hinder further expenditures if they create a capacity that is excessive, or is of inadequate scale or is located "outside" the 12-country group.

Political Factors

Standardization of marketing strategy across the EC also depends on the nature and degree of EC-wide control vis-à-vis national independence on various aspects. The first of these aspects is *product standards*. At the end of 1989, roughly 750 sets of such standards have been accepted. The EC hopes to have 2000 to 3000 of them in place by the end of 1992, but that is only a fraction of the total of machines and products sold in Europe. It will take years before the remaining product standards are enacted. Some U.S. producers, for example, have established some capacity in Europe just to have more adequate access to *standards* development information, as well as some slight voice in the process. A further concern (and barrier) for food and drug firms relates to EC 92 mandated plant inspections to insure quality and the likelihood that insufficient inspectors will be available to handle facilities outside the EC.

Marketing standardization would be more feasible if a product has EC standards (Sheth, 1986). Even then, some countries may resist certain *foreign* products and the issue of local content is significant, as we will see later. In Holland, for example, national health standards still rule out France's *baguette* bread loaf, judged lacking in nutrition. Chances are the European court ruling (assuming the French bring the matter before it) will force Holland to accept the imported bread. But such settlements may take years (Thimm, 1989).

Further, an enormous amount of work remains in standard setting for industrial goods, the largest and by far the most important class of products. Besides, the EC only sets basic health and safety standards. Beyond that, producers have to settle on industry standards–making sure that an Italian industrial robot will actually work when plugged into a Spanish auto assembly line or that a boiler inspected in Greece will be cleared for use in Denmark. In summary, where the EC and industry product standards have been enacted and finally accepted, marketing standardization throughout the EC appears practical.

Another aspect is *media standards*. The lack of availability of media because of restrictions on TV advertising in many EC countries has, until now, been a major problem. With the anticipated homogenization of laws relating to advertising in the EC, the overall availability of media should increase. As far as ad copy is concerned, language and other cultural differences will continue to discourage standardization. Interestingly, as Ryans and Rau (1990) mention, many companies are experimenting with commercials that are used across Europe with only the voice-over changed. As a matter of fact, some of the satellite networks have experimented with programming in a single language; i.e., English, which may eventually emerge as a link language across the EC.

It must be noted that the EC efforts at present are limited to the harmonization of general media standards, leaving member countries to keep their specific rules, which are abundant. For example,

Saatchi and Saatchi advertising agency prints a 52-page book listing the basic broadcast and print rules. The alcohol section alone runs into seven pages. Ireland forbids TV ads for spirits but allows beer and wine commercials–as long as they do not run before 7 p.m. Spain allows commercials only for drinks with less than 23% alcohol content, and only after 9:30 p.m. (Toman, 1989). Such local rules are likely to prove an irritant to companies planning to employ marketing standardization.

Standardization across the EC will also be affected by the extent of *national interest* at stake in a business. If standardization is likely to lead to dislocation of resources, particularly resulting in substantial unemployment, the government may step in to prevent it in the name of national interest. This is particularly true in such industries as steel and airlines in which European governments maintain major ownership. Similarly, for national security reasons a business may be discouraged from seeking a common EC-wide perspective. Related to national interest, yet slightly different, is the matter of *political importance* of the business. A firm may be provided large public subsidy or favorable tax treatment to develop itself as a Euro-champion (Vernon, 1989). Likewise, political shrewdness might prompt an active hand on the part of government through bending rules and regulations for select businesses and thus discourage standardization.

Perhaps the most significant marketing standardization barrier for many non-European firms considering the post-January 1, 1993 market is the much-discussed *fortress Europe mentality* often evidenced by Community officials and corporate executives. Rumors and speculation still prevail regarding the likelihood that the EC would ultimately employ severe local content rules and other non-tariff barriers to impede the access of non-EC firms relying primarily on export (to the EC) to serve the enlarged market. Such politically-activated uncertainty would undoubtedly prevent most non-EC firms from employing a marketing standardization strategy until the matters are clearly resolved.

Similarly, the EC has wrestled with the public procurement issue; i.e., the "right of access" to the national/local government markets question, and has yet to have it fully resolved. As in North America, the government procurement markets are sizeable for many consumer and business-to-business products, especially the latter. Virtually all the EC countries have traditionally given their local companies preferential treatment (or even a virtual monopoly) on government contracts. In the process of redefining the European marketplace, this was one of the most sensitive areas of negotiation. Since national sensitivity, country-of-origin and local content concerns abound, the firm seeking to employ a standardized marketing approach could potentially be creating unnecessary culture-related concerns. The temptation to employ standardization here, of course, lies in the fact that the various governments will generally be seeking the same product benefits, especially for business-to-business products, and will have well-defined product standards established. What may be expected are EC procurement rules that permit all Community companies, as defined by some local content limitation, to bid on any national/local government contract with the proviso that local producers have some potential slight price advantage.

Marketing Implications

The customer factors and the business factors combine to determine the potential of EC-wide marketing with standardized strategies. The corporate factors and the political factors focus on a firm's readiness to adapt to Europe 1992. The potential and the readiness capture the influence of European integration on marketing strategy (Figure 13.1). Together they determine the strategic thrust of the business. Three likely strategic thrusts could be: Euro-global, multi-focal, and locally responsive. *Euro-global* refers to the central decision on strategy, and the central management of resource commitments across national boundaries in the pursuit of a strategy. *Multifocal* is defined as centralized management of geographically dispersed strategies and activities required to implement these strategies on an ongoing basis. And finally, the term *locally responsive* refers to defining strategy in response to primarily local competitive or customer demands, and letting resource commitment decisions be managed autonomously by country managers; a system that has been popular in the pre-1992 European marketplace.

The strategic thrust serves as the summary measure of marketing strategy being employed in response to Europe 1992. Thus, a Euro-global business would be expected to choose to introduce Euro-brands, follow standardized marketing strategies that would have Euro-wide appeal, and regionalize marketing decisions. On the other hand, the locally responsive business likely would follow strategies (and tactics) which are the reverse of the Euro-global business. Typically, businesses in which there are no meaningful economies of scale or proprietary technology fall into this latter category. The need for significant local adaptation of products due to cultural differences and/or differences in distribution across national markets may also justify local responsiveness. Multifocal businesses, as a compromise among extremes, should experience a slow, evolutionary movement toward introducing one or more Eurobrands, in pursuing standardized marketing strategies, and in centralizing resource commitments.

In conclusion, the European integration program affects different businesses in different ways. Over the long run, each business will be more or less susceptible to it; but the effect for each kind of business will occur in its own distinctive fashion and at its own unique speed. Where the potential and readiness, discussed above, are high (for example; in the case of Euro-global businesses), the marketing impact is current and deeper. Where they are low (for example, in the case of locally responsive businesses), the implications will appear slowly, if at all (e.g., depending on how cultural changes diminish). Perhaps the real challenge for international marketing managers is to understand the impact of Europe 1992 on multifocal businesses, and to act on that understanding.

TOWARD A RESEARCH PROGRAM

Overcoming the limitations of the current international marketing literature is essential if marketing is to increase its global relevance. Research on regional market integration vis-à-vis Europe 1992 should incorporate, at a minimum, three major points:

- The development of conceptual frameworks or taxonomies to enable researchers to better understand the evolutionary process of homogenization of customer demand that has begun to occur in the regional market and to more clearly identify the fragments that will remain the domain of the cross-border niche markets.

- An examination of the impact that market integration has had on both intra-market firms and global firms. Has, for example, the integration led to the number of mergers and acquisitions that one would anticipate as a result of efforts to achieve scale economies in marketing and production?
- The generation and testing of hypotheses related to the impact of market integration on various types of products, promotional aspects, and channel arrangements.

The above focal points set the boundaries of major marketing concerns in the context of regional market integration. Each research focus can lead to a variety of specific projects. Illustrated below are the types of research that can be undertaken in each delineated area.

Development of Conceptual Frameworks

An important outcome of regional market integration is the emergence of a large market and a concomitant emphasis on achieving economies of scale. In fact, the major impetus for the EC was a desire to create an environment in which European companies could achieve a competitive scale comparable to that of U.S. and Japanese producers. From marketing's perspective the makeup of this market is significant. For example, after 1992, the EC will represent a market of some 320 million European consumers, the world's biggest and richest single market. But will this be a homogeneous market? In the short run, the answer is "no." But in the long run cross-border lifestyles should develop. Customers will go through an evolutionary process to begin losing their cultural bonds and start sharing common traits. They begin to exhibit similar desires, fulfilling them with similar goods and services. There will, however, be interesting cross-border niches that will be identifiable (and exploitable) from the outset. These are likely to initially be seen in rather traditional demographic clusters with the major differences being that the clusters will no longer be national-border-bound (Walsh, 1990; Vandermerwe and L'Huillier, 1989). It will be the homogenization process, of course, that will ultimately be most important for a true European consumer marketplace.

How does this evolutionary homogenization process work? Can

this process be characterized by stages? What factors highlight each stage? What factors strengthen/weaken the evolution toward homogeneity? What role is technology expected to play in this process? Which products and services are more likely to be affected early on to offer opportunities for region-wide standardized marketing? Can this evolutionary process be applicable to ASEAN countries? the newly proposed South American common market? other regions of the world?

To encourage the proper development of marketing theory for regional economic integration, it is crucial at the outset to develop a framework in which the basic terms and concepts such as evolution, homogeneity and culture are rigorously and consistently defined. To date, most theoretical discussion of economic integration has centered on the concepts relating to economies of scale and to economic integration as a means of achieving economic development. While the latter has been most appropriate for the developing nations, it is the former that was highlighted in the Cecchini Report, which was commissioned by the EC itself (Cecchini, 1988). Marketers, however, will be particularly concerned with the questions raised above and wish them incorporated in any viable framework.

Market Integration and Competition

Nations integrate regionally for their own good and the Cecchini Report suggested an average increase of 4.5% to EC G.D.P. (Cecchini, 1988). Toward this end they strengthen their firms to be competitive both inside and outside. The thrust of Europe 1992 is to make Europe more competitive. Larger and more open markets for U.S. and other foreign goods is merely a by-product of the process, not an objective. Many interesting research questions related to competition require inquiry. How do the integration efforts galvanize inside firms to become more competitive? What regulatory measures strengthen the competitive position of insiders, and what measures weaken the outsiders? What strategies may outsiders adopt to continue to be viable? In what industries is competition expected to be fierce? What factors will influence success?

The new strength of the firms within the integrated market is likely to equip them to compete well outside their home market as well. Thus the EC firms will become a major factor in the global market, competing against the U.S. and Japanese firms. In this light, how will global competition be altered? Will, in fact, the EC businesses respond to the opportunity provided by the EC 92 initiative or will it be the foreign-based firms that most fully exploit the new market?

A variety of marketing strategy concerns become relevant here. In what kind of product/market do global firms lead? What survival strategies can local firms adopt? In what way can niche marketing help? Finally, how can companies from Third World countries and the Eastern European nations compete globally? What is already evident is the ever increasing numbers of mergers and acquisitions, and in some industries the number of players is now quite concentrated. What this will mean to future marketing strategy needs to be examined.

Generation and Testing of Hypotheses

In addition to understanding the dynamics of customer and competitive environments, research programs are needed to gain insights into the effects of European market integration from the perspective of the 4 Ps. Such research programs should focus on the generation and evaluation of various hypotheses, assessing the likely impact of market integration on different aspects of the marketing mix.

Already, many of the building blocks are in place, as much of the research related to advertising standardization, the product life cycle and country of origin appear useful as starting points. However, the range of the hypotheses that might be developed is limited only by the creativity of the researchers. Such research will go a long way in the accumulation of substantive marketing knowledge globally, enriching the field of international marketing. A few of the most basic questions are given below:

- To what extent can the EC serve as a regional test for the globalization strategies that have been proposed by Levitt and others?
- In segmenting the EC market, what U.S. experience may be applicable to the EC in both consumer and industrial goods?

- On what basis can inter-market segments be formed within the EC (e.g., based on age–teenagers; based on occupation–professionals; based on lifestyle–cosmopolitans)?
- What is the value of pursuing the EC-wide standardized marketing strategies as separate from the globalization issue?
- What organizational changes and innovations are required to accommodate the power shift from country to region (i.e., emergence of European regional headquarters as the power base)?
- How does the emergence of large retailing and large distribution in general affect marketing strategies at the level of manufacturer, especially with reference to promotion logistics and price strategies?

Last but not the least important is the question of the impact of market integration on society. While, in terms of economics, market integration appears to be highly beneficial, are there any ill effects (e.g., on disadvantaged consumers) that fall within the realm of marketing? Comparative studies on societal effects of a large market among the U.S., Japan and the EC will be useful.

As these research questions suggest, the range of issues has both micro and macro elements and has firm, industry and public policy implications. As the research in this field progresses, it is expected that the general framework presented in this paper will give rise to a more detailed and developed body of theory on regional-market marketing strategy. Studies can be undertaken in a number of industries and the relative strengths of the background variables as predictors of appropriate marketing strategy can be asserted in each industry. Moreover, interactions between the potential of EC-wide marketing imperatives and readiness to adapt to 1992 imperatives are much more extensive than have been examined in this paper. These interactions need to be uncovered and examined to increase understanding of the effects that potential and readiness have on each other.

CONCLUSION

By December 31, 1992, corporations from the U.S., Japan, and other developed nations were closely following the events surrounding the single European Market. Clearly, the market opportunities created by the European Community are as dramatic as the statistics suggest; i.e., over 300 million people with a collective "buying power" that exceeds or matches the U.S. and Japan in most consumer and business-to-business categories. The "fallout" in terms of change in global markets as nations react to this new regional marketplace has been equally impressive. Certainly, the new North American Free Trade Association (U.S., Canada and Mexico) planning can be directly attributed to a desire to counter the European agenda, and the proposed Latin American alignment, featuring Argentina, Uruguay, Paraguay and Brazil, appears to be EC driven.

Adapting to the 12-country market is a concern for European firms as well as those outside the Community. In fact, a record number of joint ventures, acquisitions and critical alliances have occurred among European producers and many industries have become increasingly concentrated.

In this chapter, a taxonomy for non-EC producers has been suggested that will assist in their adapting to the new Europe. As with any proposed framework, considerable research will be needed to test the propositions that it engenders. However, this taxonomy is based on a foundation of a prior experience with economic groups, the trans-European research that has been conducted to date and the perspectives offered by knowledgeable academics and practitioners familiar with the European area.

At a minimum, the taxonomy identifies the critical factors that non-EC firms need to consider as they prepare to enter the EC or to restructure existing national market organizational structures to allow for the anticipated change. And, of course, the opportunity is present to test Levitt's globalization views on a regional basis. It is expected, however, that the conceptual framework will stimulate propositions and hypotheses as well as research designed to test them. In the decades ahead, few events are likely to precipitate more structural change in global markets than EC 92 and the response of other nations to it. To date, the framework has been applied in a large division of a *Fortune 500* firm. Most of the recommendations developed by the use of the taxonomy are now being implemented at the firm. Yet, this is, of course, not a true validation of this conceptual framework and further development and extensive testing are required. Thus, the opportunity for (and need for) significant scholarly international market research is apparent. The research agenda proposed here provides a place to begin, but additional work on the theory and practice of regional market integration, and further probing of market implications of Europe 1992 are needed.

BIBLIOGRAPHY

Baker, B.A. (1977). "International Marketing Standardization," A Presentation to European International Business Administration Annual Meeting, December: 1-21.
Boddewyn, Jean J. and Joseph John Falco. (1988). "The Size of the Market Sector Around the World," *Journal of Macromarketing*, 8 (Spring): 32-42.
Boddewyn, Jean J., Soehl, Robin and Picard, Jacques. (1986). "Standardization in International Marketing: Is Ted Levitt in Fact Right?" *Business Horizons*, 29 (November-December): 69-75.
Britt, Stewart H. (1974). "Standardizing Marketing for the International Market," *Columbia Journal of World Business*, (Winter): 39-45.
Browning, E.S. (1989). "Sticky Solutions: As Europeans Try to Set Product Standards, A Jar of Jam Becomes a Pandora's Box," *The Wall Street Journal* (September 22): R8.
Caulkin, Simon. (1988). "Ford Tunes Up Europe," *Management Today* (UK), 25 (July): 38-44.
Cecchini, Paolo. (1988). *The European Challenge*. Aldershot, U.K.: Wildwood House Limited.
EC 92: Growth Markets (Washington, DC: U.S. Department of Commerce, 1989): 7.
Friberg, Eric G. (1989). "1992: Moves Europeans Are Making," *Harvard Business Review*, 67 (May-June): 85-89.
Hamel, Gary. (1988). "1992 in a Global Context," *Multinational Business* (UK), 3 (Autumn): 1-8.
Harrigan, Kathryn Rudie. (1980). "The Effect of Exit Barriers Upon Strategic Flexibility," *Strategic Management Journal*, 1:165-176.
Harris, John M. (1988). "1992 Harmonization: A Survey of European Chief Executives," *Outlook*, 12 (no date): 39-47. (A publication of Booz Allen & Hamilton Inc.)
Higgins, James M. and Santalainen, Timo. (1989). "Strategies for Europe 1992," *Business Horizons*, 32 (July-August): 54-58.
Howard, Donald G. and Ryans, John K., Jr. (1989). "The Probable Effect of Satellite TV on Agency/Client Relationships," *Journal of Advertising Research* (December/January): 43.

Howell, James M. (1989). *U.S. Manufacturing Firms' Attitudes Toward 1992*. Boston: Bank of Boston.

Hunsicker, J. Quincy. (1989). "Strategies for European Survival," *The McKinsey Quarterly*, 25 (Summer): 37-47.

Jain, Subhash C. (1989). "Standardization of International Marketing Strategy: Some Research Hypotheses," *Journal of Marketing*, 53 (January): 70-79.

Keegan, Warren J. (1969). "Multinational Product Planning: Strategic Alternatives," *Journal of Marketing*, 33 (January): 58-62.

Kelly, M. (1988). *Issues and Developments in International Trade Policy*. Washington, DC: International Monetary Fund.

Kirkland, Richard I., Jr. (1988). "Entering a New Age of Boundless Competition," *Fortune*, 117 (March 14): 40-48.

Kotler, Philip. (1986). "Global Standardization–Courting Danger," *Journal of Consumer Marketing*, 3 (Spring): 13-15.

Laird, S. and Yeats, A. (1988). *Quantitative Methods for Trade Barrier Analysis*. Washington, DC: The World Bank.

Levitt, Theodore. (1983). "The Globalization of Markets," *Harvard Business Review*, 61 (May-June): 92-102.

McClenahen, John S. and Moskal, Brian S. (1989). "Europe 1992: The Challenge to U.S.; Unprepared for '92," *Industry Week*, 238 (April 3): 78-88.

Mitchell, David. (1989). "1992: The Implications for Management," *Long Range Planning*, 22 (February): 32-40.

Murray, Edwin A., Jr. (1989). "Entry Strategies for Europe 1992," a paper presented at a conference of The Planning Forum in Boston, October 17, 1989.

Ohmae, Kenichi. (1985). "Managing in a Borderless World," *Harvard Business Review*, 67 (May-June): 152-161.

Onto, John. (1988). "Maintain Your Market Share: Strategies for Success in Post-1992 Europe," *Export Today*, 4 (November-December): 12-17.

Pearce, John A., II and Roth, Kendall. (1988). "Multinationalization of the Mission Statement," *Advanced Management Journal*, 53 (Summer): 39-44.

Peebles, Dean M. and Ryans, John K., Jr. (1990). *Management of International Advertising*. Boston: Allyn & Bacon, 231.

Porter, Michael E. (1980). *Competitive Strategy*. New York: The Free Press, 20-21.

Quelch, John A. and Hoff, E.J. (1986). "Customizing Global Marketing," *Harvard Business Review*, 64 (May-June): 59-68.

Quelch, John A. and Buzzell, Robert D. (1989). "Marketing Moves Through EC Crossroads," *Sloan Management Review*, 31 (Fall): 63-74.

Quelch, John A., Buzzell, Robert D. and Salama, Eric R. (1990). *The Marketing Challenge of 1992*. Reading, MA: Addison-Wesley Publishing Co.

"Reshaping Europe." (1988). *Business Week* (December 12): 48.

Ryans, John K., Jr. and Rau, Pradeep A. (1990). *Marketing Strategies for the New Europe: A North American Perspective on 1992*. Chicago: American Marketing Association.

Schultz, Don E. (1989). "New Directions for 1992," *Marketing Communications*, 14 (March): 28-30.
Sheth, Japdish. (1986). "Global Markets or Global Competition," *Journal of Consumer Marketing*, 3 (Spring): 9-11.
Simmonds, Kenneth. (1985). "Global Strategy: Achieving the Geocentric Ideal," *International Marketing Review*, 2 (Spring): 8-17.
Thimm, Alfred L. (1989). "Europe 1992–Opportunity or Threat for U.S. Business: The Case of Telecommunications," *California Management Review*, 31 (Winter): 54-78.
Toman, Barbara. (1989). "Now Comes The Hard Part: Marketing," *The Wall Street Journal* (September 22): R10.
Tully, Shawn. (1989). "The Coming Boom in Europe," *Fortune*, (April 10): 108.
U.S. Department of Commerce (1989), Unpublished Report, Washington, DC.
Vandermerwe, Sandra and L'Huillier, Marc-André. (1989). "Euro-Consumers in 1992," *Business Horizons*, 32 (January-February): 34-40.
Vernon, Raymond. (1989). "Can the U.S. Negotiate for Trade Equality," *Harvard Business Review*, 67 (May-June): 96-101.
Walsh, Doris L. (1990). "Six European Trends for the Nineties," *Market: Europe* (August): 1.
Walters, Peter G. (1986). "International Marketing Policy: A Discussion of the Standardization Constructs and Its Relevance for Corporate Policy," *Journal of International Business Studies*, 17 (Summer): 55-69.
Wind, Yoram and Douglas, Susan P. (1986). "The Myth of Globalization," *Journal of Consumer Marketing*, 3 (Spring): 23-26.

Chapter 14

European Marketing: Future Directions

Pervez N. Ghauri
Erdener Kaynak

After 1992, business everywhere faced a new set of opportunities and threats due to the changing picture of Europe. The tremendous changes taking place in Europe due to the unification of the EC and due to the liberalization of Eastern and Central Europe would force public policy makers as well as the private sector to change gears in regard to their economic and trade policies. For about 40 to 50 years, the U.S. has been dictating the rules of trade and politics on the world scene; now, especially after 1992, it is Europe's turn to write the rules of trade and politics in the world. The Pacific century notion of trade will convert itself into Atlantic century trade where countries on both sides of the Atlantic ocean will dominate world trade. In this bilateral trade relationship, the importance of Europe will accelerate substantially.

The coming years will be a contest between an Anglo-Saxon recession and economic growth of German and Japanese economies. The German and Japanese investments will pull the economies of the rest of the world. This has already been experienced through a high bankruptcy rate in banking and industrial sectors, in spite of the decline in interest rates. This undesirable situation is creating a prolonged recession in the U.S. and other Western countries. The war in the Persian Gulf and its end has not helped much in the improvement of the Western economies, especially the American economy. The world has gradually been transferred from a single polar economic world centered around the U.S. to a three-polar economic world centered around the U.S., Japan, and the EC.

The next 50 years or so are definitely considered as Europe's age of economic challenges and opportunities. In spite of the transition period, German integration would stimulate European growth. The effects of German reunification are already emerging (see, for example, Table 14.1). The liberalization of Eastern Europe provides enormous opportunities. For Europe, it is not the time for diminishing expectations, it is the time for economic opportunities, or as put by Schumpeter: the time for "creative destruction" (Thurow, 1991).

At present, there are signs that the EC would also include EFTA countries such as: Austria, Finland, Sweden, and Norway. Although EFTA countries are already enjoying some benefits through the 1973 free trade agreement between the EC and EFTA, these countries and some countries from Eastern Europe, such as Poland, Hun-

TABLE 14.1. Impact of German Unification on the Growth Rate of the Other Member Countries.

	Memorandum items 1990		Impact on rate of growth in % points per year	
	Share of exports to Germany in total exports (%)	Share of exports in GDP (%)	1990[1]	1991
BLEU	19.8	75.3	+0.6	+1.0
Denmark	18.2	35.1	+0.4	+0.7
Greece	25.1	23.4	+0.2	+0.4
Spain	11.1	17.7	+0.3	+0.5
France	18.7	23.4	+0.4	+0.7
Ireland	12.2	63.5	+0.3	+0.8
Italy	17.4	20.6	+0.3	+0.6
Netherlands	28.1	56.4	+0.7	+0.9
Portugal	15.8	37.3	+0.3	+0.4
United Kingdom	12.7	24.8	+0.2	+0.5
EUR 11	12.8	28.0	+0.4	+0.6

[1]Second semester, in yearly terms.

Source: European Economy, Annual Economic Report 1991-1992 Brussels, December 1991, p. 8.

gary, and Czechoslovakia are expected to join the EC in one way or another in the near future. Two of those countries, Poland and Czechoslovakia, have already applied for EC membership. There is also an increasing expectation that the national boundaries might disappear in Europe but regional boundaries might emerge. The regional block-building might cause weakening of national economies and as a result nation states. Therefore, there is a strong motivation to prevent bilateralism and regional block-building.

It is also seen that EC must help Eastern Europe to succeed in its economic reforms. It is necessary to open doors for Eastern Europe for mutual benefits. This might lead to an enlarged EC or the formation of an outer ring attached to the EC; the countries in this outer ring might enjoy some benefits of the EC in the same manner as EFTA countries are doing today (see Figure 14.1).

THREATS AND OPPORTUNITIES BEYOND EUROPE 1992

Much has been said on threats and opportunities associated with 1992 in the previous chapters. However, beyond 1992, the companies would find it easier to do business in the European market. The obstacles, in the shape of different standards and rules and regulations, are being removed. Most of these rules and regulations were formed by national governments to protect their home markets and local firms from outside competition. The companies thus, do not have to adapt to different and unnecessary standards. The EC would also lead to rather healthy competition, at least within Europe, as the governments would not have to protect their own industries by unnecessary and heavy subsidies to agriculture, textile, telecommunication, and other local industries.

State subsidies have always been a threat to free competition because they reduce the welfare for consumers by preventing the most efficient resource allocation. Basically, state subsidies have the same effects as tariffs and other protective measures. The EC's second survey on state subsidies showed that these are at an unacceptably high level (Table 14.2). The EC is striving to weed out these unjustifiable and anticompetitive state subsidies, which disturb the market mechanisms and free competition (Ehlermann, 1991). In the community, there will be great benefits for consumers

FIGURE 14.1. Enlarged Europe Beyond 2000

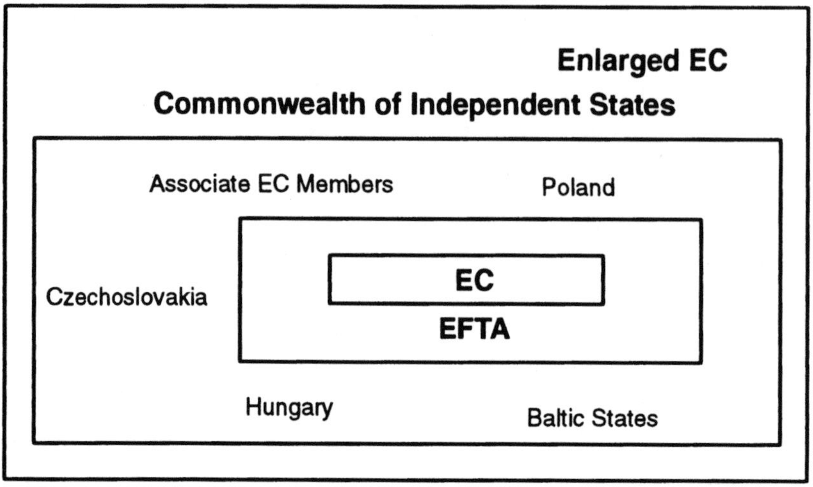

```
┌─────────────────────────────────────────────────────────────┐
│                                          Enlarged EC          │
│        Commonwealth of Independent States                     │
│   ┌───────────────────────────────────────────────────────┐  │
│   │  Associate EC Members              Poland              │  │
│   │        ┌────────────────────────────────────────┐      │  │
│   │        │            ┌──────────────────┐         │      │  │
│   │ Czechoslovakia      │       EC         │         │      │  │
│   │        │            └──────────────────┘         │      │  │
│   │        │                EFTA                     │      │  │
│   │        └────────────────────────────────────────┘      │  │
│   │          Hungary                                        │  │
│   │                                     Baltic States       │  │
│   └───────────────────────────────────────────────────────┘  │
└─────────────────────────────────────────────────────────────┘
```

with a wide variety of products and goods available to all of them. The firms, however, would have to compete harder and thereby would be forced to spend their resources on R&D and innovations, and to become more efficient. In other words, the most efficient firms would survive and prosper–the real essence of full competition.

Mergers and Acquisitions

The 1992 target date has already triggered a number of mergers and acquisitions. The firms are striving to gain economies of scale and efficiencies. For example, in 1989/1990, more than 350 national, 315 within-EC, and 165 involving the EC and an outside country, mergers took place. In the industrial sector the number is 622 where 36% of the companies involved had a combined turnover of more than 5 billion ECU. Of these mergers, 40% were exceeding the range of 5 billion ECU. This means that the EC and especially 1992 would greatly influence the structure of industries, not only in the EC but also in the rest of the world. The EC, contrary to the U.S. anti-trust policies, is not against mergers and acquisitions and it considers these activities as a necessary path towards efficiency

TABLE 14.2. State Aids in the European Community[1]

(average 1986-88)

| | As % of GDP | As % of public expenditure | Granted in the form of: | |
			public expenditure (%)	tax expenditure (%)
Belgium	3.2	5.8	89	11
Denmark	1.0	1.7	100	0
Germany	2.5	5.3	36	64
Greece	3.1	6.5	100	0
Spain	2.3	5.5	100	0
France	2.0	3.8	82	18
Ireland	2.7	5.2	63	37
Italy	3.1	6.2	64	36
Luxembourg	4.1	7.6	91	9
Netherlands	1.3	2.1	70	30
Portugal	2.3	5.3	41	60
United Kingdom	1.1	2.6	94	6

[1] *Refers to subsidies that are subject to Community rules. The total of subsidies granted is difficult to establish due to the various forms which subsidies can take and the lack of comprehensive national data.*

Source: European Economy, Annual Economic Report 1991-1992, Brussels, December 1991, p. 20.

(Ehlermann, 1991). However, the EC has shown some concern that mergers that lead to less diversity, choice, and unhealthy competition, should be controlled. Thus, some regulations on the control of mergers has been in operation since September 21, 1990.

The increasing number of takeovers and mergers can be understood as panic reactions by firms which are afraid of the future or as a chance for consultants to make money. The problem is that the EC wants to achieve two contradictory gains. First, it encourages firms to merge so that they can achieve economies of scale and efficiencies, and second, they do not want to create very large companies which can enjoy a dominant/monopoly position and thereby can abuse this position against smaller companies, consumers, and society at large. Finding a balance between the above two is the main problem. Article 86 of the Treaty of Rome clearly states:

> Any abuse by one or more undertakings of a dominant position within the common market or a substantial part of it should be prohibited as incompatible with the common market in so much as it may affect trade within its member states.

The EC has in fact already exercised its power to control such mergers and takeovers. For example, in 1973 Continental Can, a large can manufacturer, acquired majority shares in Schmalbach-Lubeca-Werke AG of Brunswick, a German producer of metal containers. It also acquired a large Dutch producer, Thaassen & Drijfer-Verblifa. At this point the EC intervened, arguing that the company already had a dominant position in the EC and after acquiring the Dutch manufacturer the competition would be disturbed. However, this intervention was not really successful, as the court of justice was not convinced this takeover would create a "dominant" position for the company. The company could thus materialize the takeover of the Dutch manufacturer (Richardson, 1989).

A surprise merger (March 1992) between UK's Midlands Bank and the Hong Kong and Shanghai Banking Corporation created a major new force in European banking. The merged entity would have more than 100,000 employees and ECU 210 billion of assets, and would rank among the world's 10 largest banks.

Opportunities

There has been a lot of discussion on the EC and on 1992. One view has been that no one actually believes that the problems have been resolved by January 1, 1993: "The wrangling will continue for some time, but as the community nears 2000 the benefits of this programme will become progressively more apparent" (*The Economist* Intelligence Unit, 1989, p. 3). At this time, however, most people believe that a lot is going to happen. There will be an internal market for the EC countries where we would have free movement of goods, services, capital, and labor. Moreover, the countries outside the EC would have to adapt new policies and strategies to cope with economic and political development across the continent. The Cecchini report that came out in 1988 containing 6000 pages, pointed out advantages and disadvantages of a single market. According to this report the firms would have to adapt their strategies to new realities coming in force. It claims that over a period of 5-6 years we would get the following macroeconomic advantages:

1. An increase in GNP between 4.5-6.5% for EC countries.
2. Around six percent lower prices for consumers.
3. Baltic State financing by 2.2% of GNP.
4. A reduction in unemployment ratios and creation of approximately 2 million new jobs.
5. Increased international trade.
6. Economies of scale.
7. Increased rate of innovations.

According to this report it is not only the EC countries but also all the countries of the world that would be influenced positively, as international trade would increase. There will be less bureaucracy, more liberal financial services, and standardization of rules and regulations.

Major objectives of the EC include: a single market for EC countries, reduced unemployment, economic and social integration, and reduced inflation. Although many scholars doubt that the EC would achieve much in these aspects, there are studies which calculated that it is possible to realize these kinds of benefits from a single market.

The standardization of standards for different products would bring about rather homogeneous consumer tastes, not only within the EC but also in other countries, as non-EC countries would rather quickly bring their own standards and technical norms into line with the EC norms and standards. It is not only the consumers who would benefit from this standardization of norms and standards. The manufacturers and their distributors would also become nearer to each other because of this standardization and because of the decrease in geographical and psychological distance due to the channel tunnel between England and France and a bridge between Sweden and Denmark. These changes would physically link the continent together.

As far as telecommunication is concerned, Europeans are already viewing the same standardized media channels such as satellite TV. It is already allowing companies to gain economies of scales as far as advertising and other consumer services are concerned. Companies like Nike, Reebok, automobile manufacturers, etc., are already making great use of these facilities. Telecommunication is an area where the major part of EC investments are going; the Community's telecommunication industry accounts for 31% of the total world production (U.S. 33% and Japan 17%). There are plans for a Europe-wide cellular telephone network, which has already started running. Now a person who has bought a mobile phone in Amsterdam can use the same phone and number in Frankfurt, London, and Oslo. The Scandinavian countries are already the heaviest users of cellular telephones, as shown by Table 14.3.

Threats

There has also been a discussion on "Fortress Europe" and whether it has been defined and completed by January 1993. Moreover, how far it would become a "fortress" and what would happen to inward investments has been a great concern. Japan and other non-EC countries such as Sweden have been trying to get in through direct investments in EC countries. An interesting aspect here is how competitive would it be? Whether outward investment and trade from the EC would also be influenced or not is contingent upon a number of factors. The EC is already losing world market share in manufacturing products such as electric goods, automobiles, and hi-tech industries. The EC manufacturers have acceptable market shares within the EC market, but how are they faring in markets outside the EC: the fast-growing Asia, Eastern Europe, the U.S., and North Africa? Although there have been increases in imports (trade) within the EC in products such as food, beverages, and tobacco, there are several other products such as electronics, office equipment, automobiles, industrial machinery and equipment, aerospace and other transport means where imports from outside the Community have increased.

The "Fortress Europe" has mostly been used as a negative term, meaning that the EC is creating a market of 325 million well-to-do people who want to protect themselves from other parts of the

TABLE 14.3. Cellular Radio Subscribers in Europe, June 1989

Country	Subscribers	Population (million)	Penetration (per 000)
Austria	44,250	7.60	5.82
Belgium	21,200	9.90	2.14
Cyprus	690	0.56	1.25
Denmark	112,830	5.20	21.70
Finland	131,610	4.80	27.42
France	135,870	55.50	2.45
Iceland	7,280	0.24	30.33
Ireland	7,570	3.50	2.16
Italy	46,850	57.20	0.82
Luxembourg	400	0.37	1.08
Netherlands	43,400	14.50	2.99
Norway	161,230	4.20	38.39
Portugal	1,400	10.5	0.13
Sweden	295,500	8.40	35.18
Switzerland	51,540	6.00	8.59
UK	650,000	56.60	11.48
West Germany	123,980	62.00	2.00
TOTAL[1]	1,857,080	345.32	5.38

Source: European Mobile Communications
Note: [1] Includes others

world, mainly Asia and North America. Moreover, it can strengthen its bargaining power to obtain raw materials and other primary products, and in the General Agreement on Tariffs and Trade (GATT). In other words, the united Europe would have a discriminatory behavior towards other nations, outside the EC. As mentioned earlier, it would also become inaccessible to outsiders. To avoid this situation, the outsiders have started investing heavily in EC countries. In 1987, Japan invested about $2.4 billion only in England and in 1989 Toyota invested $1.2 billion in a car plant in England. The scene is somewhat similar with investments from the U.S. England is attractive to the U.S. and Japan because of the language and cheap labor, while Sweden is investing in Denmark. The "Fortress Europe" however, might have its worst effects on the third world countries (Goodman, 1990).

Another burning issue is why are the unemployment figures not coming down in the EC countries? A comparison with the U.S. shows that between 1979 to 1988 unemployment in the U.S. has decreased from 5.8 to 5.3%, although it rose to 9.7% in 1982 while figures for Europe for the same period have been almost constantly increasing (see Table 14.4). It is important to note that over the last ten years the working age population (15-64) has increased at the same rate in Europe and the U.S. (Makridakis). One explanation is that a combination of social and demographic factors, and restructuring of economies/industries is leading to a "mismatch" between the supply and demand for labor.

TABLE 14.4. Duration Structure of Unemployment (as % of labor force)

	Unemployed less than 6 months	Between 6 & 12 months	Over 12 months	Total
France				
1979	2.7	1.5	1.8	6.0
1983	2.8	2.1	3.5	8.4
1987	3.6	2.2	4.8	10.6
West Germany				
1979	2.0	0.7	0.7	3.3
1983	3.7	1.8	2.7	8.2
1986	3.8	1.6	2.7	8.0
UK				
1979	2.7	0.7	1.1	4.5
1983	4.7	2.4	4.1	11.3
1987	4.0	1.9	4.4	10.4
USA				
1979	5.3	0.3	0.2	5.8
1983	7.3	1.0	1.3	9.6
1987	5.3	0.4	0.5	6.2

Source: The Economist Intelligence Unit, London 1990, p. 169.

The problem is, however, that without knowing the real cause and nature of this "mismatch," it is difficult to introduce policies which would bring down the unemployment figures. Flangen (1988) explains the unemployment problem in Europe as one of hiring: that European employers are reluctant to employ new/more workers. Therefore, there are more vacancies today in Europe while the unemployment rate is the same as in the previous years. Moreover, it leads to long-term unemployment; the longer a person has been unemployed the more difficult it is for him or her to find a job as illustrated by Table 14.4.

The table shows that in most cases long-term unemployment is a high proportion of the total unemployment in Europe while it is not the case in the U.S.

Unemployment is not the only problematic issue in EC. Different economic growth and inflation performance in different EC countries might also create problems in regard to standardization and movement of labor and capital. Table 14.5. shows economic growth statistics for EC countries. We can see that it ranges from 5% for Spain to 0.3% for Denmark. The table also illustrates the trend from 1982-1988, showing how the economic growth has developed in different countries. For example, if we look at economic growth in Denmark which has moved from 3% (1982) to 0.3% (1988), the benefits of joining the EC are highly questionable in Scandinavia, especially in Norway. Another problem is the inflation rate in different EC countries. Table 14.6 shows inflation performance of EC countries. Here we can see that the annual average percentage change in consumer price varies from 13.6% in Greece to 0.7% in the Netherlands. Trade among countries and movement of investments can be influenced due to these differences, at least in the short-run. In addition to these issues there are several other hidden aspects, not yet put forward, which force many scholars to ask the question, is the Community a tower of Babel (Goodman, 1990)?

The Community has nine official languages: English, Dutch, French, German, Greek, Italian, Portuguese, and Spanish, entailing a financial and personnel burden. All meetings would need simultaneous translations and minutes of meetings and other documents in nine languages. These translations into or out of a language are creating an enormous extra burden on the Community and its bud-

TABLE 14.5. Economic Growth (% annual average change in real gross domestic product)

	1982	1983	1984	1985	1986	1987	1988
Belgium	1.5	0.1	2.0	1.4	2.8	1.8	2.3[a]
Denmark	3.0	2.5	4.4	4.2	3.3	−1.1	0.3[a]
France	2.5	0.7	1.3	1.7	2.3	2.3	3.6
Greece	0.4	0.4	2.7	3.1	1.2	−0.5	3.5[a]
Ireland	2.3	−0.2	4.2	1.6	−0.4	4.1	2.5[a]
Italy	0.2	0.5	3.8	2.9	2.9	3.1	3.7[a]
Luxembourg	1.5	2.0	5.5	2.9	2.0	2.5	3.0[a]
Netherlands	−1.5	1.4	3.1	2.4	2.3	2.5	3.0[a]
Portugal	3.2	−0.3	−1.6	3.3	4.3	4.7	3.0[a]
Spain	1.2	1.8	1.9	2.2	3.3	5.2	5.0
UK	1.8	3.7	1.7	3.8	3.2	4.3	4.3[a]
West Germany[b]	−1.0	1.9	3.3	1.9	2.3	1.8	3.4

a Estimate. b Gross national product.
Source: *The Economist* Intelligence Unit, London 1990, p. 169.

get. We can imagine how many translations and office facilities are required for such an operation. In spite of a number of meetings to reduce the number of official languages, there is no hope for such a decision. Moreover, we have a number of countries, with new languages, waiting at the door such as Finland, Turkey, Sweden, and Norway. Would the number of languages be twelve instead of nine? Up to now the Community has been successful in restricting a number of its events and meetings to two languages: English and French. There is, however, a great resistance from other members. It will be interesting to see how Germany would react once it is done with its integration problems.

EUROPE BEYOND 1992

As predicted by the Cecchini report, there are already some positive signs in regard to control of inflation within the Community. Membership in the European Monetary System (EMS) is proving to

TABLE 14.6. Inflation Performance (% annual average change in consumer prices)

	1982	1983	1984	1985	1986	1987	1988
Belgium	8.7	7.7	6.3	4.9	1.3	1.5	1.4[a]
Denmark	10.1	6.9	6.3	4.7	3.6	4.0	4.6[a]
France	11.8	9.6	7.4	5.8	2.7	3.1	2.7
Greece	21.0	20.2	18.5	19.5	23.0	16.4	13.6
Ireland	17.1	10.5	8.6	5.5	3.9	3.2	2.1[a]
Italy	16.5	14.7	10.8	9.2	5.9	4.6	5.0
Luxembourg	9.3	8.7	4.6	4.1	0.3	−0.2	2.0[a]
Netherlands	5.9	2.8	3.3	2.2	0.2	−0.5	0.7
Portugal	22.8	21.5	28.9	19.6	11.8	9.3	9.6[a]
Spain	14.4	12.2	11.3	8.8	8.8	5.2	4.8
UK	8.6	4.6	5.0	6.1	3.4	4.1	4.9
West Germany	5.9	3.3	2.4	2.2	−0.2	0.2	1.2

[a]Estimate
Source: *The Economist* Intelligence Unit, London 1990, p. 197.

be beneficial to full member countries. The European Monetary System (EMS) is designed to eradicate market instability in Europe. It is a very simple mechanism to provide monetary stability, eliminating uncertainty in the marketplace. The idea is to fix the values of EC currencies against each other within certain bands and to force central banks to abide by these values and bands through buying and selling currencies. The currencies involved are linked through an exchange value mechanism, which would drive the Community towards European Monetary Union (EMU). However, the turbulence in financial markets in the latter half of 1992 has made the EMS rather ineffective. Countries such as England, France, Sweden, and Norway left the EMS and let their currencies float free.

The European Currency Unit (ECU)

Each country in the EMU has an exchange rate against the ECU, weighted according to the respective strength of the currencies. The ECU has four functions:

1. A denominator of the EMU.
2. An indicator of differences in currencies from their central rates within the EMS.
3. A unit of account for the international mechanisms of the EMU.
4. An instrument of settlements and exchange between different central banks in the EC.

In this mechanism, each currency has a bilateral exchange rate with each other. There are some limits on how weak or strong a currency can be as compared to the central rate. These bilateral central rates are given in Table 14.7.

The rates are also constrained through bilateral limits against other currencies. We can see from the table that Spanish Peseta has been the strongest currency within the system since 1989. The provided stability in exchange rates is due to the fact that a consistently weak or strong currency can be revalued by agreement of all the central banks. At present, ten out of 12 EC countries are members of the EMU. Greece and Portugal are not members. The biggest advantages with the EMU are that it stabilizes the exchange rate fluctuations, facilitates exports and imports among member countries, and, as there are no or very little risks involved in trade, it is easier and stimulates economic growth.

In the prewar era the European currencies competed severely with each other, as governments kept on devaluing their currencies to increase their exports. As a result, when more and more countries started devaluing, other governments became more and more protectionist and created trade barriers for imports to avoid this development. The Bretton Woods agreement was signed in 1944, which established fixed exchange rates. However, this system broke down in 1972, and a new mechanism called "Snake" was introduced in the same year. It was based on 2.25% currency bands, but it did not work as countries could not stay within their trading bands. In March of 1979, the EMS was introduced as an agreement between the central banks of EC countries. It is more efficient than the Bretton Agreement and Snake as it is also related to the ECU and the European Monetary Cooperation Fund (EMCF) which issues

TABLE 14.7. Exchange Rates to the ECU (as of September 16,1991)

Belgium and Luxembourg Franc	42.330
Danish Krone	7.917
German Deutchmark	2.051
Greek Drachma	227.490
French Franc	6.985
Dutch Guilder	2.312
Irish Punt	0.767
Italian Lira	1535.000
Portuguese Escudo	179.950
Spanish Peseta	128.590
UK Pound Sterling	0.703

ECUs to central banks in exchange for deposits of gold or other reserves. EMCF works as a European Central bank.

The usefulness of the EMS is very much discussed, as it links the EC countries' currencies which automatically links their economies with each other. It means that their inflation rates, interest rates and economic growth rates are linked and thereby dependent on each other. Although it is difficult to measure the effects of this mechanism, they are quite apparent. For example, Table 14.8 illustrates, taking just one indicator (inflation), what a significant convergence there has been after the EMS was introduced.

Another issue which is discussed widely is that the currency bands to which currencies are tied are artificial and limit the ability of different governments to develop their own policies regarding monetary issues. However, EC members who have joined the EMS are quite positive and hold that stable currencies make trade easier. It also expresses a commitment from member states towards the EC as a whole.

The Composition of the ECU

The ECU is a basket of EC currencies composed of a specific amount of each currency in proportion to the economic strength of EC members. This is illustrated by Table 14.9.

TABLE 14.8. The EMS and Economic Convergence: The Inflation Example

THE EMS AND ECONOMIC CONVERGENCE: THE INFLATION EXAMPLE

Italy
UK
France
Germany

The left-hand scale shows headline inflation rates in absolute percentage terms.

UK's entry into ERM Oct 1990

Start of EMS March 1979

Source: *The European*, September 20-22, 1991, p. 22.

330

In 1989 the president of the EC proposed a three-stage process to achieve a European Monetary Union:

1. All European currencies should be linked to the EMS, and they should trade between 2.25% bands against each other and against the ECU.
2. After all EC countries are committed to the ECU, currency bands would be narrowed and a European central bank (Eurofed, as it is known at this time) would begin to operate.
3. Currencies of EC countries would be locked together without any bands of fluctuations. Eurofed would design European monetary policies and the ECU would become a Pan-European currency.

If we look back, stage one has already been completed. However, although all EC countries are members of the EMS, Portugal and Greece are not members of the EMU. In October 1990, it was decided in Rome that the second stage should begin on January 1, 1994. In fact, there already does exist a European central bank on paper.

We should also realize that the more the EC is adapting the measures contained in the 1985 White Paper (which set out a time limit and agenda for the Single Market Program at the end of 1992) the more benefits are accruing for members. In other words, the adaption of measures have a cumulative effect, and achievement of 75% of measures is not giving 75% of the benefits; it is giving much more. Scholars in the U.S. have calculated that 1992 would regularly add 0.25% to 1% to EC annual growth. It might provide the EC with 2.25% to 10% every ten years.

When we talk about Europe, we should keep in mind that it is a continent with 10.5 million square km area and about 675 million people. Economically the different countries might consider themselves as one continent, but culturally and politically the countries are far away from each other. However, an interest for economic cooperation has always been there. European history is full of economic cooperations and political conflicts. The Second World War and its effects brought a new Europe, where this economic cooperation among nations disappeared and two major powers, the U.S. and the Soviet Union took control over Europe, and a new boundary line between East and West Europe emerged.

TABLE 14.9. Composition of the ECU

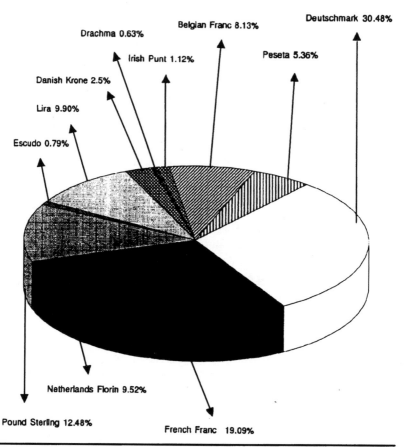

Source: *The European,* September 20-22, 1991, p. 22.

Later we have also experienced a division of western Europe in the form of EFTA and the EC. Moreover, we have also experienced efforts to unite these two parts of Western Europe, at least as regards to economic cooperation through the European Monetary System. In more recent years the liberalization of Eastern and Central Europe and the independence of Baltic States has opened up new dimensions to Europe and its economic cooperation. There should not be any doubts that Europe as a whole is heading towards an economic and political integration.

The map of the EC is definitely going to change immediately after 1992. East Germany has already been automatically incorporated in the EC; next is Austria and the Nordic countries, especially Sweden, Norway and Finland, and even Switzerland. The recent changes in Eastern and Central Europe would also influence the outlook of Europe. The independence of Baltic States is already bringing them nearer to the EC and to Nordic countries in particular.

MANAGERIAL IMPLICATIONS

To a member of European Managers, the unified market looks uneven and untidy. These managers believe that "social dimensions" of doing business in Europe are more ambiguous than ever. The European Company Statute is proposing measures for cross-border mergers which would force employers to choose among three different models of worker participation. One is a two-tier board system, based on the German "Mitbestimmung" approach, where workers in companies with more than 1,000 employees would "elect" half of the company's advisory board. The second model is the Benelux-style, where employee representatives, independent of company boards, receive reports on financial performance and should be consulted in advance of board meetings. The third alternative involves more traditional collective bargaining to arrive at a mutually acceptable system of representation (Friberg, 1989).

Other than these managerial problems, it is quite difficult to predict precisely how doing business in Europe would change after 1992. However, a price competition is inevitable, as at present there are enormous price differences in industries such as chemicals, consumer packaged goods, financial services, and automobiles. A Volkswagen Golf (before tax) is 55% more expensive in Britain than in Denmark and 29% more expensive in Ireland than in Greece. Different tax rates in different countries can make the price differences even more dramatic. However, it is important to realize that the post-1992 EC does not mean that differences which exist between different countries would disappear. For example, Table 14.10 illustrates some of the differences which prevail in the gro-

TABLE 14.10. The West European Retail Market in 1988

	Population (mn)	Retail Sales Total (ECU bn)	Food (ECU bn)	Sales per person Total (ECU)	Food (ECU)	Retail outlets Total ('000)	Food ('000)	Persons per food outlet No.	Sales per food outlet (ECU '000)
Belgium	9.9	34.8	16.9	3,519	1,708	113.7	35.4	279	562
Denmark	5.1	17.7	10.2	3,442	1,987	41.7	15.1	340	675
France	55.8	207.6	82.2	3,724	1,474	418.2	134.3	415	612
W. Germany	61.1	233.0	66.7	3,810	1,090	415.0	95.8	638	696
Greece	10.0	17.6	11.2	1,759	1,123	171.5	63.6	157	176
Ireland	3.5	7.1	3.2	2,017	907	31.5	11.5	308	278
Italy	57.4	182.3	100.4	3,176	1,749	871.3	312.0	184	322
Luxembourg	0.4	1.4	0.7	3,750	1,842	3.7	1.1	336	636
Netherlands	14.7	39.3	15.8	2,670	1,071	156.2	43.7	337	362
Portugal	10.2	18.8	11.1	1,838	1,083	97.5	45.0	227	247
Spain	38.9	81.9	41.9	2,107	1,076	540.0	268.5	145	156
UK	57.1	156.9	58.7	2,750	1,028	345.4	98.4	580	597
Total	324.1	998.4	419.0	3,081	1,293	3,205.7	1,124.4	288	373

Source: "Retailing in Europe" (1990), published by The Corporate Intelligence Group Ltd.

Notes: (1) Estimates are for 1988 sales and have been adjusted to exclude motors and fuel.
(2) 'Food' in the above analysis includes drink but so far as is possible excludes tobacco.
(3) The number of outlets is based on the latest year for which data are available.
(4) ECU exchange rates have been taken as the Eurostat 1988 annual average.

334

cery retailing business in different countries. The table illustrates that Germany has the highest number of retailing outlets per capita and highest level of sales per outlet. The annual expenditure on food per person varies from a low of 907 ECU in Ireland and 1,028 ECU in UK to a high of 1,842 in Luxembourg and 1,987 ECU in Denmark. In regard to market structure the actual number of food outlets varies from 1,100 in Luxembourg to 312,000 in Italy (Gary and Nathan, 1990). In recent years there has been consolidation of power by retailers across Europe to boost their buying power further. This trend toward further concentration would increase after completion of the unified Europe. This particular trend will not only affect consumer goods companies, it will also have an impact on the producers of industrial goods and services who supply them as illustrated by Table 14.11 (Mazur, 1991).

The main impact of 1992 would, however, be on the production and processing of grocery items/products. Due to centralization, it is expected that the industry would restructure through mergers and

TABLE 14.11. European Retail Market, 1989

	Population (mn)	Total retail sales[a] ($ bn)	Sales per person ($)	Total retail outlets[b] ('000)	Persons per outlet
France	56.0	253	4,518	418	134
West Germany	62.0	273	4,403	415	149
Italy	57.7	278	4,818	871	66
Spain	39.1	107	2,737	540	72
UK	57.2	215	3,759	343	167

[a] Estimates are for 1989 sales and have been adjusted to exclude motors and fuel.

[b] Number of outlets based on the latest year census data for separate fixed retail businesses.

Source: Laura Mazur, "Marketing 2000—Critical Challenges for Corporate Survival," *The Economist* Intelligence Unit, Special Report No. 2126, London 1991, p. 16.

acquisitions and a central production unit would emerge to achieve economies of scale.

The countries would have to approximate the VAT and excise duties. In some countries, for example in Sweden, Norway, and Finland, there are enormous VAT and duties on products such as tobacco, beer, and spirits. The standardization of VAT and duties seems impossible. However, two levels/types of duties can be established. A lower one for food and necessities and a higher one for luxury and non-essential products. We do not, however, foresee a general rush of grocery products between EC countries, mainly because the customers are already used to their national brands and standards and it would take a long time for a new brand to develop a position in a new market. Especially in Nordic countries concentration in grocery retailing has resulted in a small number of large retailing organizations which dominate their national markets. For example, in Sweden there are only three main retailers which are vertically integrated both backwards and forwards. The intense competition between a small number of big dominating retailers makes entry into these markets by a newcomer rather impossible.

Although it is difficult to forecast the patterns of competition, the managers cannot just sit and wait for these new realities to emerge. The forward-looking managers from different countries are thus quite active in influencing these emerging new patterns. Italian companies such as Benetton, Fiat, and Olivetti are focusing on lower distribution costs and effective logistics. Germans are very much labor-cost aware and are making investments in Eastern Europe, while British companies are also working hard to achieve efficiencies. Most of the industries in Europe are fragmented and need restructuring; developments described in earlier chapters of this volume reveal that both companies and national governments are working to reduce this overcapacity.

Electrolux, for example, has closed or reorganized every factory it has acquired over the past ten years. At present it is manufacturing front-loading washing machines only in Pordenone, Italy, all top loaders in Revin, France and all microwave ovens in Luton, England. In the telecommunication industry, for example, for central-office telephone exchanges, there are 11 companies for an 8 billion dollar European market, while in the U.S. there are only four companies (Friberg, 1989).

The restructuring of industries and economies of scale would allow the companies to spend more resources on research and development. To achieve these economies of scale and R&D advantages even big companies like ASEA (Sweden) and Brown Boveri (Switzerland), AT&T and Italel, as well as a number of banks and insurance companies are merging or forming strategic alliances. These alliances need not influence European marketing, but are necessary for general international competition. Alliances between Delta Airlines and Lufthansa, SAS and Thai Air, SAS and Texas Air are typical examples. The EC, with its regulations and the larger companies are actively working to homogenize the tastes of European consumers. There are huge economies of scale to gain in advertising through satellite television and companies like Benetton and Gucci, as well as beverage and cosmetic producers, are already benefitting from this.

Table 14.12 presents the types of strategies available to EC as well as non-EC country companies to cope with an integrated European market. Here we can see which alternative strategies are available for different companies. This also explains recent mergers and alliances between EC and non-EC country companies.

Speed, in regard to innovation and new product development, has also become much more important. Now one has to introduce a product almost at the same time at home and in other countries. It is not that the product life cycle thinking has become absolute, but that product life cycle of products and new ideas has become so short. At the same time investment in new product development has increased.

These changes and an integrated market have thus created a new manager: a manager without any nationality, perhaps a European or global manager. It was not too long ago when all the managers of Philips subsidiaries were Dutch. Now it is quite common that their top manager in Canada is a German, in Brazil a Norwegian, and in France a Swiss. The situation has been quite similar in Swedish firms. Not only are the managers in international operations different, but even the members of management boards come from different countries.

TABLE 14.12. Firm Strategies Toward the Single European Market

Headquarters location	Current position	Alternative strategies	Comments
EC Companies	Single country focus	• Consolidate domestic market position through mergers, acquisitions, alliances	• Vulnerable to large European competitors
		• Identify local market niches and tailor products/ services to local needs	• Vulnerable to lower-priced standard Euro-products
		• Sell out to an expanding pan-European company	
		• Become a pan-European company by identifing a specialized customer segment with common needs throughout Europe	
		• Become an OEM supplier in multiple markets to pan-European companies	
	Pan-European	• Fill in gaps in European product market portfo-lios (via acquisitions, alliances) to create a more strategically balanced pan-European company	• Sales of many so-called pan-European companies are today weighted heavily to-ward the headquarters country market
		• Develop European plan in context of global strategy	• Avoid European myopia as markets be-come more global

Non-EC Companies	Weak EC representation	• Consolidate domestic market position	• Stronger European competitors will attempt further penetration of non-EC markets
		• Establish alliances with EC firms (especially for mutual distribution of products)	• Easier to penetrate multiple EC countries with trade barriers removed
		• Sell out to EC firm expanding overseas	
		• Establish initial or additional offices and manufacturing plants within EC before 1992. Acquire or invest if large company; joint venture if small company	• EC protectionism, local content, and reciprocity requirements may impede exports into EC after 1992
	Strong EC representation	• Fill in gaps in European product/market portfolios to become even more strategically balanced	• Already see EC as one market—need to consolidate further as EC companies develop same perception

Source: John A. Quelch and Robert D. Buzzell, 'Marketing Moves through EC Crossroads', *Sloane Management Review*, Vol. 31, No. 1, 1989.

We have also seen privatization of several industries in Europe, such as telecommunication, and these private enterprises are no longer favoring their local suppliers. In the case of British Telecom, we have clearly seen orders going over to non-British companies, e.g., Ericsson. It is, therefore, more and more the companies who compete and not the countries. The companies have to be better, cheaper and faster in providing benefits to their customers. They can no longer learn from their experiences as there are no second chances.

The competition between the three blocks is becoming more and more severe. Table 14.13 illustrates the main economic indicators of the three blocks. The Japanese have already started talking about a future scenario where the United States will be the granary of the world, and would supply food to the rest of the world. The Far East would produce and supply hardware to the world and Europe will be the cultural museum and playground.

If we look at the performance of European companies in the last decade, we are tempted to believe the above statement. For example, the combined result of the 100 largest companies in Europe, excluding oil companies, showed a profit of zero percent. However, the performance of all the blocks have been rather weak and over the years 1990 and 1991 the Community has had to operate in an increasingly unfavorable economic climate. After peaking in 1988 at around 4%, the growth of world output, excluding the EC, has been going down and was near 0% in 1991. The growth in the volume of world trade (excluding the EC) has declined even more, from a rate in excess of 7% in 1988 to less than 2% in 1991. Real GDP, compared with domestic demand and world trade in the three blocks is presented in Table 14.14. This means that the previous assessment of the economic outlook has been clearly too optimistic (Euromonitor, 1990).

In light of the foregoing discussion, we can state that a unified Europe of 1992 offers both opportunities as well as threats for the companies of Europe and overseas countries. To be able to be least affected by this transition, companies need to prepare strategic working plans and programs. This planned approach should be implemented in view of the two scenarios available to decision makers within which they have to work.

If the EC allows as many members as possible, for example,

TABLE 14.13. Main Economic Indicators, 1989-1993 (Community, USA, and Japan)

(a) GDP at constant prices[1]
     (annual % change)

	1989	1990	1991[2]	1992[2]	1993[2]
Belgium	3.9	3.7	1.3	2.25	2.5
Denmark	1.2	2.1	1.8	3.0	3.25
Germany	3.3	4.7	3.3	2.25	1.75
Greece	2.8	−0.3	0.7	1.25	2.0
Spain	4.8	3.7	2.5	3.0	3.25
France	3.6	2.8	1.3	2.25	2.5
Ireland	5.9	5.7	1.3	2.25	2.75
Italy	3.2	2.0	1.1	2.0	2.5
Luxembourg	6.1	2.3	3.0	3.5	3.5
Netherlands	4.0	3.9	2.3	1.25	2.0
Portugal	5.4	4.0	2.0	1.75	2.0
United Kingdom	2.2	0.8	−1.8	2.0	2.75
EC	3.3	2.8	1.3	2.25	2.5
USA	2.8	0.9	−0.4	2.0	2.25
Japan	4.9	5.6	4.6	3.5	3.5

Source: European Economy, Annual Economic Report 1991-1992, Brussels, December 1991, p. 20.

most Eastern and Central European countries as well as all EFTA countries, there is a great risk that it becomes too big and bureaucratic to achieve any efficient decision making. On the other hand, if it remains somewhat smaller, say at the most around 15 countries, the objectives of the EC and its benefits are easier to achieve. Another implication of these two scenarios is that if only EFTA countries like Austria, Finland, Norway, Sweden, and Switzerland are allowed in, the standard of living of a combined EC will be much higher and the rules and regulations (e.g., for pollution and other issues) will be higher in order to effect a better quality of life, as standard of living and rules regarding pollution, etc., are higher

TABLE 14.14. Real GDP, Domestic Demand, and World Trade (annual % change)

	1981-85	1986-89	1990	1991[1]	1992[1]	1993[1]
			GDP			
World (excluding EC)	2.6	3.8	1.8	−0.2	2.1	3.1
USA	2.9	3.5	0.9	−0.4	2.1	2.2
Japan	3.9	4.4	5.6	4.6	3.5	3.5
EC	1.5	3.2	2.8	1.3	2.2	2.4
			Domestic demand			
USA	3.7	3.0	0.5	−1.0	2.1	2.1
Japan	2.9	5.6	5.8	3.4	3.7	3.7
EC	0.9	4.2	2.9	1.1	2.2	2.6
			World trade			
World imports (excluding EC)	3.0	6.0	3.0	1.8	5.1	6.1
German imports	1.6	6.1	11.4	12.8	5.0	4.7
EC imports[2]	2.0	8.8	4.7	2.5	5.2	5.5
			Current account (% of GDP)			
USA	−1.2	−2.8	−1.6	−0.1	−0.7	−0.6
Japan	1.9	3.2	1.2	1.5	1.6	1.7
EC[3]	−0.1	0.5	−0.2	−0.8	−0.9	−0.8

1 Economic forecast, autumn 1991.
2 EC excluding Germany
3 EC including unified Germany from 1991 onward

Source: European Economy, Annual Report 1991-1992, Brussels, December 1991, p. 9.

in these countries than in the EC. On the other hand, if other countries, such as Turkey, Poland, Hungary, and Czechoslovakia are included, all these standards and consequently the standard and quality of life, as a whole, will be much lower. The ultimate action will hinge upon what kind of a market and society EC countries would like to see in Europe beyond 1992.

BIBLIOGRAPHY

Boddewyn, J.J. and Hansen, D.M. 1977. "American Marketing in European Common Market," *European Journal of Marketing* (11), pp. 548-563.
Cecchini, P. 1988. *The European Challenge 1992*, Wildwood House.
de Chernatony, L. 1991. "Prospects for Grocery Brands in The Single European Market." A study prepared for the Coca Cola Retailing Research Group Europe.
The Economist Intelligence Unit. 1989. European Community: Economic Structure and Analysis; London.
Ehlermann, Claus-Dieter (1991), "Competing to Win," *European Affairs*, 5:2 (April) :63.
Euromonitor. 1990. *Europe in the Year 2000*, Euromonitor Publication Ltd., London.
The European, September 20-22, 1991, London, p. 22.
European Economy, Annual Report 1991-1992, Brussels, 1991.
Flangen, Robert J. Autumn 1988. "Unemployment as a Hiring Problem," OECD Economic Studies No. 11.
Forsell, Leif. 1991. Regional Politikk i EF, Universitetsforlaget, Oslo.
Friberg, Eric. May-June 1989. "1992: Moves Europeans are Making" *Harvard Business Review*, pp. 85-89.
Gary, D.A. and Nathan, H. 1990. "Grocery Retailing and 1992," A study prepared for the Coca Cola Retailing Research Group Europe.
Goodman, S.F., 1990. *The European Community*, Macmillan: London.
Magee, J.F. May-June, 1989. "1992: Moves Americans Must Make," *Harvard Business Review*, pp. 78-84.
Makridakis, Spyros G. 1991. "Single Market Europe: Opportunities and Challenges for Business," Jossey-Bass Publishers, San Francisco and Oxford.
Mazur, L. 1991. "Marketing 2000 Critical Challenges for Corporate Survival," The Economist Intelligence Unit, Special Report 2126, London, pp. 15-16.
Richardson, G. 1989. "EC Attitudes Towards Mergers and Acquisitions," in *European Community*, Vol. 2, pp. 32-38.
Stone, Nan. May-June 1989. "The Globalization of Europe: An Interview with Wisse Dekker," *Harvard Business Review*, pp. 90-95.
Strøm, Bjorn. 1991. Veien til EØS fra OEEC til EØS, Universitetsforlaget, Oslo.
Thurow, C.L. April/May 1991. "Europe Will Write The Rules of Trade. In The 1990s, Europe Will Set The Economic Agenda" in *European Affairs*, Vol. 5, No. 2, pp. 30-33.
Vernon, R. May-June 1989. "Can The US Negotiate for Trade Equality?" *Harvard Business Review*, pp. 96-101.

Index

Page numbers preceded by "f", "n", or "t" represent pages containing a figure, footnote, or table.

Acquisitions. *See* Mergers and
    acquisitions
Act VI. *See* Company Act, The (Act
    VI).
Act XXIV. *See* Investments by
    Foreigners in Hungary Act
    (Act XXIV)
Advertising
    agencies, 102-103
    communications and, 151-153,
        293
    pan-European campaigns of,
        150-151,t151,153-154
    positioning in, 154
    public relations, sales promotion
        and, 154-155,165
    television media and, 102,103,
        152-153,158-159,176,297,
        299-300,302
Aircraft industry
    airline mergers in, 95,337
    national interest in, 303
    protectionism in, t276,280
Aldi retail chain, 79
Artificial fibers industry, 38
ASEA-Brown Boveri merger, 8,337
Association Act, The, 210-211
AT&T, 337
Austria
    cellular radio subscribers in, t323
    cultural, geographical proximity
        growth strategy and, n167
    European Community (EC)

        membership of, 59,333,341
    European Free Trade Association
        (EFTA) membership of, 5-6,
        t6,316
Automotive industry
    Minimum efficient technical scale
        (METS) and, 38-40
    price comparisons in, 37,298,333
    protectionism in, 270-271
Avery International Europe, 297

Balassa, B., 86
BASF, 60
Bayer, 60
Beck, Tamas, 211
Belgium
    cellular radio subscribers in, t323
    economic growth statistics in, 325,
        t326,t341
    European Community (EC)
        membership of, 58,t59,60,61
    European Currency Unit (ECU)
        and, t329,t332
    food, beverage retail market
        statistics in, t334
    food industry cooperative
        agreements in, 95
    inflation statistics of, t327
    state subsidies in, t319
Benelux, n167
Benetton, 100,296,336
BMW, 99

345

Bond (U.S. joint venture company),
    f242,243-250,t245-246,f249,
    261-262
Bretton Woods Agreement
    (exchange rates), 328
Britain. See United Kingdom
British Telecom, 340
Brown Boveri Company
    (Switzerland), 8,337
Bulgaria
    joint ventures in, 209,t212
    marketing affected by economic
        factors in, t201,202,203
Business firm
    advertising by, 300
    commitments of, 301
    competitive advantages of,
        298-299
    distribution channel access and,
        297-298,299
    economies of marketing scale and,
        296-297
    financial resources of, 301
    industry concentration and, 299
    internal environmental changes
        affecting, 94-95
    management talent, orientation of,
        300-301
    product benefits and, 299
    product standardization and, 297
    profit economics and, 298

Campbell Soup, 150
Capitalism, xxvi
Carrifaur retail chain, 79
Cecchini Report, 91-92,t92,101,270,
    321,326
Central European trading bloc
    Hungary membership of, 5-6,t6
    trading links of, xxix-xxx,
        5-6,t6,30
Central Planning Bureau (CPB)
    (Netherlands), 91-92,t92,101

Clothing and textiles industry
    expected developments in, 92,t93
    minimum efficient technical scale
        (METS) affecting, 38-40
    protectionist policies in, 271,275,
        t276-279,281,283
Coca-Cola
    advertising standardization and,
        154,300
    product standardization and,
        40,99,291
Cockfield, Lord, 87
Colgate-Polmolive, 150
Comecon. See Council for Mutual
    Economic Assistance
    (Comecon)
COMETT. See Community Action
    Programme in Education for
    Technology (COMETT)
Commission White Paper of 1985.
    See European Community
    commission
Common Agricultural Policy, 68
Commonwealth of Independent
    States, 185-186
Communications
    advertising and, 151-153,293
    distribution improvement and, 157
    telecommunications, 32,217,
        t278-279,281,322,t323
Community Action Programme in
    Education for Technology
    (COMETT), 29
Company Act, The (Act VI),
    206,210-211
Competition. See also Price
    Competition
    low-cost, narrow geographic scope
        strategy of, 43-44,f44,f47,
        49-50,f51
    low-cost, broad geographic scope
        strategy of, 44,f47,49-50,f51
    differentiation, broad geographic
        scope strategy of, 45,f47-48,
        49-50,f51

differentiation, narrow geographic
scope strategy of, 46,f48-49,
49-50,f51
European Community commission
policy of, 18
generic competitive strategies,
96-97
pricing and, 36-37,81,96-97,101,
148-150,t149,165
product differentiation strategy
and, 42,96-97
state subsides affecting, 317-318,
t319
tariff removals affecting, 36-37,
f39
technical barriers affecting, 38
Completing the Internal Market
(European Community
Commission), 57,63,66,273
key steps outlined in, 87
Consumers
differentiation strategy and, 42,76,
81
direct marketing and, 158-159
"Euro-consumer" myth and,
141-144,f142-143,173-175,
f174
homogeneity vs. heterogeneity of,
72-77,t75-76,175-176,n175,
291
lifestyle segmentation and,
293,296
local vs. global marketing and,
169-173,n172,175-178
nationality vs. regionality and,
70-71
product image and, 291-293
standardized products and, 40-41,
74-75,81,92-93,99,101-102,
141-144,f142-143,144-147,
t146,168,178,178-179,321
total spending of, 71-72,t73
usage patterns of, 291
Continental Can, 320
Cost. *See* Price competition

Council for Mutual Economic
Assistance (Comecon),
206-207,n207,219-220
Csepel Iron Works, t208,218
Culture
joint venture factor of, 217
market clusters and, 141-144,
f142-143
marketing implications of, 71,
73-74,82,102
product standardization and, 41
trade barrier of, 66,82
Currency. *See also* European
Currency Unit (ECU);
European Monetary Union
(EMU)
marketing implications of, 74,t75,82
unification of,.86
Cyprus
cellular radio subscribers in, t323
European Community (EC)
associate member, xxx, f6
Czechoslovakia
Central European trading block
member, 5-6,t6
European Community (EC)
membership of, 316-317,342
joint ventures in, 209,210,t212
marketing affected by economic
factors in, t201,202

Decision systems analysis (DSA),
12,230-232
Hungarian/Japanese joint venture:
phase 1,250-252,f251
Hungarian/Japanese joint venture:
phase 2,252-255,f253-254
Hungarian/Japanese joint venture:
phase 3,256-257
Hungarian/US joint venture: phase
1, 241-244,f242
Hungarian/US joint venture: phase
2, 244-248,f245-246
Hungarian/US joint venture: phase
3, 248-250,f249

interview form of,
232-240,f237-239
procedure of, 240-241
Dee retail chain, 79
DELTA. *See* Developing European
Learning through
Technological Advance
(DELTA)
Democratic government
European Community (EC)
membership requirement, 61
impact of, xxvi
Denmark
automotive prices in, 298,333
cellular radio subscribers in, t323
economic growth statistics of,
325,t326,t341
European Community (EC)
membership of, 58,t59,60,61
European Currency Unit (ECU)
and, t329,t332
European Free Trade Association
(EFTA) membership of, 5-6,t6
food, beverage retail market
statistics in, t334-335
German economic growth and, t316
industrial standards of, 302
inflation statistics of, t327
state subsidies in, t319
Sweden bridge to, 321
Developing European Learning
through Technological
Advance (DELTA), 29
Distribution
direct marketing and, 158-159
networks of, 100,t295,297-298,299
retailers and supermarkets and,
157-158
transportation and, t146,155-157,
n156,165,176,t294,296-297
Drink and tobacco industry,
minimum efficient technical
scale (METS) affecting, 40
DSA. *See* Decision systems analysis
(DSA)

EAEC. *See* European Atomic Energy
Community (EAEC)
East Asian trading bloc, xxix
East and Central European countries.
See also Hungary; United
States/Hungarian joint
venture; specific country
Hungarian marketing potential to,
199-203,t200-201
marketing characteristics of,
185-186,288
trading links of, xxix, f6,30,333
Western investment in, 199,t200
East Germany. *See* Germany
Economic change, growth, xxvi. *See
also* Hungary
in East and Central Europe,
185-186
economies of scale benefits and,
38,40,108,140,141,144,164,
169,267,269,t294,296-297,
318-319,336
European currency Unit (ECU) of,
327-333,t329-330,t332
growth strategies for, 165-169,
f167,340-342,t342
marketing impact of, xxi
mergers, acquisitions and, 78,95,
97,140,158,179,271-272,299,
318-320,337
state subsides and, 317-318,t319
statistics of, 325,t326,329,t330
unemployment and, 324-325,t324
Economic integration definition, 85
Economies of scale
benefits of, 140,141,164,169,267,
269,t294,296-297
industry comparisons of, 38-40
price reductions through, 108,164
through mergers and acquisitions,
140,318-319,335-336,337
through television advertising,
322,337
Economist Intelligence Unit, The
(Mazur), 8,71-72,95,320

Economist, The, 234
ECSC. *See* European Coal and Steel
    Community (ECSC)
ECU. *See* European Currency Unit
    (ECU)
Education, xxvi
    European Community commission
        support of, 19,24,29
    trade barrier and, 66
    Treaty on European Union
        position on, 33-34
EEC. *See* European Economic
    community (EEC)
EES. *See* European Economic Space
    (EES)
EFTA. *See* European Free Trade
    Association (EFTA)
EIM. *See* Small Business Economic
    Institute (EIM)
Electrolux, 336
Electronic data exchange, 157
Electronics and Information
    Technology (IT) industry
    European Community commission
        guidelines affecting, 25-27
    European market segmentation of,
        27
    human resources training in, 28
    industrial diversity in, 28
    research and development
        difficulties in, 27-30
EMCF. *See* European Monetary
    Cooperation Fund (EMCF)
EMS. *See* European Monetary
    System (EMS)
EMU. *See* European Monetary
    Union (EMU)
Energy industry, 32
Engineering industry, 38
Environmental protection, xxvi
    European Community commission
        policy of, 19-20
ESPIRIT. *See* European Strategic
    Programme for Research and
    Developing in IT (ESPRIT)

Ethnocentric geographic marketing
    strategy, 98
Euro Russia, f6. *See also* Russia
Euro-brands, Europroducts. *See also*
    Product development;
    Standardization
    identification of, 77-78,289
    marketing mix strategies for,
        145-147,t146
    nationality vs. regionality of,
        70-71
    promotion decisions and,
        101-102
    retail alliances and, 100-101
"Euro-consumer" myth, 141-144,
    f142-143,173-175,f174
Euro-market. *See* Internal market
Eurogroup, 95,99
Europe 1992. *See* Internal market
European Act, 57
European Atomic Energy
    Community (EAEC), 61
European Coal and Steel Community
    (ECSC), 60-61
European Community commission,
    10,57
    change catalysts and, 20-23
    change prerequisites and, 18-20
    coherence and effectiveness
        ensured by, 24-25
    commercial trade policy of, 23
    Electronics and Information
        Technology (IT) guidelines
        of, 25-31
    industrial policy expectations of,
        34
    internal market of, 20-23
    objectives of, 17-18
    public procurement policy of,
        21-22
    role of, 16-17
    trans-European network
        promotion by, 22-23,29
    Treaty on European Union at
        Maastricht affected by, 31-34

European Community (EC). *See also*
  European Community
  commission; Internal market;
  Marketing strategies;
  Strategic marketing planning
  benefits of, 63-65,t64-65
  common external tariff and, 85
  composition of, 58-60,t59
  development, organization of,
    60-63,f62
  economic growth statistics of,
    340-342,t341-342
  economic integration of, 85-88
  European Free Trade Association
    (EFTA) trading links with,
    xxvi,xxix, 5-6,t7,8,30,85,
    316-317,332-333
  Foreign Direct Investment (FDI)
    into, 9
  homogeneous vs. hetogeneous
    marketplace and, 71-77,t73,
    t75-76
  impact of, xxvi
  marketing implications of,
    68-71,t69-71
  obstacles to, 65-68,t67
  socio-economic indicators for, t59
  statistics of, xxix
  suppliers to, 77-78
  total consumer spending and,
    71-72,t73
  triad trading block membership of,
    3-5,f4,t5,f6,340,t341
  unification of Europe plausibility
    and, 63-68,t64-65,t67
European Currency Unit (ECU), 86
  composition of, t322,329-333,
    t329-330
  functions of, 327-329
European Economic Community
  (EEC), 61
European Economic Space (EES),
  formation of, xxix
European Free Trade Association
  (EFTA)

European Community (EC)
  trading links with, xxvi, xxix,
    5-6,t7,8,30,316-317,332,
    341-342,t341-342
  tariff removals within, 85
European Monetary Cooperation
  Fund (EMCF), 328-329
European Monetary System (EMS),
  85,326-327
European Monetary Union (EMU),
  327-328,331
European Retail Alliance, 95,99
European Round Table of
  Industrialists, 16
European Strategic Programme for
  Research and Developing in
  IT (ESPRIT), 33
European, The (newspaper), 300
Expansion growth strategy, 166-168

FDI. *See* Foreign Direct Investment
  (FD)
Fiat, 336
Finland
  cellular radio subscribers in, t323
  European Community (EC)
    membership of, 59,333,341
  European Free Trade Association
    (EFTA) membership of, 5-6,
    t6,316
  state subsidies in, t319
Food and beverage industry
  expected developments in, 93,t93
  joint ventures, alliances in,
    79,t80,94,95,99-100,299,336
  market research available on,
    94,n175,333-336,t334-335
  product standardization in, 99,
    n175,177
  supermarket chains and, 95,
    157-158
Foreign Direct Investment (FDI), 9
"Fortress Europe". *See* Internal
  market

France
  advertising in, 153
  automotive industry protectionism
    in, 271
  cellular radio subscribers in, t323
  cultural, geographical proximity
    growth strategy and, n167,168
  economic growth statistics in,
    325,t326,t341
  electronics industry viewpoint of, 31
  English channel tunnel to, 321
  European Community (EC)
    membership of, 58,t59,60,61,67
  European Currency Unit (ECU)
    and, t329,t332
  food, beverage retail market
    statistics in, t334-335
  German economic growth and,
    t316
  inflation statistics of, t327
  state subsidies in, t319
  television commercials in, 152
  trade barriers of, 65
  trading status of, xxvi
  unemployment statistics in,
    324-325,t324
Furukawa (Japanese joint venture
  company), 250-257,f251,
  f253-254,262

GATT. *See* General Agreement on
  Tariffs and Trade (GATT)
GDP. *See* Gross domestic product
  (GDP)
General Agreement on Tariffs and
  Trade (GATT), 323
Geocentric geographic marketing
  strategy, 98
Germany
  advertising in, 153-154
  automotive industry in,
    37,101,271
  cellular radio subscribers in, t323
  companies restructuring in, 336
  cultural, geographical proximity

  growth strategy and, n167
  economic growth statistics in,
    315-316,t315,325,t326,
    t341-342
  European Community (EC)
    membership of, 58,t59,60,61
  European Currency Unit (ECU)
    and, t329,t332
  food, beverage retail market
    statistics in, t334-335,335
  food industry cooperative
    agreements in, 95
  high quality products of, 97
  inflation statistics of, t327
  state subsidies in, t319
  television commercials in, 152
  trading status of, xxvi
  unemployment statistics in,
    324-325, t324
  unrestricted capital flow into/out
    of, 85
Gillette Company, n153
Goodyear International, 300
Greece
  advertising in, 154
  automotive prices in, 101,298,333
  capital flow restrictions into/out
    of, 85-86
  economic growth statistics in, 325,
    t326
  European Community (EC)
    membership of, 58,t59,60,61
  European Currency Unit (ECU)
    and, 328,t329
  food, beverage retail market
    statistics in, t334
  German economic growth and, t316
  industrial standards of, 302
  inflation statistics of, t327
Gross domestic product (GDP). *See
  also* Economic change,
    growth
  anticipated changes in, 109
  statistics of, 5,t5,94

Heinekin Breweries, 103
Hoechst, 60
Holland
advertising in, 154
ECU exchange rates of, t329
nutritional standards of, 302
Hong Kong and Shanghai Banking
Corporation, 320
Hoover Corporation, 293
Hungarian/Japanese joint venture
description of, 235-236,240
interview procedure, 240-241
management implications of,
259-262
phase 1 of: solution-opportunity
identification, 250-252,f251
phase 2 of: evaluation, 252-255,
f253-254
phase 3 of: design,
implementation, 256-258
U.S./Hungarian joint venture
compared to, 257-259,t258
Hungary. *See also* Hungarian/
Japanese joint venture;
United States/Hungarian joint
venture
Central European trading bloc
membership of, 5-6,t6
domestic markets of, 189-190
Eastern European bridge function
of,219-221
Eastern European markets of,
190,199-203,t200-201
economic facts, history of,
186-190,t188,205-207
European Community (EC)
membership of, 316-317,342
importance of, xxx
labor market, costs in, 209,217-218
marketing affected by economic
factors in, t201,202
mixed marketing course forecasts
in, 192-193,f194,196-197
radical marketing course forecasts
in, 191-192,193-195,f194

reforms in, 205-207
retrograde marketing course
forecasts in, 193,f194,197
slow marketing course forecasts
in, 192,f194,195-196
Soviet Union trade with, 188,198,
206,219-220,222
state-ownership in, 189
U.S. debt of, 186,189
Western markets of, investment in,
190,191-193,195-199

IBM, 291
Iceland
cellular radio subscribers in, t323
European Free Trade Association
(EFTA) membership of, 5-6,t6
IJV (International Joint Ventures).
See Hungarian/Japanese joint
venture; International joint
venture (IJV); United States/
Hungarian joint venture
Ikea, 100,296
Internal market. *See also*
Competition; European
Community (EC); Marketing
mix strategies; Marketing
strategies; Price competition;
Protectionism
barriers to, 38,64-66,t67,82,108,
268,287-288
characteristics, effects of, 3-6,15,
35-37,57-58,85-88,107-109,
139-141,163-164,185-186,
205-207,225-226,267-272,
315-317
economic growth statistics of, 325,
t326,329,t330
economies of scale benefit of, 38,
40,108,140,141,144,164,169,
267,269,t294,296-297,
318-319,336
European currency Unit (ECU) of,
327-333,t329-330,t332

future of, 315-317,t318,333-342,
t334-335,t338-339,t341-342
global manager in, 337
low cost strategy of, 41-42
managerial implications of,
333-342,t334-335,t338-339,
t341-342
market integration effects and,
36-37,109,139-140,163-164,
n163,288-290
marketing mix affected by, 165,
n165
mergers, acquisitions and, 78,95,
97,140,158,179,271-272,299,
318-320,337
opportunities of, 320-322
state subsides affecting, 317-318,t319
statistics of, 57-58,287-288
strategies: low-cost, narrow
geographic scope competitive
strategy, 43-44,f44,f47,f51
strategies: low-cost, broad
geographic scope competitive
strategy, 44,f47,f51
strategies: differentiation, broad
geographic scope competitive
strategy, 45,f47-48,f51
strategies: differentiation, narrow
geographic scope competitive
strategy, 46,f48-49,f51
strategies: growth strategies
affected by, 165-169,f167,
340-342,t342-342
threats of, 322-326
unemployment and, 324-325,t324
uniform consumer preferences of,
40-41
International joint venture (IJV). *See
also* Hungarian/Japanese joint
venture; United States/
Hungarian joint venture
decision process: components of,
226-230
decision process: design model of,
f237-239

decision process: interview form
of, 232-233
decision process: national
environment surrounding,
233-236,f237-239,240
decision process: procedure of,
240-241
decision process: study method of,
230-232
decision process: summary of,
257-259,t258
management implications of
examples, 259-262
motivations for, 228-230
organizational knowledge,
learning motivation for,
229-230,250-252,f251,262
problems encountered in,
236,240,248,250,257
solution-opportunity driven
decision process, 228,241,
243,260-262
strategic behavior (competitive
position) motivation for,
229-230,250-252,f251,
261-262
transaction cost motivation for,
229-230,261-262
Investments by Foreigners in
Hungary Act (Act XXIV),
206
Ireland
advertising regulations in, 303
automotive prices in, 298,333
cellular radio subscribers in, t323
economic growth statistics in, 325,
t326,t341
European Community (EC)
membership of, 58,t59,60,61
European Currency Unit (ECU)
and, t329,t332
food, beverage retail market
statistics in, t334,335
German economic growth and,
t316

inflation statistics of, t327
state subsidies in, t319
IT. *See* Electronics and Information
    Technology (IT) industry
Italel, 337
Italy
    advertising in, 153,154
    automotive industry protectionism
        in, 271
    cellular radio subscribers in, t323
    companies restructuring in, 336
    cultural, geographical proximity
        growth strategy and, n167,168
    economic growth statistics in, 325,
        t326,t341
    European Community (EC)
        membership of, 58,t59,60,61
    European Currency Unit (ECU)
        and, t329,t332
    food, beverage retail market
        statistics in, t334-335,335
    German economic growth and,
        t316
    industrial standards of, 302
    inflation statistics of, t327
    low labor costs in, 97
    state subsidies in, t319
    trading status of, xxvi

Japan. *See also* Hungarian/Japanese
    joint venture
    competitive advantages of, 30
    EC protectionism against
        (automotive), 271
    economic growth statistics of,
        t341-342
    Electronics and Information
        Technology (IT) industry of,
        26-31
    Europe 1992 interest of, 87
    European investments of, 8,t9,96,
        322-324
    triad trading block membership of,
        3-5,f4,t5,f6,315,340,t341

Johnson & Johnson, n153
Joint ventures. *See*
    Hungarian/Japanese joint
        venture; United States/
        Hungarian joint venture

Kawasaki, 300
Kaynak-Ghauri proposition, xxvi

Language
    common market communications
        and, 151-152,302,326
    joint venture factor of, 217
    marketing implication of, 68-69,
        t69,74,102,103-104,393
    trade barrier of, 66,74,82
Levi Strauss, t208,209,217,293
Lotus software company product
    improvement case history,
    121-122
Luxembourg
    automotive tax in, 101
    cellular radio subscribers in, t323
    cultural, geographic proximity
        growth strategy and, n167
    economic growth statistics in,
        325,t326,t341
    European Community (EC)
        membership of, 58,t59,60,61
    food, beverage retail market
        statistics in, t334,335
    inflation statistics of, t327
    state subsidies in, t319

McDonalds
    joint venture of, t208,209,217
    uniform consumer preferences
        and, 40
Malta, xxx, f6
Market clusters, 141-144,f142-143
Market research
    components of, 305-306
    conceptual framework
        development of, 306-307

on "Euro-Consumers", 94-95
hypotheses generation, testing in,
   308-309
market clusters and, 141-144,
   f142-143
market integration, competition
   and, 307-308
Marketing mix strategies
advertising strategy and, 153-154
benefit segmentation and, 146
communications strategies and,
   151-153,293
direct marketing strategy and,
   158-159
"Euro-consumer" myth and,
   141-144,f142-143
"Euro-market" characteristics
   and, 139-141,165
Euro-product, Euro-brand strategy
   and, 145-147,t146,289
market management strategy,
   146-147,n147
national product standard strategy
   and, 144-145,t146
packaging strategy, t146,147-148
Pan-European promotion
   campaign and, 150-151,t151
pricing strategies and, 148-150,t149
product positioning strategy and, 154
public relations, sales promotion
   and, 154-155
retailers and supermarkets and,
   157- 158
transportation distribution and,
   155-157,t156
Marketing News, 96,98,102
exporting vs. marketing, 140-141
Marketing strategies. *See also*
   Consumers; East and Central
   European countries; Hungary;
   Internal market; Market
   research; Marketing mix
   strategies; Product
   positioning; Strategic
   marketing planning process

advertising agencies and, 102-103
attack strategies, 109-111
business factors affecting,
   t294-295,296-300
consumer product differentiation
   and, 76,141,291-293,t294,296
corporate factors affecting,
   300-301
culture differences affecting,
   70-71,73-74,76,102,291
currency differences affecting,
   74,t75
distribution decisions in, 99-101
"Euro-consumer" myth, 141-144,
   f142-143,173-175,f174,
   304-305
geographic marketing strategies
   and, 98
global strategies and, 169-173,
   175-177
growth strategies and, 165-169,
   f167,337,t338-339
industrial product standardization
   and, 74-75
language differences affecting,
   68-69,t69,74,102,293
local strategies and, 169-173,
   177-178
market research of, 94-95
media product promotion and,
   79-80
political factors affecting, 301-304
pricing decisions in, 81,101
product decisions in, 98-99
product/customer matching and,
   81
promotion decisions in, 101-102
standardized products and, 40-41,
   74-75,81,92-93,99,101-102,
   141-144,f142-143,144-147,
   t146,178,178-179,289-290
total consumer spending,
   71-72,t73
Marks and Spencer, 100
Marlboro, 150

Maytag Corporation, 293
Media
  changes in, 102
  common market communications
    and, 151-152,165
  satellite channels and, 152-153,
    158-159,290,297,300,322
  television advertising, 102,103,
    152-153,176,297,299-300,
    302,322
Mergers, acquisitions
  blockage of, 158
  increase of, 78,95,97,140,158,179,
    271-272,299,318-320,337
  protectionism and, 271-272
  tariff removals affecting, xxii
Midlands Bank, 320
Mill, John Stuart, xxiii-xxiv
Minimum efficient technical scale
    (METS)
  low-cost, narrow geographic scope
    competitive strategy and,
    43-44,f47,49-50,f51
  low-cost, broad geographic scope
    competitive strategy and,
    44,f47,49-50,f51
  differentiation, broad geographic
    scope competitive strategy
    and, 45,f47-48,49-50,f51
  differentiation, narrow geographic
    scope competitive strategy
    and, 46,f48-49,49-50,f51
  economies of scale and, 38,40

National Renewal of the Hungarian
    Democratic Forum, 191
Nestlé, 82,158,179
Netherlands
  automotive prices in, 37,101
  cellular radio subscribers in, t323
  Central Planning Bureau (CPB) of,
    91,91-92,t92,101
  economic growth statistics in, 325,
    t326,t341

European Community (EC)
  membership of, 58,t59,60,61
European Currency Unit (ECU)
  and, t332
  food, beverage industry in, 95,t334
  German economic growth and, t316
  inflation statistics of, t327
  retail internationalization and, 100
  Small Business Economic Institute
    (EIM) of, 97
  state subsidies in, t319
  television commercials in, 152
  trade barriers of, 65
  unrestricted capital flow into/out
    of, 85
Networking
  distribution networks, 100
  European Community commission
    promotion of, 22-23,29
  Treaty on European Union policy
    on, 32-33
Nike, 322
North American trading bloc, xxix
Norway
  cellular radio subscribers in, t323
  European Community (EC)
    membership of, 59,333,341
  European Free Trade Association
    (EFTA) membership of,
    5-6,t6,516

OECD. See Organization for
    Economic Cooperation and
    Development (OECD)
Olivetti, 336
Opel, 300
OPIC. See Organization for
    International Economic
    Cooperation (OPIC)
Organization for Economic
    Cooperation and
    Development (OECD), 221
Organization for International
    Economic Cooperation
    (OPIC), 221

Packaging strategy, 146,t146,147-148
Pangus Rubber, t208,218
Pannanplast (Hungarian joint venture
   company), 250-257,f251,
   f253-254,262
Paper and printing industry, 38
Patent system, of European
   Community commission,
   22,147
Patten, C., xxv
Penetration growth strategy, 166,
   168-169
Pepsi-Cola, 150,154,291
Perrier Water, 145
Philips, 82,297,337
Poland
   Central European trading block
     membership of, 5-6,t6
   European Community (EC)
     membership of, 86,316-317,342
   joint ventures in, 209,210,t213,
     225,234,259-260
   marketing affected by economic
     factors in, 199,t201,203
Polifoam
   joint venture establishment of, 235
   problems encountered by, 236
Political factors affecting marketing.
   See also Protectionism
   impact of, xxi, 82
   national interest and, 303
   product standards, 301-303
Polycentric geographic marketing
   strategy, 98
Population, population growth
   market clusters and, 141-144,
     f142-143
   marketing implications of, xxvi,
     69-70,t70-71,93
   mobility of, 176
   statistics of, 5,t5,69-70,t70-71
Portugal
   cellular radio subscribers in, t323
   economic growth statistics in,
     325,t326,t341

European Community (EC)
   membership of, 58,t59,60,61
European Currency Unit (ECU)
   and, 328,t329
food, beverage retail market
   statistics in, t334
German economic growth and,
   t316
inflation statistics of, t327
low labor costs in, 97
state subsidies in, t319
Price competition. *See also*
   Competition
decreased costs and, 148-150,
   n148,t149
different price structures and,
   149-150
factors affecting, 96-97,t295,298
internal market integration effects
   on, 36-37,333-334
marketing mix strategies and,
   148-150,t149
marketing strategies and, 81,101,
   150,165,t295,298
product positioning and, 119-122,
   f120,125-127,t126-128,129
Procter & Gamble, 150
Product development. *See also*
   Product positioning
consumer usage patterns affecting,
   291-296,t294
differentiation strategy and, 42,76,81
European conservativeness and, 27
homogeneity vs. heterogeneity of, 72
industrial product standardization
   and, 74-75,141
marketing strategy component of,
   98-99
media promotion of, 79-81
pricing and, 81
standardization and, 40-41,74-75,
   81,92-93,99,101-102,
   141-144,f142-143,144-147,
   t146,165,169,178-179,
   291-296,t294,297,321

Product positioning
  attack strategies and, 109-111
  concept of, 107-109,131-133
  defensive strategies of, 110-112
  image and, 291-293,299
  marketing mix strategies and, 154
  new product revolutionary attack
    and, 119-124,f120,f123,
    129-131,t130
  packaging, t146,147-148
  price cutting and, 119-122,f120,
    125-127,t126-128,129
  product improvement and,
    119-122,f120,124-127,
    t126-128,129,299
Protectionism. *See also* Trade
  against Japanese products, 271
  foreign direct investment and,
    282,322-324
  of internal market, 267-272
  product standardization barrier of,
    303-304
  strategic implications of, 284-285,
    322-324
  vulnerable products: definition
    methodology, 272-275,t275
  vulnerable products: high,
    t277-279,281-282,283
  vulnerable products: low,
    275,t276-278,280-281,284
Public procurement policy, of
    European Community
    commission, 21-22

Quaker Oats Co., 158
Qualiplastic, t208,217

RACE. *See* Research and
    Development in Advanced
    Communications
    Technologies for Europe
    (RACE)
Reebok, 322

Regiocentric geographic marketing
    strategy, 98,102
Research and development
  European Community commission
    promotion of, 29
  Treaty on European Union Policy
    on, 33
Research and Development in
    Advanced Communications
    Technologies for Europe
    (RACE), 33
Romania
  joint ventures in, 209,t213
  marketing affected by economic
    factors in, t201,202,203
Russia. *See also* Euro Russia
  economic reforms in, xxvi
  Hungarian economy and, 188,198,
    206,219
  joint ventures in, 209,210,t213,
    225-226
  Levi Strauss in, 393
  marketing affected by economic
    factors in, t201,202-203

Saatchi & Saatchi, 150,153,n153,303
Schwinn-Csepel, t208,218-219
SKY television channel, 102,103,153
Small Business Economic Institute
    (EIM), 97
Socioeconomic change, xxi,
    69-71,t71. *See also* Economic
    change, growth
Soviet Union. *See* Russia
Spain
  advertising in, 154,303
  capital flow restrictions into/out
    of, 85-86
  cultural, geographical proximity
    growth strategy and, n167
  economic growth statistics in,
    325,t326
  European Community (EC)
    membership of, 58,t59,60,61

European Currency Unit (ECU)
and, 328,t329
food, beverage retail market
statistics in, t334-335
German economic growth and, t316
industrial standards of, 302
inflation statistics of, t327
low labor costs in, 97
price increases in, n148
Standardization of products
business factors affecting,
t294-295,296-300
consumer factors affecting, 92-93,
289-290,291-296,t294
corporate factors affecting,
t295,300-301
vs. customization, 178-179
growth strategy and, 168
internal market result and, 321
marketing mix strategies and,
74-75,81,99,141-144,
f142-143,165,297,304-305
political factors affecting,
t295,301-304
product/price differentiation and,
40-41
promotion decisions and, 101-102
Strategic alliances. *See*
Hungarian/Japanese joint
venture; United States/
Hungarian joint venture
Strategic marketing planning process
annual marketing plan of, 89,f90
environment analysis and, 88,f90,
91-95,t92-93
evaluation of, 89,f90
implementation of, 89,f90,103
marketing strategies of, 89,f90,
97-103
mission statement, generic
competitive strategies, 88,
f90,95-97
steps in, 88-91,f90
Super Channel television channel,
102,103,153,300

Supermarket chains, 95,157-158
Swatch watch product positioning
case history, 122,124
Sweden
cellular radio subscribers in, t323
Denmark bridge to, 321
European Community (EC)
membership of, 59,322,333,
341
European Free Trade Association
(EFTA) membership of, 5-6,
t6,316
multinational corporations in,
n178
Switzerland
cellular radio subscribers in, t323
cultural, geographical proximity
growth strategy and, n167
European Community (EC)
membership of, 59,333,341
European Free Trade Association
(EFTA) membership of, 5-6,
t6

Tariff removals
examples of, 85
price competition and, 36-37,f39,
108
takeovers because of, xxii
Taxation
economic integration barriers of,
87
of Hungarian profits, 210-211,t213
pricing decisions and, 101
value-added tax (VAT) and,
65-66,81,87,101,149,336
Telecommunications,
telecommunications industry
cellular telephone network and,
322,t323
in Hungary, 217
networking in, 32,322,337
privatization in, 340
protectionism of, t278-279,281

Television
  advertising media and, 102,103,
    152-153,176,297,299-300,
    302,322
  satellite channels and, 152-153,
    158-159,290,297,300,322
Throw, Lester, xxv-xxvi
Trade. *See also* Protectionism
  barriers to, 38,64-66,t67,82,108,268
  EC with U.S., 269-270
  global trade map, f4
  protectionism factors and,
    272-275,t275
  triad trading bloc and, 3-6,f4,t5,f6,
    315,340,t341
Transport goods industry
  aircraft protectionism and, t276,280
  airline mergers in, 95
  consumer standardization in, 99
  expected developments in, t93
  minimum efficient technical scale
    (METS) affecting, 40
  networking in, 32
  technical barriers affecting, 38
Transportation (distribution),
    155-157,n156,t156,165,t294,
    296-297
Treaty on European Union at
    Maastricht, 10
  education and training issue of,
    33-34
  industrial policy of, 31-32
  research and technological
    development issue of, 33
  trans-European networks issue of,
    32-33
Treaty of Rome, 58,66,158,268,320
Triad trading bloc, 3-6,f4,t5,f6,315,
    340,t341
Turkey, xxx, f6,86,342

UD. *See* United Distillers (UD)
Ukraine, xxvi
Unified Europe, xxix-xxx. *See also*
    Internal market

Unilever, 82
United Distillers (UD), 41
United Kingdom
  advertising in, 153,154
  automotive industry in, 271,298,
    333
  cellular radio subscribers in, t323
  companies restructuring in, 336
  cultural, geographical proximity
    growth strategy and, n167
  decreased prices in, n148
  economic growth statistics in, 325,
    t326,t341
  European Community (EC)
    membership of, 58,t59,60,61,
    67
  European Currency Unit (ECU)
    and, t329,t332
  food, beverage retail market
    statistics in, t334-335,335
  French channel tunnel to, 321
  German economic growth and,
    t316
  inflation statistics of, t327
  mergers, acquisition in, 320
  state subsidies in, t319
  tariff removals by, 85
  trade: barriers of, 65
  trade: status of, xxvi
  unemployment statistics in, t324
United States. *See also* United
    States/Hungarian joint
    venture
  competitive advantages of, 30
  economic growth statistics of,
    t341-342
  Electronics and Information
    Technology (IT) industry of,
    26-31
  European Community (EC)
    exports from, 59
  European investments of,
    96,323-324
  geocentric marketing strategy in,
    98

Hungarian debt to, 186,189
interest in Europe, 1992,87
triad trading block membership of,
   3-5,f4,t5,f6,340,t341
unemployment statistics in,
   324-325,t324
United States/Hungarian joint
   venture, 225-226
aspects of, 208-211
Hungarian/Japanese joint venture
   compared to, 257-259,t258
Hungary as Eastern European
   bridge, 219-221
interview procedure of, 240
investigation techniques of,
   207-208,t208
management implications of,
   259-262
managerial views, both sides,
   211-216,t214,t216
phase 1 of: solution-identification,
   241-244,f242
phase 2 of: evaluation, 244-248,
   f245-246
phase 3 of: design,
   implementation, 248-250,
   f249
problems encountered in, 216-219,
   t216,236,248,250,257

repatriation of profits and, 210,t213
U.S. comparison to other joint
   ventures, t214
USSR. *See* Russia

Value-added tax (VAT)
   food and beverage retail industry
      and, 336
   pricing and, 81,101,149
   trade barrier of, 65-66,87
Vendex retail chain, 79
Volkswagen, 298,333

West Germany. *See* Germany
White Paper of 1985. *See*
   *Completing the Internal
   Market* (European
   Community Commission)

Yol (Hungarian joint venture
   company), f242,243-244,
   243-250,t245-246,f249,262
Yugoslavia
   joint ventures in, 209,210,t212,234
   marketing affected by economic
      factors in, 199,t201,202